SOUTH DEVON COLLEGE LIBRARY

HEINEMANN
GNVQ

D1649723

2000
STANDARDS

FOUNDATION

Health and
Social Care

Lynda Mason • Penelope Gresford

WITHDRAWN

**Compulsory Units
Plus Options**

Edexcel
Success through qualifications

Heinemann Educational Publishers,
Halley Court, Jordan Hill, Oxford OX2 8EJ
A division of Reed Educational & Professional Publishing Ltd.

Heinemann is a registered trademark of Reed Educational & Professional Publishing

OXFORD MELBOURNE AUCKLAND
JOHANNESBURG BLANTYRE GABORONE
IBADAN PORTSMOUTH (NH) USA CHICAGO

First published 2000

05 04 03 02
10 9 8 7 6 5 4

A catalogue record for this book is available from the British Library on request

ISBN 0435 45601 6

Cover designed by Sarah Garbett

Typeset by 🅐 Tek-Art, Croydon, Surrey

Printed and bound in Great Britain by The Bath Press Ltd., Bath

Acknowledgements
The publishers wish to thank the following for permission to reproduce the photographs in this book:
p.7 Sally & Richard Greenhill; p. 10 T. Hill; p.12 Barnaby's Picture Library/Anne Crabbe; p.27 Format/Ulrike Preuss;
p.40 Oxford and County Newspapers; p.55 SPL; p.62 Niquitin; p.82, 93, 96, 104 Sally & Richard Greenhill;
p.147 Health Education Authority; p.148 MAFF; p.162 Format; p.190 Sally & Richard Greenhill; p.207
J. Allan Cash; p.213 SPL; p.217 Chris Ashford/Camera Press; p.229 Age Concern

Website: www.heinemann.co.uk

Contents

Unit 1 Investigating Health and Social Care   1

1.1   The main types of service   1
Health services: doctors' surgeries 2; health centres 3;
dentists 5; hospitals 5; community health care 7;
health services for people with disability 8
Personal social services: residential care services 9;
sheltered accommodation 10; day care services 11;
foster care and adoption 13; domiciliary care 14;
support groups and voluntary groups 14; charitable
groups 16
Early years services: day nurseries 17; child minders
17; playgroups 18; nannies 18; after school and holiday
care 18; early years education services 18

1.2   Main jobs in health and social care services   19
Direct care: nurses 20; doctors 21; occupational
therapists 21; social workers 22; care assistants 23;
nursery nurses 23; early years curriculum 23
Indirect care: laboratory technicians 25; catering
assistants 26; informal carers 26

1.3   The care value base   27
Respect in practice 27; principles of the care value
base 27

1.4   How people can gain access to use the services   29
Referral 29
Barriers to the use of services: physical barriers 30;
psychological barriers 30; financial barriers 31;
environmental barriers 31

Assessment   32

Unit 2 Understanding Health and Well-being   36

2.1   Defining health and well-being   36
Physical aspects of health 38; intellectual aspects of
health 39; emotional aspects of health 40; social aspects
of health 42
Different groups and their health needs: infants 42;
young children 43; adolescents 43; adults 44; older
people 45

2.2 **Factors affecting health and well-being**   47
Diet 47; exercise 49; recreation 52; monitoring and prevention 54; environment 56; social class 57; employment 58

2.3 **Risks to health and well-being**   59
Recreational drugs 59; drinking alcohol 60; smoking tobacco 61; diet 62; personal hygiene 63; exercise 64; sexual behaviour 65; unsafe practices in the home and the workplace 67

2.4 **Indicators of good physical health**   68
Height and weight charts 68; peak flow 69; body mass index 70

Assessment   71

Unit 3 Understanding Personal Development and Relationships   76

3.1 **Human growth and development**   76
Infancy 78; childhood 80; adolescence 84; adulthood 86; old age 89

3.2 **Factors that affect growth and development**   92
Physical factors 92; genetic factors 92; diet 94; environmental factors 95; social factors 95; economic factors 99; the effects on growth and personal development 101

3.3 **Effects of relationships on personal development**   101
Friendships 102; family relationships 103; sexual relationships 104; working relationships 104; barriers to effective relationships 105

Assessment   106

Unit 4 Investigating Common Hazards and Health Emergencies   111

4.1 Hazards and risks in health and social care settings   111
Human factors 112; environmental factors 112; unsafe equipment 113; hazardous substances 114; infections 115; moving and handling people and equipment 117; fire 118
Identifying and reducing risks in the workplace: environmental safety surveys and audits 119; staff

training 120; regular checking and servicing of
equipment 121; putting in place rules and regulations
122; personal and general hygiene 124; provision
of safety and warning notices 125

4.2 **Dealing with emergencies**   125
Asthma attack 126; choking 126; head injury 127;
burn and scald injuries 128; fits 128; electric shock
129; broken bones 130

4.3 **Basic first-aid procedures**   130
When breathing stops 131; no pulse or heartbeat 133;
loss of consciousness 134; bleeding 135; the recovery
position 137; summoning the emergency services 137

Assessment   139

Unit 5 Planning Diets   143

5.1 **A healthy balanced diet**   143
Food groups for a balanced diet 144: malnutrition
144; the balance of good health 145; health problems
resulting from an unbalanced diet 148

5.2 **The nutrients in food**   150
Proteins 150; carbohydrates 151; fats 151; vitamins
152; minerals 153; water 153

5.3 **Different diets for different needs**   153
Vegetarian diets 153; cultural differences 154; special
diets for weight loss or weight gain 155; dietary needs
of children 155; dietary needs of elderly people 157;
pregnancy and lactation 157

5.4 **Planning meals**   158
Budget 158

5.5 **Preparing meals**   160
Before you start 160; use of kitchen equipment 160;
choosing a cooking method 161; mixing ingredients
and following recipes 162; following instructions on
food packaging 163.
Good hygiene in food preparation: bacterial food
poisoning 163; preventing cross-contamination 163; the
kitchen environment 164; personal hygiene 164;
prevention of direct contamination if you are ill or unwell
165

5.6 **Presenting meals**   165
Taste 166; texture 166; appearance 166; portion size
166.
Groups with special nutritional needs: older people
167; children 167; the client who is ill or recovering
from illness 167

Assessment   169

Unit 6 Exploring Recreational Activities for Clients   174

6.1 **Benefits of recreational activity**   174
Improving mobility through physical activity 175;
improving relationships 177; keeping the mind
active 180

6.2 **Local recreational facilities and activities**   182
Places for social activities 183; sources of intellectual
activity 183

6.3 **Recreational activities for different client groups**   184
Children 186; adolescents 187; adults 189; elderly
people 190; people with special needs 191; therapists
who use recreational activities 193

6.4 **Barriers to recreational activities**   196
Cost 196; physical access 197; availability of
recreational facilities 198; specialist equipment 198;
specialist clothing 199; transport 199; social pressure
200; cultural pressure 201; stereotyping 201

6.5 **Health and safety factors in recreational activities** 203

Assessment   206

Unit 7 Exploring Physical Care   210

7.1 **Reasons why people need physical care**   210
Age-related reasons for needing physical care 210;
deteriorating sight and hearing 212; memory loss 213;
long-term illness 213; after-effects of a stroke or
heart attack 214; accidents 215; acute illness 216;
long-term disabilities 216.
Types of activity requiring help: getting up and going
to bed 217; personal hygiene 218; getting out and
about 218; shopping 218; gardening 219; social

activities 219; moving about the house and outside 220; preparing meals, eating and drinking 220; housework 220; hearing and answering the telephone and doorbell 221; seeing to read and write and take part in hobbies 221; going to work 221; taking part in education 222

Providing physical care: settings 222; specialist equipment 224

7.2 **Settings, agencies and personnel involved in physical care**   226

Informal carers 226; formal carers 227; voluntary organisations 228

7.3 **Relevant health and safety issues**   228

Legislation 228; safe practice in moving and handling techniques and use of equipment 229; personal, general and food hygiene 230; dealing with body waste 231; demonstrating the skills of physical care 231

Assessment   233

Answers to questions   237

Glossary   238

Introduction

How to use this book

This book has been written as a brand new text for students who are working to the 2000 national standards for Foundation GNVQ in Health and Social Care. It covers the three compulsory units and four option units for the award.

These units are:

1 Investigating health and social care

2 Understanding health and well-being

3 Understanding personal development and relationships

4 Investigating common hazards and health emergencies

5 Planning diets

6 Exploring recreational activities for clients

7 Exploring physical care.

Within each unit, the text is organised under exactly the same headings as the GNVQ units, to make it easy for you to find your way round the unit. By working through the units, you will find all the knowledge and ideas you need to prepare your assessment.

There is also an introduction to two further options. These are:

8 Preparing for employment in health and social care

9 Working as part of a team.

If you decide to choose these options, you will find the full text on the Heinemann GNVQ website www.heinemann.co.uk/gnvq (password FOUNDTWO). This is a free service.

Assessment

Assessment in the new GNVQ is carried out on the whole unit, rather than by many smaller pieces of work. The methods of assessment are:

* one major assignment, for example carrying out an investigation into the health and care provision in your local area

* an external test, set and marked by the awarding body, for example Edexcel.

At the end of each unit in the book, you will find a **unit assessment** section which provides you with practice for both these forms of assessment. The first part is a series of carefully planned tasks. By working through the tasks you will have an opportunity to obtain a *pass* grade. Further sections then guide you towards obtaining *merit* and *distinction* grades. The second part is a short unit **test**. This can be used to check your knowledge of the unit and also to prepare for the external test.

Special features of the book

Throughout the text there are a number of features which are designed to encourage discussion and group work, and to help you relate the theory to real work in health and social care.

Think it over:

Thought-provoking questions or dilemmas about people in health and social care. They can be used for individual reflection or group discussion.

Talk it over:

Health and social care issues are raised for you to discuss with another person.

Did you know?:

Interesting facts and snippets of information about the health and social care sectors.

Remember!:

Reminders of what you should know and what practices you should follow in health and social care.

Try it out:

Activities that encourage you to apply the theory in a practical situation.

Look it up:

Tasks for finding out more about some of the issues in health and social care.

Case studies:

Examples of real (or simulated) clients in health and social care with real needs. Questions on the case studies will enable you to explore the key issues and deepen your understanding of the subject.

Other features, included at the end of the book, are: **answers to questions** in the unit assessment section and a **glossary** of key terms.

This unit explores the various services for health and social care and early years education. You will find out about the many different kinds of services in your own area. These are the medical services, such as hospitals and GPs; the personal social services, such as day care centres for elderly people; and the early years education services such as nursery schools. You will discover how the services provide help and support to those who use them. You will also learn about the way people use the services and about some of the barriers that stop people using them.

You will also explore some of the main job roles involved in these services. Some of the roles involve direct contact with clients (people who use the services) and others provide help and support without close contact with clients. We will also explore key values that underpin the work of all those employed in health and social care and early years education. These values are called 'the care value base' and the principles of good practice.

For the unit you need to learn about:

* the main types of health, social care and early years services

* the main jobs in the health, social care and early years services

* the care value base

* how people can gain access to and use the services.

It is important to remember throughout that the care value base is an essential part of the caring role. Health and care workers should always implement the principles of good practice in all the work that they do. This is especially important in the case of carers working directly with clients. They should always promote the values of equality and diversity. This means not preferring to work with one client rather than another because of age, race, religion, ability etc. and always respecting the differences in people.

Remember the principles of good practice and the care value base as you work towards your qualification.

1.1 The main types of service

Health services

In 1948 the government of the time set up the National Health Service (NHS). For the first time everyone in the country would have free access to all the services needed to maintain their health and well-being.

These are some of the services available in 1948.

* nurses

* dentists

* opticians

* health centres

* family planning.

All of them and many more are available to us today. The government department responsible for health services is called the **Department of Health**. The money to pay for the services comes mostly from our taxes and it is the Secretary of State for Health who decides how the money should be spent each year.

Look it up

Find out who the present Secretary of State for Health is.

Managing the NHS in your area

The government gives a range of organisations, such as health authorities, social services and voluntary or private businesses, the authority to run our health and social services on its behalf.

The government gives each service a framework to work to. This framework guides each organisation as to the kind of services they should be providing and which client groups they should be working with.

Local health services are purchased by groups of doctors, nurses and other professionals on our behalf. They decide what kind of health care we need in our local area. These groups are called **primary care groups** and their job is to make sure that all the services we need are available.

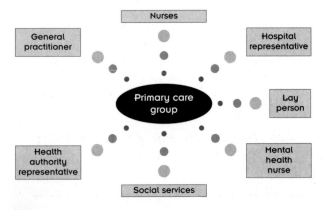

Primary care

The word 'primary' is often used to mean 'first'. Primary care is usually our first point of contact with the health service. It is mainly provided at a health centre or a doctor's surgery.

Look it up

Working with another person find out about the primary care group in your area. Find out which health care workers are members. You could ask at your doctor's surgery or a health centre. You will even find the information in a library or on the Internet.

There are many different health and social care professionals involved in the delivery of primary health care. In general, these are:

- general practitioners (doctors in the community)
- health visitors
- practice nurses
- social workers
- community midwives
- community psychiatric nurses
- district nurses.

Many of these health and social care professionals can be found in a health centre or doctor's surgery. The difference between a health centre and a doctor's surgery is that a health centre can usually provide a wider range of services, such as a dentist, as well as a doctor. A doctor's surgery usually only has the doctor and the nursing and administration staff.

Doctors' surgeries

It is likely that at some time you will have visited a doctor's surgery. Here the main purpose is to provide medical care. A surgery however also provides a wider range of services. These can include:

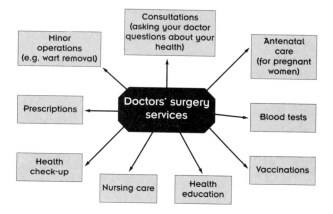

Doctors' surgery services

- Consultations (asking your doctor questions about your health)
- Minor operations (e.g. wart removal)
- Antenatal care (for pregnant women)
- Prescriptions
- Blood tests
- Health check-up
- Nursing care
- Health education
- Vaccinations

Talk it over

Jenny was visiting her doctor's surgery today to have a small, raised freckle removed from her scalp. She had noticed every time she brushed her hair that it got caught in the bristles and started to bleed.

When she arrived at the surgery the receptionist took her name and personal details. The nurse then came to take her through to the surgery when the doctor was ready for her.

The doctor gave Jenny an injection in her scalp so that she could not feel the freckle being removed. Once the minor operation was complete the nurse stitched the little cut and Jenny was ready to go home.

Working with another person discuss the service Jenny received at her doctor's surgery. Which health professionals helped to treat her? Make a list of them in your portfolio.

Health centres

The main purpose of a health centre is to provide medical and health care, however many also provide support and personal welfare services as well. The range of services provided depends on the kind of care

Look it up

Working with another person find out about the services offered in your doctor's surgery. It is likely that there will be a leaflet describing the services offered. If not, you could ask the receptionist. A good time to call is when the surgery is finished and staff have a little more time to talk to you.

required in your local area, how many people live there, how old they are and the amount of money available for the primary care groups to spend.

By building health centres, health service planners can organise most of the required health services under one roof. This is what has happened over the years in most towns.

Did you know?

The first health centres were started in the 1930s.

SNAPSHOT

The primary care group of Anytown was meeting to decide how to spend the funding they had available for the primary care services.

'We have a lot of older people in this town so we need to think about buying services that will help them', said Dr Smith. 'Agreed', said the nurse, 'but we also have a lot of young mothers and children, so we will need to think about the kind of services they will require.'

'When the new health centre opens we will be able to put these services in for everyone to use,' said the doctor.

CASE STUDY – Anytown's New Health Centre

A local Story by Andy McAllister, our roving newspaper reporter.

At last, the new health centre is open to the public. I went along to the opening ceremony to find out exactly what services you, the customer, will be able to access.

Shirley Smith, the chief executive of the hospital trust which had built and staffed this centre, greeted me at the door. She was keen to show me around the facilities. Our first port of call was the large, modern reception area. Computers seemed to stretch as far as the eye could see. Shirley explained that such a large well-equipped area was necessary to accommodate the six large GP practices that were going to share the premises and the reception area. In fact, receptionists were hard at work answering the phone and making appointments, and the centre had only just opened!

The waiting area has comfortable seats and plenty of health information literature for clients to read. Some of the leaflets and posters describe the services on offer from the GPs, others explain how to look after your health.

On the other side of reception there is a series of rooms dedicated to providing a comprehensive range of services. There is a physiotherapy room, a speech therapy office, opticians and a dental service.

There is a bright, well-designed play area for children adjoining the health visitor's office. The antenatal and postnatal care rooms look to be particularly well planned, with four separate consulting rooms for the midwives.

Shirley Smith explained that the bright, attractive treatment room, staffed by qualified nurses, should save patients having to travel to the hospital for minor surgery or dressings care.

When I asked one of the older visitors to the centre what she liked best she said, 'the chemist shop is wonderful. I will be able to come out of the doctor's and pick up my prescription right away. No need for a bus journey!'

Questions

1   How many services are offered at Anytown Health Centre? Make a list of as many as you can.

2   Name two services offered by this health centre which you would not find at a doctor's surgery.

Look it up

There may be some services in the Anytown health centre case study that you do not know very much about. Choose one service and find out as much as you can about it.

Present your findings to your colleagues for discussion.

Try it out

In groups or pairs locate your nearest health centre and find out from them what range of health services they offer. Make a list of these to keep with your class notes.

Dentists

Dental care is part of medical care. This is because the mouth is so important to our health and well-being. Imagine not being able to chew and digest food properly due to lack of teeth, or having constant toothache!

Dentists are also part of the primary care service because they are usually the first ones that anyone with a mouth problem goes to.

Dentists are based in either a health centre or a dental surgery. Sometimes they share their surgery premises with other dentists and sometimes they work alone. They usually offer a wide range of services, such as:

- treatment (fillings, extractions, false teeth)
- check-ups
- oral health education
- hygienist treatment

Talk it over

> Annie lives in a residential care home for older people. She has been having trouble with her dentures (false teeth) for about a fortnight. She cannot chew her food properly and now she has got mouth ulcers, which are very painful.
>
> Shamim, her care worker, noticed Annie leaving most of her meals. When she went to talk to her she realised that Annie was in pain. She rang the dentist and asked if he would come to the care home to see Annie.
>
> When the dentist arrived he examined Annie and said she needed some new dentures because her old ones were worn out. He took an impression and started the process of making new ones for her there and then.
>
> He also prescribed a mouth wash for her which would help to heal her mouth ulcers.

Working with another person discuss the service being offered to Annie by this dentist. What role did the care worker play in Annie's treatment?

- fluoride treatment
- orthodontics (making teeth straight)
- minor oral surgery.

Some dentists offer NHS treatment, which is free to some people or at a reduced cost. Others only offer private treatment, which clients must pay for. Some do both. All treatment to children under the age of 16 is free.

Look it up

Working with another person find out about the way your dentist is funded. Are they an NHS practice or are they a private practice? They will most likely have leaflets that tell you about their service.

Look it up

Find out what a health service is called when the health professional visits the client's home. You could ask your teacher or a health professional who carries out visits to a client's home.

Hospitals

Hospitals are also known as 'Trusts'. They provide secondary care, that is, the stage of care following primary care. Clients usually go to the hospital because a health

Try it out Divide into groups of three or four. Discuss together what you know about hospitals from your own or other people's experiences, or even from reading or watching television dramas. In these groups, draw a spidergram on a large piece of paper, and write down everything that comes to mind when you think about hospitals. For example, you might think of operations, nurses or ambulances. Make one large group spidergram for display.

professional has referred them there. The main purpose of hospitals is to provide medical treatment, however they also provide support, education and training.

SNAPSHOT

John has had an accident on his pushbike. He fell off when he skidded on wet leaves. He has got a bad cut on his knee. His mother has washed the wound but thinks he really should be seen by a health professional.

When they get to the hospital a receptionist takes John's personal details and then asks him and his mother to sit and wait until a nurse comes to see them.

After a few minutes a nurse arrives to see John. She explains that the wound is not serious but will need to be seen by a doctor.

The doctor will see John as soon as possible for the required treatment.

Think it over There are times when a client might use a hospital without being sent by a health professional. When do you think this might be?

Look at our spidergram – is yours similar?

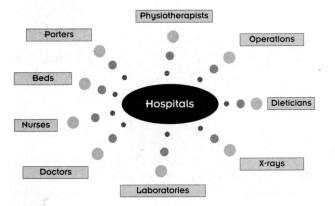

The care offered by a hospital is for everyone. Many hospitals will care for anyone who needs to use them – there are no conditions as to age, race or state of health. Clients use hospitals for:

- operations and consultations
- treatment for infections, accidents or illness
- health education
- rehabilitation after an operation or illness.

Sometimes a client who needs special treatment or help will have to go to a specialist hospital. These hospitals are often called 'centres of excellence', because they specialise in certain kinds of care or treatment, such as:

- heart transplants
- terminal illness (care of people who are dying)
- paediatric care (children's specialist)
- mental health care
- maternity and women's health.

All treatment in NHS hospitals is free. But there are also some private hospitals too, for example, the Nuffield hospitals.

Look it up

Find out more about the services provided by:

- outpatient departments in a hospital
- hospice care
- orthopaedic departments in hospitals.

Research these in the library, or on the Internet, or contact your local health authority or hospital. Are these services provided in your local area? Keep the information you find in your class notes.

Community health care

Clients can have health care in their own home as well as in hospitals, health centres and doctors' surgeries. The services provided in the community are often based at a health centre or surgery and are carried out by primary health care teams. Services can also be provided by a community health care trust attached to a hospital.

Read the case study to find out about the health care that Nell receives.

You may have identified these services in the case study:

* district nurse
* physiotherapist
* hospital transport
* day hospital nurse.

These are all community services.

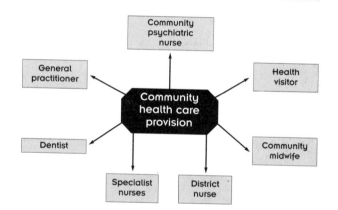

Many other community services can be provided for people who need them. For example, Nell's neighbour Julie recently had a baby and is suffering from postnatal depression. She told Nell that she was crying all the time but has been feeling much better since a community psychiatric nurse started visiting regularly to help with her medication and problems.

CASE STUDY – Nell

Nell is 79 years of age. She lives by herself with her two cats. She has very bad arthritis and leg ulcers that will not heal up. She cannot get around much by herself. Once a day she is visited by a district nurse who treats her leg ulcers and gives her a weekly vitamin injection.

Every evening a care worker comes at about seven o'clock to help her wash and get changed for bed. She also makes sure that Nell has remembered to take her tablets. On Wednesdays Nell is taken by hospital transport to the day centre at the local community hospital. A physiotherapist helps her with exercises to keep her joints mobile. She has lunch with her friends and really looks forward to the day.

The nurse at the day hospital always has a chat with Nell to make sure that everything is going well at home.

Question

From this case study you can see that Nell receives a wide variety of services. What are they and who provides them?

Look it up

Working with another person find out how the community services are provided in your area. Is the service attached to a local hospital trust or is it part of the service provided from primary care teams? Make notes for your portfolio of your findings.

Health services for people with disability

People who have physical or learning disabilities require the kind of care that enables them to live as full a life as possible. We need a wide range of services for these people. Primary health care teams and community services, as well as hospitals, often provide these services. The kinds of service you might come across are:

- Supported community living – people with special needs sharing a house in the local community and being supported by health care workers.

Talk it over

Maureen and Andrew both have physical disabilities. They have been married for four years and without the help of the community nursing service they would have had to be separated long ago.

They both need to have medication every day. Maureen has been catheterised and this needs to be changed regularly. A nurse helps with their personal hygiene routines and helps them to prepare for bed last thing at night. A care worker also attends during the day to make sure that everything is all right.

Working with another person discuss the support being provided to Maureen and Andrew by the health service. What are the benefits to Maureen and Andrew of this service?

- Day care centres – often based in local hospitals, providing, for example, assessment, treatment and occupational therapy.

- Hospital care – to treat specific illness or disability.

- Home care – medical care provided in the home to allow the client the opportunity to stay within their own community.

Personal social services

The main purpose of personal social services is to provide personal welfare and support to clients who need it. Some clients will not have health problems but will need help with personal things, such as cleaning their home, preparing meals or transport. The government pays for the work of social services in the same way that it pays for health services. The money is collected through taxes and handed out to local authorities. In each area the local authority or county council runs the social services department for the local people. They are able to offer a wide range of services, such as:

- residential care
- day care centres
- fostering and adoption
- domiciliary (home care)
- support groups and voluntary groups
- charitable groups.

Social service departments have a 'duty to care'. This means that it is part of their statutory work to provide care and assistance for those people who need their support, such as older people, people with learning disabilities, children and people with mental or physical disabilities.

Social services have a legal duty to purchase (buy) the services that a client might need to support them. They have to buy the service required from the public services, for example the NHS, voluntary services or private companies. An example of services purchased is long-term nursing care or residential care for older people with health care needs, who cannot be cared for in their own home.

Residential care services

In social care services the term 'residential' often means a client living in a care home with other people. This could be a residential home where care workers are on duty at all times.

The social services and the independent sector (private business) provide residential services. Residential care is also provided by charitable groups. There are wide ranges of people who live in residential care homes. For example:

- older people who can no longer care for themselves

- people with physical disabilities who need practical help with moving, eating and dressing

- children with no carers – e.g, children whose parents have died or cannot care for them

- people with learning disabilities who need support managing their own lives.

CASE STUDY – A residential home for older people

Hello, my name is Cath and I am a care worker at a residential home for older people. I only work 15 hours a week because I am also a student at my local college. When I go into work first thing in the morning, the night duty staff tell me about our residents and what sort of night they have had. They tell me if Mrs Hall has not been able to sleep or if Mr Bancroft had a good night out with his daughter. They make sure that all the clients' records are up to date before they leave duty.

The first thing I have to do is awaken the clients I work with. Sometimes I find Mary already up and dressed (usually waiting for her breakfast!). I always have to help George. He can't get out of bed easily, so with the help of other staff, I use the hoist to get him up and on to his favourite chair. Some of my clients eat their breakfast in bed if they are not feeling too well. If this is the case then I take them their breakfast.

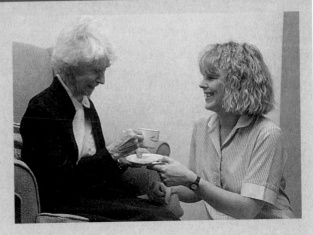

Activities

1 Identify three ways in which Cath helps her clients.

2 Identify the differences for the clients living in residential care compared with living in their own homes. Why do you think somebody might need to go into residential care?

Long-term care homes	Most long-term care homes are for older people, although some exist for children and people with severe mental health needs or learning disabilities.
Short-term care (respite) homes	This kind of care is often for clients who need care all the time and usually live at home with their carer. Respite care allows the carer to have a short break or holiday from the caring role they are doing every day.
Short-stay care homes	These are different to respite care homes because the service they offer is different. Very often short-term care homes are used to assess an individual client to help identify their personal and social care needs. This helps the personal social services plan the help the client will need with daily living when they go home.

Residential care is different for different people. The table shows the main differences in residential care.

Sheltered accommodation

There is also another kind of residential care. This is sheltered housing. Clients live independently in their own home (rented or purchased) and help is immediately available if they need it. A warden is on duty at all times. Their job is to make sure that the clients are safe and well. The clients are also encouraged to join in with a range of social activities that are planned and provided for them, usually by the residents and warden of the accommodation.

Clients do not have to join in unless they want to. They are still completely independent and make their own choices about their lives.

Talk it over

Doreen has been on the social service waiting list for 12 months for a sheltered home. She fell and broke her hip last year and has felt unsafe in her own home since.

She went to visit four different sheltered home complexes, in different areas of her town. The first one she saw was 10 small separate bungalows built in a square around a small garden. The second one was a row of small terraced cottages all connected to each other. When she had seen the others she had to select the two she liked the best.

She has just received a letter to say that a small bungalow in the square has become available (her first choice). She is delighted.

Although she has only one bedroom, her family can still come to stay because there is a guest's room attached to the complex. All the residents take turns in letting family members use it.

Discuss with another person the benefits to Doreen of living in sheltered accommodation. How important do you think the visitor's accommodation is? What kind of a difference will living there make to Doreen's life?

Day care services

You have read about day care centres provided by the health service in the case study about Nell on page 7. Day care services are also run by the social services. The main purpose is to provide social support for the client, not to provide medical treatment and health care. Social support can include:

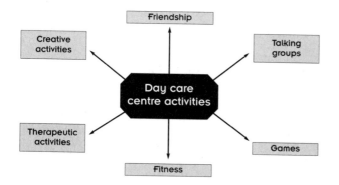

Day care centres can provide a range of activities

Day care centres are very important in the lives of many older clients or those with special support needs. Often clients are collected from their own homes or residential homes and taken to the day care centres in minibuses run by social services or voluntary groups.

Look it up

Find out what the word 'therapeutic' means. Make a note in your portfolio of your findings.

Day centres for people with learning disabilities

These have a range of supporting activities for their clients. Read the case of Stephen to get an idea of what this might mean for him.

CASE STUDY — Winston

Winston is 83 years old. Two years ago his wife died and his children have long since grown up and moved away. He now lives alone and can manage his own cooking and shopping. But he gets lonely. 'I don't need no help', he says, 'but I like to meet people now and then'.

Winston's social worker has arranged for him to go to the local day centre twice a week from 10am to 3pm. There Winston plays cards with friends, listens to music and has a hot lunch. 'I'm much happier now', says Winston. 'But I lost £3 to that Jack Thompson playing canasta last week.'

Questions

1   Why do you think Winston was lonely?

2   Why do you think the day care centre might be an important service?

Talk it over

Stephen is 17 years of age and has Down's syndrome. He lives at home with his parents. Every day he takes the bus to the Woodlands Centre, five kilometres from where he lives. At Woodlands he is able to take part in a range of sporting and recreation activities, which he thoroughly enjoys.

These include horse riding at the local riding centre. Stephen is also part of the horticulture group, which raises plants for sale at a garden fair twice a year. The money they raise helps to pay for extra facilities the centre needs.

Each day a group of the clients at the centre work out a menu for lunch and then walk to the super-market to buy the ingredients. Then with the support of one of their carers they cook lunch for everyone.

Stephen is also learning computer skills. This is very useful as he has his own computer at home.

Working with another person discuss the services that are available to Stephen at this centre. How does each service help Stephen achieve a better standard of life? Make notes of your discussions for your portfolio.

Talk it over

Ahmed has been 'Statemented', which means his learning needs have been identified.

He lives at home with his parents and attends primary school along with all his friends.

His learning disability means that he needs extra help with his speech, reading, writing and sometimes his behaviour. He has been given some help in the classroom but the education authorities feel that he could benefit from attending a day centre where he could be given one-to-one tuition without any distractions. He will also be able to spend some time with an educational psychologist.

He is looking forward to going, as long as it is just for one day a week.

Discuss with another person why Ahmed might benefit from attending the day care centre. Why do you think he is keen not to increase his attendance at the day centre to more than one day per week? Make notes for your portfolio.

Foster care and adoption

Fostering can be divided into three kinds:

- short-term fostering
- long-term fostering
- teenage fostering.

A child or teenager is usually fostered in someone else's home because the social services and sometimes the parents or carers believe there is a need for help. This can be because:

- the child's parents or carer is ill or unable to look after the child and there is no one else to care for them
- the child has been abused in some way (either physically or mentally)
- the child has been neglected.

Foster parents are paid for looking after a child or teenager. The money is used to support the child with clothes and other expenses. The foster parents take only a small amount to cover the cost of their caring

work. Very often a child is able to return home after a period of time. Occasionally, a child will never return home. This can be for a variety of reasons. Instead a child may be adopted (this means living with someone else permanently), sometimes by the foster family.

Look it up

- Find out about legislation called The Foster Placement (Children) Regulations, 1991. In groups make notes of your findings. How will this legislation help to safeguard children in foster care?

- Working with another person find out which organisations might help foster parents with special training in the care of children with disabilities. A good place to start is with the library.

Talk it over

Mike and Janet have decided to foster children now that their own three children have grown up and left home. They feel that they would like to help other people who have difficulties with their own children.

They have applied to social services to become foster parents. They are undergoing checks to make sure that they are suitable as carers of young children.

If they are accepted as foster parents, a voluntary organisation has offered them special training on how to care for children with disabilities.

Discuss with another person the importance of social services checking the suitability of people who want to become foster carers. Make notes for your portfolio.

Talk it over

Mina is seven years old and lives with her mother in a small village in Cumbria. She attends the local primary school with her friends.

Her mother has just been told that she has to go into hospital for a major operation but should be home again in about two weeks. Her next door neighbour has said that she will look after Mina while she is in hospital.

After Mina's mother had the operation she was too poorly to come straight home, so the hospital staff arranged for her to go to another hospital, called a convalescence home, to rest and build up her strength again.

Unfortunately Mina's next door neighbour could not look after Mina any longer because they had arranged to go on holiday, so they had to ask social services to find a foster home for Mina until her mother came home.

In pairs use the case of Mina to help discuss some of the possible reasons why a child might not be able to return home after being placed in foster care.

Domiciliary care

Domiciliary care is care that is provided in the client's own home. This can include:

- help with personal hygiene – e.g. bathing, dressing and using the toilet.

- household care and cleaning

- transport

- shopping.

The availability of these services usually varies from one place to another. It often depends on the amount of money the social services has to spend on client care. In some

Try it out

Can you find a person who uses any of the above domiciliary services? Perhaps you could ask them about the kind of help they get and who does the work. You could write your own case study and share it with other members of the group.

places clients are asked to contribute a small amount to the cost of the service provided.

Look it up

Find out who the disability living allowance is for and how it is usually spent. Make notes for your portfolio. Remember that some clients are asked to make a financial contribution to the cost of their home care.

Talk it over

Violet is 28 years old. She has recently moved into her own flat for the first time. She is a wheelchair user with some loss of mobility in her neck and shoulders.

She has a computer, which means that she can work from home for the company who has employed her for the last 10 years.

She needs extra support because of her disabilities. Her care worker visits every day and helps to clean those parts of the flat that Violet cannot reach very easily.

The care worker also collects Violet's disability living allowance while she is out doing her shopping.

Transport can be made available for Violet when she wants to go visiting her friends and family, but she has to organise this ahead of the time it is needed.

Discuss with another person the services that Violet is using in her own home. Make a list of them for your portfolio.

Support groups and voluntary groups

Support groups

Support groups are groups set up by individuals to give mutual support through difficult times. They may react to a particular local disaster or tragedy, or they may give more long-term support, such as helping support carers of people with Alzheimer's disease, or mental health problems, or chronic diseases, such as motor neurone disease. Support may also come from friends, family or professionals such as nurses, doctors or counsellors.

Here is an example of a support group advertising its presence to those who might need them. This notice was put up in the entrance of the outpatient department of the local NHS Mental Health Care Trust.

> ## Are you a relative, friend or carer of someone suffering from depression?
>
> *Yellow Room Support Group*
>
> We are a support group who meet in the Yellow Room (Room D105) every Thursday evening 7–9 pm. We discuss problems and solutions. Please feel welcome to join us – you don't have to come regularly, but we would love to meet you. Contact Jenny on 01966-815712 x233 for more information. Tea, coffee, soft drinks available.

Wider support organisations include:

- Citizens Advice Bureau, which provides free information on a range of personal and legal issues.

- Relate, which provides guidance for people undergoing difficulties within a marriage or partnership.

- British Red Cross, which can provide information, equipment and even occasional 'sit in' volunteers, and help people deal with physical and emotional problems of caring.

- Samaritans, who provide telephone guidance, in strict confidence, for people in distress.

- Gingerbread, a national organisation whose principal aim is to support one-parent families.

- Childline, a confidential telephone helpline for children in distress or seeking advice.

Some support organisations are local but might have links to a wider organisation. For example, the Yellow Room Support Group possibly has links with a national mental health charity such as MIND.

> **Think it over**
>
> In what other situations could people benefit from a support group being formed? Think about certain diseases or illnesses or even about accidents and crises that families and individuals can experience. Make a note of some you have heard of.

Voluntary groups

The voluntary sector (area) is that part of the health and social care services that are provided by voluntary organisations or groups. These groups are not paid for by the government, but by donations from the public. A voluntary organisation however might apply to the government (or the lottery fund) for a grant to help them provide more services to the public and their client groups.

Voluntary groups often have a leader or manager who runs the group and organises the different jobs for the volunteers to do. Sometimes groups have staff who are paid to carry out certain jobs – for example, administration and office work. However most

> **Think it over**
>
> Lizzie is homeless. She has been on the streets since she was 64 years old. She is now 72 and still plans to stay on the streets. She has no intention of being put in an 'old biddies' home.
>
> She is well known at the Salvation Army, where she sometimes goes for a hot meal and a bed for the night. She has also used the facilities at a Shelter hostel, where she can get a bed for several nights.
>
> The Night Safe worker often visits her when she is curled up in a shop doorway, to see if she wants a hot drink or a blanket for the night.
>
> *Name the three organisations involved in the care of Lizzie whilst she is on the streets of London. Make a note of them for your portfolio. Find out if you have a similar voluntary organisation in your area.*

Think it over

Ronnie is 68 years old and has just had a liver transplant. He is in hospital in a specialist centre in Leeds. His wife lives over 60 kilometres away and cannot drive.

The Wheels for Support group have been organising voluntary drivers to take Hilda to Leeds every day so that she can visit Ronnie in hospital. She is so grateful to them.

What would have been the effects on Ronnie and Hilda if this voluntary group had not existed?

of the people who work in a voluntary group give their time and effort free of charge. They want to use some of the time they have available to help those who need support.

Many voluntary organisations provide practical help, such as sitting services, respite care, cleaning and shopping assistance, as well as transport for people who need help to get around.

Voluntary organisations do not try to make money (profits) out of what they do, however they do need money to run their services. Sometimes they apply for lottery grants and sometimes they request funds from the personal social service or the health service. Most of their money however comes from fund-raising events.

Talk it over

What kinds of voluntary service have you got in your area? You could use the Internet to find out or ask at your local library.

Charitable groups

Some voluntary groups become charitable organisations (sometimes called Foundations) with large paid staffs and many volunteers. They provide practical help and assistance to the people who use their services.

Money comes from donations, fund-raising events and often grants from the health and personal social services. Some of the charitable voluntary organisations that you know of could include:

- Age Concern
- MIND
- Kidscape
- Mencap
- NSPCC.

Try it out

Working with another person choose one of the organisations listed and find out as much as you can about the way they work. Try and collect information about the way the service is paid for and who the main client groups are.

Early years services

The early years service provides care and support for children under eight years of age. A wide range of services is available to the children and their parents or carers – for example, care of the children while parents are working. Social services, the private sector and voluntary groups all offer the services provided. Here are some examples of early years services.

- Day nurseries
- Nursery education
- Playgroups
- Child minders
- Nannies
- After school and holiday care
- Early years education.

In 1996 the government identified six desirable learning outcomes for children aged under five. Each of the early years services should be working towards these outcomes to help the child grow fully in all parts of its development. The areas the government identified for action are:

- language and literacy
- maths and numeracy
- creativity
- knowledge of the world
- personal and social development
- physical development.

Now that we know the areas of growth and development required for children aged under five years, we can explore those services that help to provide that care and support.

Day nurseries

Day nurseries usually provide care for children not old enough to attend school, whose parents or carers are out at work all day. The opening hours of nurseries varies, with some open for as much as 12 hours a day.

Child minders

A child minder looks after children in their own home. The parents pay them for the service. Child minders must be registered by social services and often have training and qualifications in child care, such as NVQ Level 2 in Care.

Talk it over

Sophie is 18 months old. Every morning, Monday to Friday, she is taken to the Sticky Fingers nursery owned by Mrs Bancroft. She arrives at 7.30am so that her parents can leave and get to work on time.

Sophie has her breakfast in the nursery and her lunch and evening meal because her parents cannot collect her until 6.00pm.

Sophie's parents pay £80.00 per week for her nursery care, but don't mind the cost because they know that qualified nursery nurses are caring for Sophie.

Sophie is learning so much by being with other children. She is beginning to play with the other children as well as joining in with the painting activities organised by the nursery nurses.

Discuss with another person the following:

1　Is the nursery privately owned or not?

2　What kind of service is being offered to Sophie and her parents?

3　What are the benefits to Sophie and her parents of using the nursery provision?

4　How are the activities organised by the nursery contributing to the desirable learning outcomes?

Try it out Working with another person try to find someone who is a child minder and interview them about their work. Include the rules and regulations that apply to child minding and the sort of qualifications a child minder might need. Make notes of your findings for your portfolio.

Talk it over

Elaine has three children in her care. She looks after Ben who is four years old and attends nursery school every afternoon, Monday to Friday. She makes sure that he is taken there and collected again. She also looks after Rachael who is only six months old. She cares for her all day. She feeds her and cares for all her personal needs.

The third child, Rahima, is seven years old, so she only stays with Elaine in the early morning (before school starts) and again when school has finished. She has her breakfast before she comes and eats her evening meal at home with her parents.

Discuss with another person the caring role that Elaine has for each of the children. What kind of support is she providing for their parents?

Playgroups

A playgroup is held in either a morning or an afternoon (or sometimes both). They are for children aged between three and five. They are provided and run by voluntary workers, often parents of some of the children, who are supported by trained workers. Children have a good range of play and learning opportunities and learn to mix with other children. It prepares them for when they start school. Parents pay for the service.

Talk it over

Victoria attends the Mill Hill playgroup two afternoons per week. She starts at 1.00pm and finishes at 3.00pm. She loves going.

There is a sand pit full of sand, and buckets, spades and other plastic toys. Some days the play leader puts out the water tank, which means that Victoria can play with bottles and tubes and pipes.

At about 2.30pm the children all sit down for a drink and a biscuit. Singing and story time follow this activity. Victoria's favourite song is the one about the 'wheels on the bus go round and round'.

When her mum comes to collect her Victoria usually does not want to go home.

Victoria's paintings cover the walls at home and models made from cardboard boxes and tubes are on every available shelf.

Working with another person identify the different activities carried out by Victoria on her two half days per week. What are the benefits to Victoria and her parents of attending play school? How do Victoria's activities contribute to the desirable learning outcomes?

Try it out Working with another person try and arrange a visit to a play school in your area. Make notes of the activities that the children participate in. You could present your findings to the rest of the group.

Nannies

A nanny is employed by parents to care for a child or children in the family home. They commonly work a 9–10 hour day. Some nannies 'live in', especially in London, and do some work on a daily basis. There is no limit as to how many children a nanny can look after, however a maximum of three under school age is advisable. A nanny's job description is known as 'Nursery Duties': personal care and feeding of the children, children's laundry, keeping the children's bedrooms, playroom etc. clean and tidy, organising a routine and activities to promote good physical, intellectual, emotional and social development. It is also a nanny's job to liaise between parents, school, pre-school, health visitor and others, and to keep a log of the children's day.

After school and holiday care

After-school clubs look after children over the age of five after school has finished during term time. Holiday clubs or playwork centres offer activities and care for children between the ages of 5 and 15 during the school holidays. Both are staffed by trained workers who may be nursery nurses or playworkers.

The main purpose of these early years services is to provide children with the best possible 'start in life'. Some experts think that it is never too early for a child to start their learning and education experiences.

Early years education services

Schools

The local education authority provides most of the schools in a community. Some nursery schools however are provided by a private organisation or by local churches. Nursery schools provide care and education from the ages of three to five. Children must start infant or primary school in the term after their fifth birthday. The children are taught by qualified teachers and they follow the 'Early Learning' goals which provide guidelines as to what children should learn to do at the ages of three, four and five. Children learn music, songs and dance, and about water and outdoor play and painting and modelling.

SNAPSHOT

Leonard is attending nursery school. He feels very grown up because he is going to the same school as his big sister who is eight years old.

When he comes home he has to practice writing his name in his workbook. He calls it his homework because he likes to think that he is doing the same kind of school work as his sister.

By the time he moves up a class he will have to be able to write his name using his letters properly.

Think it over Discuss with another person how learning about play, music, dance and songs can help children learn about the world around them.

Schools for children with specific needs

Some children have specific learning needs that cannot be met in the usual school environment. In these cases children can attend schools that will help them develop necessary skills at their own pace. These schools have specially trained staff to assist the children with their learning and development.

Read the case of Mirriam to get some idea of the provision offered to a child with special needs.

Talk it over

Miriam is six years old and attends a special school for children with cerebral palsy. At the school the toys and equipment she uses are especially adapted so that she can play with them easily. The jigsaws are big and bright with chunky pieces. Miriam also takes part in a music group every morning, using the instruments helps with her co-ordination. Miriam has a special chair at school which supports her body whilst she is sitting down. She does most of her work from the supported chair.

The school has a swimming pool which the children use every day. This helps them with their mobility as well as being lots of fun.

A physiotherapist and an occupational therapist visit the school and the children twice a week to help organise therapeutic activities for them.

Working with another person identify the differences between the special school and a mainstream school for children of Miriam's age.

1.2 Main jobs in health and social care services

There are many different jobs in health and social care settings. Probably too many to deal with in this book! We are going to explore some of the main jobs that you might be interested in finding out more about.

There are three main groups of care workers in health and social care services. These are known as:

- direct carers (provide care straight to the client)
- indirect carers (provide a service to the direct carers in order to benefit the client)
- informal carers (usually relatives or friends of the client).

Direct care

Nurses

All nurses share the same basic training and can work in a wide range of care settings. Some work on hospital wards or hospital departments, others work in doctors' surgeries or health centres. The two Snapshots give you some idea of the variety of roles in nursing.

SNAPSHOT

Nursing in a busy GP practice

Pen is a practice nurse working for Dr Murray in a large GP practice. Her days are very full. These are some of the nursing activities she carried out yesterday.

1   *She vaccinated two students going on holiday to Africa.*

2   *She removed the stitches from Lynda's cut arm and advised her to keep it covered for two days to keep it free from infection.*

3   *She weighed and took the blood pressure of Mike who is in his 40s and at risk of developing coronary heart disease.*

4   *She took some blood to test a patient for glandular fever.*

5   *She did a routine cervical smear for Jasmine who is 37.*

6   *She attended the practice team meeting with GPs to discuss the new computer system.*

7   *She completed patient records at the end of each consultation.*

8   *Between 4 and 5.30pm she held a diabetic clinic to monitor and provide advice to her clients.*

9   *Discussed with a young couple their contraceptive needs.*

SNAPSHOT

Nursing in a busy hospital ward

Serge is a fully qualified nurse on a busy medical ward at his local teaching hospital. When he arrives at work he meets with the other nurses to discuss the care given to the patients during the night. He is part of the Blue Team and has responsibility for a certain number of patients. This morning he will be caring for six patients but will have a care assistant to help him.

First, he gives tablets, which have been prescribed by the doctor, to each patient, and makes sure that each of them has had breakfast. His first priority is to care for Mr Desai who has a chest infection and needs particular care with his breathing.

After he is satisfied that Mr Desai is comfortable and has easy access to his oxygen mask, if he needs it, he checks the drip on Mr Smith. Mr Smith has had diarrhoea and vomiting for three days and needs extra fluids regularly.

As Mr Smith is quite weak Serge decides to give him a bed bath with the help of the care assistant.

Think it over

Lillian is 86 years old and lives alone. She recently developed leg ulcers that will not heal. She is being visited by a district nurse, who comes to check the ulcers and change the dressings every day.

Lillian looks forward to the nurse coming. She always has a cup of tea ready for her and welcomes a chat to break the monotony of the day.

What caring role is this nurse providing to Lillian? Think about more than just medical care!

Try it out

Think about the nurses in the Snapshots and others that you have come into contact with either as a patient or as a care worker. What kind of activities do they do as part of their role? Make a list of job roles for your portfolio.

Doctors

Doctors all have the same basic training before they go on to specialise in different aspects of medicine. Part of a doctor's job is to diagnose (identify) the illness a client is suffering from or to reassure them there is nothing wrong!

When treatment is required a doctor has a wide range of tasks to perform, depending on their role.

- **Oncologist** – cancer specialist.
- **Cardiologist** – heart specialist.
- **Surgeon** – performs operations.
- **Pathologist** – examines blood and tissue specimens and provides a diagnosis.

These specialists usually work in a hospital.

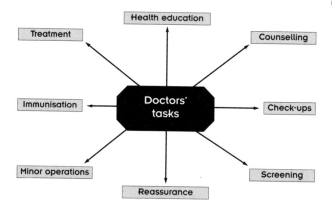

Think it over

Shanaz is four months old. It is time for her visit to the doctor for a check up and her next immunisation treatment.

Her father has prepared her for the visit. Because she has to be weighed he has dressed her in easily removable clothing. He is not looking forward to her being immunised. Last time she cried for ages.

What is the doctor's role in this case? Find out what the immunisation is for a child of 16 weeks. Make a note of your findings for your portfolio.

Talk it over

Dr Minski is very busy. He has to see 30 patients before 11.00am. Barbara has made an appointment to see him today. As soon as the doctor sees her name he knows that he will have to spend a great deal of time with her.

Barbara is suffering from mental illness that means her confidence is very low and she always worries about her ability to cope with everyday life situations. This has resulted in panic attacks.

Sometimes the nurse sees Barbara but today she wants to talk to the doctor about her panic attacks in case there is something seriously wrong with her physical health.

Working with another person identify the major roles that Dr Minski has to carry out to provide a good standard of care for Barbara. Make a list of them for your portfolio.

The doctor that most patients see first is the general practitioner (GP), who works in a local surgery or health centre. Depending on their needs, the patient may be referred to one of a number of specialists. Here are some examples:

- **Paediatrician** – specialises in children's diseases.

Occupational therapists

Occupational therapists work in hospitals, day centres, the community and sometimes for the social services and the voluntary sector. They are trained to provide specific activities to help people who have had an accident or illness to recover full strength and use of their bodies. They may choose to specialise in either the physical care or the mental health care of clients. In some cases occupational therapists work in both physical and mental health care.

The main aim of an occupational therapist is to help their clients to live as independently as possible. Once qualified, they provide a wide range of services to their clients that will help them to meet this aim. For example, if there was an occupational therapist available in the day centre to work with Nell (see page 7) she would have devised ways of getting Nell's hands mobile, for example by getting her to sew or make pottery.

An occupational therapist also identifies ways of making a client's home and life easier to manage. They might do this by identifying the sort of equipment and the kind of environment the client needs – for example, a client with hands which are stiff and painful might need special equipment to help with eating, dressing (doing up buttons) and so on.

Some of the jobs of an occupational therapist are:

* adaptations to the client's living environment

* organising equipment

* assessing need

* training for everyday living

* health and safety for clients before they go home after illness.

Social workers

Social workers are key workers who are trained to help people overcome personal, social and environmental problems so that they can live more satisfactory lives. They deal with a variety of family and community issues.

A social worker can be part of an area health team, dealing with several different families or individuals, or may work with groups of people in, for example, a child guidance clinic, or hospital or in the community with people in their own homes.

Talk it over

Anthony is a social worker specialising in the care of older people. His clients are referred by GPs, health visitors, the hospital and sometimes by friends and family of the older person.

Albert has been referred by a hospital to the social services department where Anthony works. Albert was in hospital being treated for an illness caused by drinking too much alcohol (alcohol abuse). Anthony plans to help Albert cut down on his drinking to avoid serious problems in the future.

Anthony knows that Albert has not claimed the benefits that he is entitled to and has been using his small savings to pay for his drinking instead of paying his bills and buying food. So he is going home to no electricity. Anthony is dealing with that before Albert goes home.

Anthony knows that Albert has a son and daughter somewhere but does not think they have much contact with their father.

Using the case above identify Anthony's role as Albert's social worker. Make a list of the roles involved.

(a) Light, thick-handled cutlery – people with arthritic hands will find these easy to hold

(e) A person who is frail, or who only has the use of one arm, will find it possible to carry several items at once on a non-slip tray with a handle

(b) An alternative to the feeding cup is to improvise with a glass with an angled straw or a teapot (not a metal one)

(f) Specially-designed gadgets exist to help with taking the lids off jars

(c) A feeding cup – remember that the liquid at the bottom is drunk first, so no tea leaves!

(g) Someone who only has the use of one hand will be able to butter bread or peel potatoes using a spiked board

(d) A person with the use of only one arm may find a deep bowl or a plate guard useful, especially when they are used with a combined knife and fork or a pusher spoon

Some of the aids clients may need

Care assistants

Care assistants work in hospitals, residential and nursing settings, and also in the community. Those who work in the community are also known as home care assistants. They are essential to the success of community care. They are key workers enabling many clients to live their lives in their own homes. Look at the job description for the care worker based in a hospital (page 24).

(page 24).

Talk it over

Read the job description for a care assistant at Anytown Hospital (page 24). Discuss the roles that the care assistant is expected to carry out.

- Look at the Person Specification.

- Why do you think the skills required are split into 'essential' and 'desirable'?

- Are you surprised by any of the information in the job description?

- Are you interested in applying?

Talk it over

Present your information back to the group before producing your own job description for a nursery nurse. Use the example included for care assistants to guide you.

Nursery nurses

Nursery nurses can be employed in:

- private homes as a nanny

- nursery schools

- children's residential homes

- schools in the reception year

- private day nurseries

- hospitals caring for sick children.

The main job roles of a nursery nurse are:

- helping to care for young children

- helping with hygiene routines

- providing early years education including planned play activities

- helping to develop independent skills in the child

- helping with language development

- helping children to learn to mix and play together.

Early years curriculum

As we have already said this is a government initiative to ensure that children at pre-school have an introduction to intellectual as well as social skills.

The areas included in the Early Learning curriculum are:

- language, literacy

- mathematical development

- creative development

- personal, social, emotional development

- knowledge and understanding of the world

- physical development.

Try it out

In pairs, can you match the Early Learning curriculum areas with the activities Jodie has outlined in the Snapshot on page 25? You might even be able to think of other activities Jodie has not mentioned which might be part of a pre-school playgroup you have visited.

Keep these notes for your portfolio.

ANYTOWN NHS HOSPITAL TRUST
ANYTOWN HOSPITAL
Job Description

Job title: Health Care Assistant
Salary grade: Grade A or equivalent
Department: Infectious Diseases Unit
Accountable to: Staff Nurse

Purpose

1 To assist nursing staff with direct patient care.

2 To keep the ward environment tidy and well maintained.

3 To provide administrative/technical/clerical support to the nursing team which will contribute to the efficiency and smooth running of the ward.

Specific responsibilities

Patient Care

1 To assist qualified nurses with the care of patients.

2 To carry out the following aspects of patient care under the direction and supervision of a registered nurse:

providing reassurance and comfort by establishing good relationships with the patient, family and friends whilst maintaining their dignity, privacy and confidence at all times, including social 'chat', especially for isolated patients

maintenance of patients' hygiene, including bathing of the patient in bed or in the bathroom, care of the skin, hair, mouth, eyes, hands and feet, care of clothing and assisting dressing

minimising the risk of pressure sores by relief of pressure through assisting the patient to change position or the use of mechanical aids or appliances

1

---

positioning of patients who are unable to help themselves by using the appropriate lifting and handling technique, including the use of mechanical aids

helping with elimination needs by giving and removing bedpans, urinals and commodes, assisting patients to walk to the toilet, assisting with the care of incontinent patients and recording urine output and bowel action

assisting with nutrition by helping patients into a comfortable position at meal and beverage times, feeding patients by mouth as needed, making drinks and snacks to supplement patients' diets, helping patients choose from the daily menu, recording fluid and food intake and distributing and collecting menus

assisting with the care of the dying and last offices

to observe the patient's condition and anxieties and feedback information to the nursing team, including formal observations of temperature, pulse and respirations

to escort patients within the hospital area when no nursing needs are identified which require a registered nurse.

Ward Environment

to keep patient lockers and other furniture surfaces in the ward clean and tidy

to keep the relatives' kitchen and bedroom clean and tidy

to be responsible for general bed-making, including stripping, cleaning and remaking beds of discharged patients, and preparing for the admission of new patients

to keep the ward storage areas clean, tidy and appropriately stocked

to check, clean and store equipment, ensuring faulty equipment is reported

to be aware of and comply with the relevant Trust, Clinical Centre and SDU policies

to assist with relocating patients and their belongings within the ward area.

2

Support for the Nursing team

to answer the telephone and take messages when the ward clerk is not available

to be available to collect and deliver ward equipment and pharmacy within the hospital as necessary

to undertake specific administrative tasks as delegated by the qualified staff, including ordering of patients' transport

to contribute to the life and development of the ward, including the maintenance of a good working atmosphere.

Personal Development

to be aware of own limitations and seek assistance and guidance of a qualified nurse as appropriate

to participate in review of performance with the SDU Manager/Team Leader and negotiate development opportunities

to keep up to date with statutory study days.

To adhere to Anytown Hospital NHS Trust policies with regard to:

Minimal Manual Handling
Infection Control
COSHH
Fire and Accidents
Patients Property

3

PERSON SPECIFICATION
Health Care Assistant

The Employee	Essential	Desirable
Physical attributes	Good health record Good attendance record Neat and tidy appearance	
Education/Qualifications	General level of education	Potential to complete NVQ Level 1/ Foundation GNVQ Health and Social Care
Previous experience		Some experience of caring in any setting
Personal characteristics	Positive and enthusiastic Friendly personality Hard working Reliable and punctual Flexible and adaptable Non-judgmental Good sense of humour	
Special aptitudes	Good communication skills – written and verbal Willing to learn Willing to accept constructive criticism Ability to organise own work load Ability to work within a team Aware of own limitations Tolerance of others' limitations Good telephone manner	

SNAPSHOT

Jodie, Nursery Nurse at Riverside Nursery

Hi, I'm Jodie, and I work at Riverside Playgroup. I qualified last year, and this is my first job. I work with children in the 3–4 years group. There are eight at the moment. My title is Nursery Nurse.

We usually start the day with a song, and then I set up activities for them to do. We have a theme each month: it is autumn colours this month (September), so we do lots of work on colour, trees, season changes, and songs and stories with the theme of autumn.

I have one structured activity in the morning, so the children will all be able to take something home. Today it was bubble painting with autumn colours – I had to make sure they 'blew' the paint not drink it up!

I have a sort of checklist to help me make sure we cover a range of activities over a two-week period. These activities include:

- *creative and imaginative play – daily*

- *something with music or song – daily*

- *stories – daily*

- *a chance for the children to each contribute to a group talk about something they have done – daily*

- *outside play – daily, unless it's really very wet or dangerously cold or icy*

- *visits or trips out – possibly once a month. It might be a simple trip down to feed the ducks, or it might be a bigger expedition when parents come too.*

- *we also look at the Calendar of Festivals, because we have lots of children of different ethnic groups*

- *natural play, with stones, sand, leaves.*

- *home corner – we change parts of it regularly, but keep in favourites like cooking, animals, dressing up clothes*

- *water play*

- *cooking – once a week*

So you can see, it is important to give the children a wide variety of activities. Most of the activities can be included in the Early Learning curriculum. We have fun!! The children are always curious, and are great to be with. I am tired at the end of the day, though.

Indirect care

Indirect care workers often provide the support that direct care workers need to carry out their job effectively. This support also helps the client with the services they need. For example, a laboratory technician who tests blood is helping the client and their doctor to find out what is wrong with them.

Laboratory technicians

Laboratory technicians work under the supervision of a pathologist (a doctor who specialises in identifying disease). The laboratory technician helps the pathologist to identify which bacteria, virus or fungi has caused the disease.

Laboratory technicians work in special laboratories usually located in a hospital. They are specially trained to carry out this important work. They test samples of blood, body tissue, cells or body fluids taken from the client. The laboratory technician's work usually involves:

- performing scientific tests on the samples

- using the results of the test to identify the disease or illness

- following strict health and safety regulations

- keeping accurate records of everything they do

- recording accurate results of tests

- reporting their findings to the appropriate health care professional.

Catering assistants

The catering staff in health and social care settings are usually well trained and qualified in food hygiene. Because they have to make up special diets for clients they have to know about different food groups and their effects on the human body. It is important that catering staff understand how their service can affect clients who are in hospital or in need of special care. For example, poorly presented food will not encourage a sick person to eat and food that is contaminated with harmful bacteria could make their condition worse.

Their work is wide and varied and includes:

- cooking food to meet the needs of different religious groups

- cooking food to meet the needs of special diets

- making sure food does not lose its vitamins and minerals by overcooking it

- providing meals that are well balanced and look attractive

- delivering food to different areas of their working environment

- providing a food service to relatives who are staying in the care centre

- following good hygiene practice

- following safe food storage practices.

Informal carers

This is care carried out by people who have had no training in health and social care work. They are usually looking after a friend, neighbour or relative who is in need of extra care. They are not paid a wage for the work they do.

An informal carer is identified and acknowledged by social services as caring for

Think it over

Trisha is an active 18-year-old girl who is a wheelchair user. She attends college full time doing a health and social care course. She lives in a self-contained flat on her own. But the flat is next to her parents' house.

She loves going to the weekly disco in her local town but needs help getting there. Claire and Pooja are her best friends and they regularly collect her on a Friday night to take her with them to the disco.

Claire and Pooja can be classed as informal carers. Why do you think this is?

more than 20 hours a week. They can get help and support for themselves and the person they are caring for.

Most of us have carried out some kind of informal care by the time we are 16 years of age. For example, making a meal for a younger brother or sister, cleaning or shopping for an older grandparent, or looking after someone with the flu.

> **Think it over**
> What kind of informal care have you provided at some time in your life? How long did you do this for, who was it for and did you enjoy it?

> **Think it over**
> Before you look at the care value base, as outlined in this unit, take some time to write down what you might expect from a carer. You might like to use an experience you or someone you know have had (it does not have to be a good experience!) to prompt your ideas. Write them down so you can refer to them later in this section.

1.3 The care value base

All of us who work in health and social care need to develop a set of principles of good practice to help us to give the kind of care each individual client or patient requires. These principles are called the care value base. They describe the kind of attitude towards care that you would appreciate if you were being cared for as a patient or client.

The main basis for the care value base is showing respect for each person as an individual. Care workers also have a responsibility to show respect towards other members of the care team with whom they are working.

Respect in practice

When you work in care you are working with people who may be ill, who may have problems in their personal lives, or who may simply need your help and support. It is particularly important for these people to be respected, even if they may sometimes make life difficult for their carers! Respect takes many different forms. Look at the example in the picture.

Respect for a client is the essential part of caring. If a carer cannot demonstrate this, then they may be in the wrong job! A carer should be able to put aside their own attitudes when caring for others, if that attitude gets in the way of caring with respect.

The principles of the care value base

In the early 1990s, a group of professional care workers met to decide what kind of care values all care workers should bring to their work. These values include all of those on the spidergram, and several more. Carers who work with these values in mind not only give clients the respect they deserve, but also help clients to have confidence and trust in all care workers.

The care value base has three main parts.

1 Making sure that the services promote and foster people's rights and responsibilities

This means that the service provider (e.g. health or social services) has a responsibility to make sure that clients know about the services available to them. They must also help clients to have access to the services and make sure that any problems clients have in obtaining these services are sorted out.

Each carer also has a responsibility to make sure that their client is able to continue having the care they need for as long as they need it.

2 Supporting and promoting equality and diversity

All clients should be given the care they need according to their individual health and care requirements. That is, everyone should have an equal opportunity to receive care and support, no matter their colour, age, sex (male or female), culture or religion, whether they have a particular kind of illness or not (for example AIDS), or whether they have a disability.

3 Maintaining the confidentiality of information

Keeping information confidential – i.e. not telling others what people tell you about themselves – is a very important part of care. It enables your client to trust you and have confidence in you as their carer. Your relationship with your client depends on this.

Sometimes you may have to tell a more senior worker or manager about information you

receive, for example when you believe that a client or other people are at risk. This is the only time when you should pass on confidential information.

Think it over

Nan and her friend Jack are waiting to see the physiotherapist at the local health centre when two staff came in having a loud conversation about one of their clients. Nan knew the client – she was the friend of her neighbour. The staff talked about personal matters relating to the client's family. They were now standing by Nan and Jack, and although Nan 'coughed' to let them know they were there, the staff members just kept on talking.

Nan said later that she had to walk away because she felt so embarrassed.

Think it over

Samina was taken into respite care for two weeks. She asked her carer for a private place to pray during the day. She explained that she would need to use the prayer place at least three times during the day. She was happy to use her bedroom in the morning and again at night, but she could not get back to her room without help.

The carer found her a quiet room and always came back to Samina in time to help her get to the prayer room.

Think it over

Ted is just about to be discharged from hospital after having had a hip replacement. He is quite worried because he doesn't know how he will cope, and no-one has had time to talk to him. His wife is quite active, but he doesn't want her rushing around after him. The nurse who is packing up his belongings notices that he seems worried. When she asks him what the problem is, he explains his concerns. The nurse realises that for some reason Ted was not given the discharge advice which is usual after an operation. She then spends time with Ted explaining everything to him and uses a booklet with illustrations to help her. Ted is much less worried now and feels confident that he will cope at home.

Try it out

In pairs, read the following three cases, each one describing a situation that relates to the care value base. Match each case to the value base represented.

1.4 How people can gain access to and use the services

Referral

Clients can gain access to the health and care services they need in a variety of ways. For example, they can arrange an appointment with the doctor themselves, or a health worker or a family member can do it for them. Whichever way the client receives the service, it is called a 'referral'.

There are three kinds of referral:

- the client goes to the service themselves (self-referral)

- a professional sends them to the service (professional referral)

Talk it over

Jim lives alone in his two-bedroomed bungalow. Since his wife died last year he has not been able to cook and clean very well for himself.

He has a very good neighbour, Mrs Parker, who often calls in and gives him a meal that she has made for him whilst cooking for her own family.

The last time Mrs Parker visited Jim she noticed that he was looking poorly and he said that he thought he had a chill coming on. When she visited yesterday, he was in bed coughing, his breathing was very noisy and seemed to be hard work for him.

She went home and called his doctor.

Working in pairs discuss the case of Jim. What kind of referral is being used?

Think it over When you visit the dentist what sort of referral are you using? Does it depend on who makes the appointment – yourself or another person?

Talk it over

Mrs Shah was worried about her legs. She had noticed that by the end of a working day they were really aching. She knew that they had never done this before. She decided that she needed to visit her doctor.

She telephoned the surgery and spoke to the receptionist. She was given an appointment to see her GP on Wednesday morning at 9.30am.

When Mrs Shah saw the doctor she explained the problem. Dr Smith examined her legs and said she thought Mrs Shah needed to see a specialist.

Dr Smith said she would write to the hospital and ask for an appointment for Mrs Shah. She said the appointment would be sent to her directly.

Working with another person discuss the case of Mrs Shah. What kind of referral is being used? You will need to think about two different kinds of referral being used in this case.

- someone else contacts the service for them (referral by friend or neighbour).

Barriers to the use of services

We might think it is easy to use the services that are available to us, and for most of the time it is. But sometimes clients do not find it easy to use health and social care services themselves. There are a variety of reasons for this. The main ones are:

- physical barriers

- psychological barriers

- financial barriers

- environmental barriers.

The following chart explains these barriers.

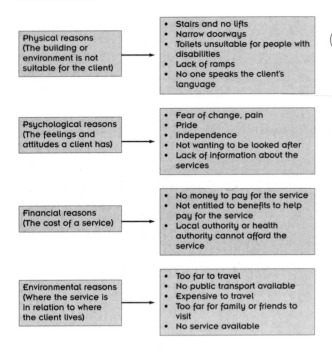

Physical reasons (The building or environment is not suitable for the client)	• Stairs and no lifts • Narrow doorways • Toilets unsuitable for people with disabilities • Lack of ramps • No one speaks the client's language
Psychological reasons (The feelings and attitudes a client has)	• Fear of change, pain • Pride • Independence • Not wanting to be looked after • Lack of information about the services
Financial reasons (The cost of a service)	• No money to pay for the service • Not entitled to benefits to help pay for the service • Local authority or health authority cannot afford the service
Environmental reasons (Where the service is in relation to where the client lives)	• Too far to travel • No public transport available • Expensive to travel • Too far for family or friends to visit • No service available

Physical barriers

These are the problems that building designs often present for clients. Older buildings are especially difficult for some people to get into. If a person cannot get into the building they cannot access the service in there. Once inside the building they need to be able to move around easily.

Language barriers are another form of physical barrier. If someone cannot make themselves understood, either because they speak a different language, or because they have had a stroke and their speech is slurred, then they will avoid using a service. In this case it is important that interpreters or specialist 'translators' are provided.

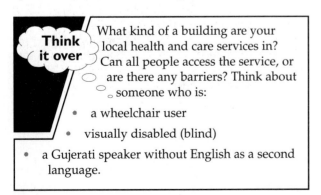

Think it over
What kind of a building are your local health and care services in? Can all people access the service, or are there any barriers? Think about someone who is:

• a wheelchair user

• visually disabled (blind)

• a Gujerati speaker without English as a second language.

Talk it over

Mike is a wheelchair user. He has just started attending his local college to study for a degree.

He is going to the education authority to organise his financial benefits and make arrangements for his home care service to change, as he will now be out of the house at different times.

When he gets to the building he wheels himself to the front door, only to find ten steps leading up to the front of the building. There is no other way in. Mike asks a passerby to go in for him to ask a member of staff to come out and speak to him.

The security man came out and arranged to carry Mike and his wheelchair up the stairs so that he could talk to a member of staff in the reception area. Mike was so embarrassed at being carried. He felt everybody was staring at him.

Working with another person, discuss how you think Mike would have felt about the service he was given.

Psychological barriers

Fear is a very powerful barrier to people using the health and social care services.

Some older people may be scared of hospitals because they knew them as workhouses when they were young. Poor people were sent to live in these before the NHS started. Some older people still think hospitals are shameful, scary places. Others are frightened to know what is wrong with them and many fear having their homes taken away from them or losing their independence.

As a care worker you may be able to help people get over their fears by explaining things to them carefully.

Sometimes people are too proud to use the health and social care services. For many older people personal pride is very important. Not having to ask for help is part of the pride they have in themselves. Some of them may see it as personal failure if they have to ask for help.

Many people like to be as independent as possible. Asking for help can be difficult for clients if they feel that the health and social care services will take over their lives. As a health and social care worker it is important that you allow clients as much independence as possible. Clients should always be given a choice about their care needs whenever possible.

Talk it over

Emily is 42 years of age. She has just found a lump in her breast. She is terrified of having developed cancer.

She will not make an appointment with the doctor and she has not told her partner. What would she do if they told her it was cancer? She would rather not know, besides if she ignores it, it might go away!

Discuss with another person how fear is making Emily react. What should she be doing? How would you encourage Emily to get over her fear?

Financial barriers

Lack of money can be a major barrier to people using health and social care services. Many services have to be paid for these days, especially if the social services do not have enough money to pay for all the needs of their clients.

Some clients may not be able to afford to pay for the bus or train fares to reach the service they need. If they need a taxi then the cost can be even higher!

Also the services clients need may not be available in their area because the health and social services simply do not have the money to provide the service.

Talk it over

Agnes has missed her hospital appointment again. She has to catch two buses and then use a taxi from the bus station to the hospital. Her pension just won't run to it.

How is the lack of money affecting Agnes' health? What might be the outcome if Agnes keeps missing her appointments? Make a note of your thoughts for your portfolio.

Environmental barriers

Having too far to travel can be a major barrier to using the services, and so can having no public transport system. Some clients live in rural (countryside) areas where public transport is limited.

Talk it over

Ahmed is 77 years old, he lives in Bury-on-Troutbeck and has to visit his doctor every two weeks for iron injections. He has a major problem with transport because there are only three buses a day: two in the morning and one in the evening.

This means that when his appointment is at 4.00pm he has to get the 11.00am morning bus and wait four hours for his appointment.

Working in small groups discuss ways in which Ahmed could get help with his transport problems. Make a note of your solutions in your portfolio.

Unit 1 Assessment

For this unit you need to produce a report on local health and social care services. You will have the opportunity to work towards a pass, merit or distinction grade.

Below are some activities, based on a scenario, which will guide you through this assessment. The level of assessment for each activity is clearly indicated as:

- P for Pass
- M for Merit
- D for Distinction.

You may wish to discuss with your tutor the activities you do.

All students must complete the first three P activities to achieve the minimum for Unit 1.

SCENARIO

Your local services: All you need to know

You are a group of health and social care students who are settling into your studies at your local school or college. A group of students from one of the European community countries is coming to stay with you for two weeks on a student exchange. They have to explore some aspects of the services in your local area. In your base room you are going to create an easy-to-read display which they will be able to refer to so they can find out about the local services, what kinds of jobs there are in them, and how people are able to access the services.

Working towards a pass grade

Activity 1P Where are the services?

You may work in groups for this activity. The members of your group should ideally be those who live quite close to each other, as you will be working on **your** local area.

- Make a list of the main health, social care and education services in your area. 'Your' area means those services that you or your family would normally use.

- On a large-scale map, identify at least six of the main local health, social care and early years education services. You could do this by attaching labels, creating drawings or taking photographs … or any other idea you might have to identify these services. Make sure that the map is to scale as much as possible, so that the visiting students will have a realistic idea of where things are.

Activity 2P What sort of work is involved?

Choose two jobs from each of the services and write a description of what each of these people do. You could do this in a number of ways – for example, interviewing a nurse or dentist, or providing an illustration of a worker as part of a spidergram of his or her work roles. Include these descriptions as part of your display.

Activity 3P How can you access the services?

Choose at least two services that you have placed on the display and indicate how you could be referred to these services. For example, you may choose the dentist and indicate that the usual way to use the services of a dentist is through self-referral – that is, you simply visit or telephone the dentist yourself to make an appointment. Use everyday language to describe this process. However, you must describe two different kinds of referral.

Working towards a merit grade

To achieve a merit grade you must carry out the activities for the pass grade, plus the additional steps to Activities 2 and 3 below.

You should also demonstrate that you have carried out some of the activities independently. You could, for example, investigate the job descriptions yourself rather than as part of a group.

Activity 2M

Write a description of the principles of the care value base, and relate it to the jobs roles that you outlined on your display in Activity 2P. Refer to pages 27–28 in the book for information on the care value base.

Activity 3M

Identify the four barriers that affect the ability of a person to make use of a service. You could relate these barriers to the referrals that you outlined in Activity 3P.

Working towards a distinction grade

To achieve this grade you must be able to complete the work at pass level, with the additions described at merit level. You must also carry out the additional steps for Activities 2 and 3 below.

Activity 2D

Describe each job role, clearly showing how the care value base would apply to each particular role. To help you in this, look back to the cases on page 28. You need to give specific examples to show you understand why health and social care workers should apply the care value base to their daily work.

Activity 3D

Having identified the barriers to services, describe how these services and their staff could attempt to reduce barriers to access.

Check your knowledge

Questions 1–11 require short answers.

Questions 12–22 are multiple choice questions. There is only one correct answer.

Short answer questions

1 List four services you could find at a health centre.

2 Describe two services provided by social services departments for:

 a older people

 b people with learning disabilities.

3 Give two examples of support groups and briefly describe what they do.

4 What is the difference between the care an older person might receive in residential accommodation and the care an older person might receive in a nursing home?

5 List three health services which might be found in a hospital and the job role(s) of carers providing this service. List them under the following headings:

Service in hospital	Role of carer providing service

6 Describe one way in which the care value base can ensure people are treated with respect.

7 Name two health or social care services that you could access by **self-referral**.

8 Within the daily routine of a nursery nurse, describe:

 a one activity that might require skills of patience and understanding

 b one that might require listening skills

 c one that she could carry out to promote equality and diversity.

9 Where might a laboratory worker work? Describe one activity he or she might perform as part of the job role.

10 One barrier to accessing services might be that the service (a GP surgery, for example) only has steps leading up to its entrance. Can you say:

   a what kind of barrier it is

   b how the service can be improved to remove this barrier.

11 Suggest two ways in which the work of voluntary organisations might support the care provided by the National Health Service.

Multiple choice questions

12 A social worker providing information to a client about her benefits is an example of:

   a early years educational services

   b health services

   c support groups and voluntary services

   d personal social services.

13 Jane has multiple sclerosis (MS), a disease which is making her very weak. She hears about a local group of people suffering from MS who meet every month to talk and discuss their problems. This group is an example of:

   a a health service group

   b a recreational group

   c a support group

   d personal social services group.

14 An example of an indirect care role is:

   a an occupational therapist

   b a catering assistant

   c dental hygienist

   d a care assistant.

15 Respite care means:

   a having a well-earned holiday

   b being cared for 'from the cradle to the grave'

   c allowing the carer to have a break from caring

   d providing a health check.

16 Care given by friends and relatives is an example of:

   a indirect care

   b informal care

   c the Community Care Act

   d personal social services.

17 A health centre is providing information in more than one language for its clients. This is an example of:

   a direct care by the GP and his staff

   b the care value base in promoting equality and diversity

   c maintaining confidentiality of information

   d support groups giving information to their members.

18 A client is referred to the hospital by her dentist. This is an example of:

   a self-referral

   b referral by contact with an informal carer

   c professional referral

   d promoting the care value base.

19 A person who provides daily help in the client's own home is most likely to be

   a a social worker

   b a care assistant

   c a district nurse

   d meals-on-wheels service.

20 Mrs Lear has received a letter from her GP inviting her to have a cervical smear. She does not want to go because she thinks this means she has cancer. This is an example of:

   a a physical barrier to accessing services

   b a financial barrier to accessing services

   c an environmental barrier with transport problems difficult to overcome

   d a psychological barrier to accessing services.

21 The care value base is essential to all care workers. This is because:

   a it is the law and you will be prosecuted if you don't keep to it

   b you learn about it when you do your GNVQ Health and Social Care qualification

   c it helps clients have confidence and trust in the care worker

   d it is part of the citizen's charter.

22 One example of a voluntary group is:

   a the National Health Service

   b the Royal College of Nursing

   c the Alzheimer's Disease Society

   d the Seaview Residential Home, Southend-on-Sea, Essex.

UNIT 1 ASSESSMENT

Understanding Health and Well-Being

This unit helps you find out about good (and poor) health and well-being. You will find out about the different things (factors) that can affect our health. You will discover what contributes to good health and what causes poor health. You will learn about the way people's health and well-being change as they become older. We will also explore some of the ways of maintaining good health for life.

The unit gives you the chance to find out about the different needs of people as they go through life. We will be looking at the health needs of infants, young children, adolescents (teenagers), adults and older people.

The whole of the unit aims to help you carry out an in-depth investigation into health and well-being for those people who may need your care in the future.

You need to learn:

* how to define health and well-being

* what is meant by good health

* what can cause poor health

* how to explore risks to health

* how people can stay healthy.

2.1 Defining health and well-being

There are many different ways of understanding what is meant by health and well-being. What one person calls healthy another person might say is unhealthy. For example, is a person unhealthy when they have a cold but can still manage to go to work, or are they unhealthy only when the cold makes them take to their bed?

Health is not a fixed condition, it changes all the time. One day you feel well, the next day you feel unwell. This is because our health is affected by everything around us, even the people we live with!

Health and social care professionals tell us that there are four parts to our health and well-being. These four parts are based on common basic health needs that all human

Think it over
Think about your health right at this moment. How are you feeling? Do you feel full of energy or are you tired? Have you got a headache or are you feeling better than you have ever felt before?

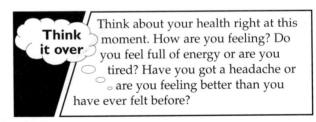

Talk it over

Discuss with another person why you are feeling the way you do. (Do not reveal confidential information if you do not want to.) Make a list of all the things that you think are making you feel as you do.

Remember to include the food that you eat, people you meet and the environment around you, as well as whatever else you think of. They could all affect how you are feeling right now.

beings share. They are called **Physical, Intellectual, Emotional** and **Social** needs.

Maslow's pyramid of needs

In the 1930s the psychologist Abraham Maslow designed a pyramid to explain 'basic health needs'. He used the pyramid to arrange health needs in order of importance.

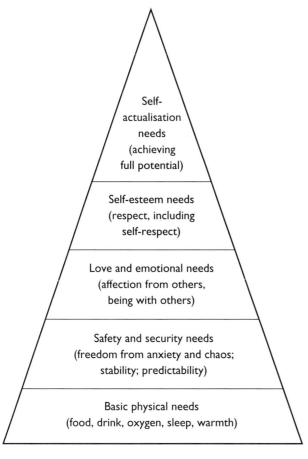

Self-actualisation needs (achieving full potential)

Self-esteem needs (respect, including self-respect)

Love and emotional needs (affection from others, being with others)

Safety and security needs (freedom from anxiety and chaos; stability; predictability)

Basic physical needs (food, drink, oxygen, sleep, warmth)

When Maslow designed his pyramid he placed physical needs at the bottom of the pyramid to show that they are the most important. These needs are supporting all the other health needs. If our physical care needs are not met, it is impossible for our other health needs to be met.

When people talk about health and well-being they often only think about physical health needs and what directly affects them. But as Maslow has shown, there is more to health and well-being than the physical.

In 1946 the World Health Organisation gave a good definition of health and well-being based on Maslow's work:

'Health is complete physical, mental and social well-being and not just the absence of disease or infirmity.'

In other words, every part of the pyramid needs to be in good working order before we can say we have 'good health'.

| Try it out | Find another definition of health by looking up the word in a dictionary. Don't forget to write the definition down in your portfolio. |

It is easy to remember the different parts to health if we use the word PIES to help us.

P = Physical

I = Intellectual

E = Emotional

S = Social

The safety and security need that Maslow identified is included in the physical part of health and well-being.

The spidergrams show examples of the different parts of health.

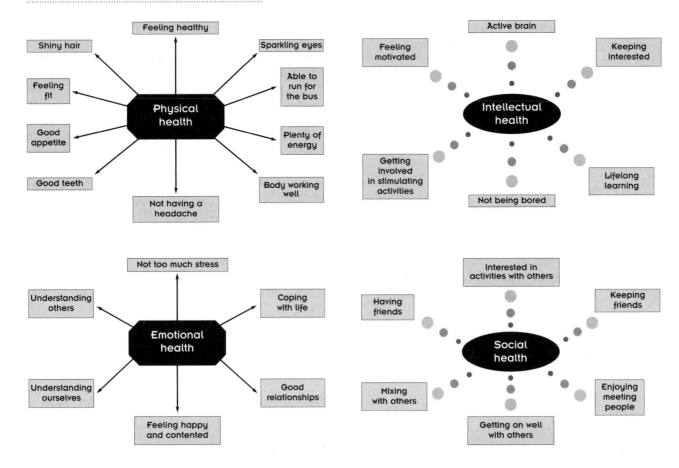

Physical aspects of health

Having good physical health means your body is working to the best of its ability. Every person's body is different, not just in the way it looks but in what it can do. Even so there are certain things we all need in order to be as physically healthy as possible.

Shelter and warmth are needed just to survive. If we could not keep our bodies sufficiently warm we would die from hypothermia (when the body becomes too cold to live). Keeping ourselves warm is even more important as we become older.

Talk it over

Discuss with another person how shelter and warmth helps to keep the body physically healthy.

Food and water are also essential. It is possible to live without food for several weeks, but the body cannot survive for very long without water.

Exercise is an important part of keeping physically healthy. Some kind of regular physical exercise is needed to prevent the body breaking down, just as a car might develop mechanical problems if it is not used regularly.

Talk it over

Discuss with another person why using our muscles and bones regularly is important to physical health.

Everything identified in the physical spidergram is very important if we are to keep physically healthy. If our physical health is poor it can affect other aspects of our health. Read the case of Rob to find out how his lack of physical fitness affected other parts of his health.

Like Rob many people simply do not realise how unhealthy they are until they try to do something they are not fit for. If people keep fit and healthy for everyday life, they will be able to do many other things they need to be fit and healthy for. In other words they are 'fit for life'.

> **Think it over**
>
> Take the time now to think for a few minutes about your own fitness levels. How would you describe your fitness? Do you know someone who is fitter than you or someone who is less fit than you?

There are certain basic requirements to being physically healthy, such as being warm and having enough food and drink. However, it is also important that we do not do anything that damages our health, such as not eating a balanced diet, smoking and drinking too much alcohol.

Intellectual aspects of health

Keeping our mind active and being interested in the world around us is part of good mental health. If we do not have enough interests we can become bored and depressed. Look at the list of things we can all do to keep our mental health in good condition.

- Reading
- Painting
- Making visits to places and people
- Learning new skills
- Watching the television (but not too much!)
- Using the Internet.

SNAPSHOT

Rob is 18 years old and very overweight. He gets very embarrassed about his weight. He feels he does not look his best and that it stops him doing things he would like to do. He has a girlfriend, Marian, who is a keen walker. She is very worried about him and gets 'fed up' that he never joins her in what she likes doing!

One day the walking club that Marian belongs to decided to do a long-distance walk. The walk was to go along the Dales Way (which is 135 kilometres long) through the Lake District in the North of England. They decided to do the walk over five days.

Rob insisted on going as well. He decided not to walk the first day because it was much too far for him (25 kilometres). So he stayed in the car and watched the others set off. He felt miserable by himself, waiting for them to come back, so he had a quick smoke and then pie and chips to cheer himself up.

On Day 2 Rob walked – 14 kilometres. He was very tired and his feet were sore but he was glad he had managed it. He hated being left behind.

Day 3 and Rob decided he was going to walk the 18 kilometres, even though he had not recovered from the day before. Now the problems really started. He could not keep up with his group, and he felt very tired and ill. He was half way up a mountain pass when he had to sit down.

As Rob sat there trying to recover, he watched other people going past him. He noticed that some of them were 20 and 30 years older than him and they were going over the pass without any problems at all. He decided there and then that he had to do something about his own fitness and weight. He looked and felt like an old man.

If he ever got off this mountain pass alive he was definitely going to change his lifestyle before it was too late!

Think it over

Have you ever been bored? How did you feel? What did you try to do to overcome it?

Talk it over

In groups, choose two of the items in the list and discuss how they can stimulate (improve) intellectual health.

It is never too late to learn

One way to keep mentally healthy as we grow older is to keep doing and learning a variety of new things. The government programme called 'Lifelong Learning' is designed to encourage people to keep using their intellectual skills for as long as they live. Medical research has shown that people who use their brains regularly are more likely to keep their 'wits about them' for longer, as

Talk it over

In pairs, discuss why people who keep their brains active are more likely to stay alert in older age than those who do not stimulate their intellectual ability.

well as live longer and have more fulfilling lives.

It is important for carers to recognise the importance of intellectual health and to help clients to keep interested in their world. Use the case involving Naomi to explore how intellectual health is stimulated in the Marybee Residential Home.

Emotional aspects of health

This can be described as how we feel about ourselves and others. For example, when we have to say 'goodbye' to a friendly neighbour because they are moving away from the area, we may feel sad because we don't want them to

A library can provide a key to intellectual health

An activities organiser, Naomi, visits the Marybee Residential Home for retirees three times a week to organise activities for the residents. She tries to arrange something different at regular intervals to keep her clients interested.

Last week, she started a 'memories diary'. She asked the residents to talk about some of their old photographs. This led to very interesting discussions about the places where residents had lived and the changes they had seen taking place over the years.

This week, tapestry-making is on the agenda. Some of the residents said they would be interested in re-creating some of their own pictures. Naomi is going to have the pictures enlarged and copied onto material so that the residents can go over them with wool stitches.

Everyone is looking forward to the activity, including Naomi, as this is an activity she has not tried out in this way before. So she will be learning the process as well.

- Discuss with others how Naomi's activities keep the residents intellectually stimulated.

- How else might the residents' health be improved through these activities?

- Do you think there are any benefits to Naomi's health as well?

leave. On another occasion we may feel happy because we have succeeded in achieving a goal or getting something we really want.

Being loved and accepted by those we love is an important part of emotional health. We have other emotional health needs as well, such as:

- privacy

- freedom

- choice

- independence

- dignity

- respect.

All of these are important to our emotional health.

Contributing to positive emotional health is an important part of a carer's work. Once again, it is part of the care value base, which is discussed in Unit 1. Sometimes it is easy to forget how our own actions and attitudes can affect someone else's emotional health.

All age groups enjoy their privacy, especially when carrying out personal hygiene tasks, like going to the toilet or having a bath.

It is true that all age groups deserve respect. No matter what a client says or does we should try to treat them politely and be as helpful as possible.

Try it out

Read about how Aden affected his client's emotional health and answer the questions that follow.

Albert Edwards had just started attending the day care centre for people who need to rehabilitate after having a stroke. Albert was having difficulties speaking but his hearing and understanding were perfect.

Aden greeted Albert. He spoke to him in a very loud voice, saying all his words very slowly. He asked Albert what he wanted for his lunch and then without waiting for an answer ordered some food for him. Albert felt very annoyed and upset. He told his wife when she came to collect him that he was never going back there!

- *Why do you think Albert was so annoyed?*

- *How could Aden have done things differently?*

- *How can Aden encourage Albert to come back to the day care centre?*

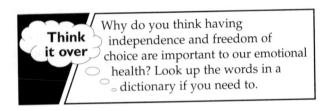

Think it over Why do you think having independence and freedom of choice are important to our emotional health? Look up the words in a dictionary if you need to.

Social aspects of health

Social health means making and keeping good relationships with others. This is an important part of our health and well-being. Examples of what is needed for good social health include:

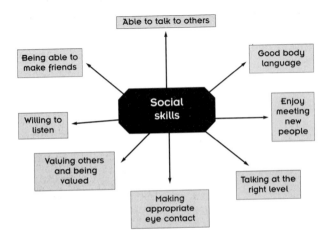

It is our social skills that enable us to develop good relationships with people around us. The skills shown in the spidergram are central to the care value base. They are all about good communication skills, valuing clients and other individuals, such as friends, work colleagues, relatives and others that we come across in everyday life.

For us to be accepted in society is important for our social health. We need to recognise the rules of our society so that we can be a part of

Think it over Very often we can improve our social health at the same time as we are improving our physical, intellectual and emotional health!

How do you think this is possible?

it. This means behaving and responding to others in a way that is acceptable to them.

Different groups and their health needs

Everyone should have good health and well-being if possible, no matter what their age or what stage of life they are at. However, people's health needs change as they pass through the different life stages.

Each 'life stage' can be given an age range to help us understand the difference between each one. For example:

0–3	3–10	10–18	18–65	65+
Infant	Young child	Teenager	Adult	Older adult

Each life stage has different needs for keeping people as healthy as possible. We will now explore some of these differences.

Infants aged 0–3

Physical needs	Intellectual needs	Emotional needs	Social needs
Warmth	Play	Bonding with carer	Develop routines
Shelter	Stimulation	Love	Meet people
Balanced diet	Toys	Encouragement	Play with others
Protection	Experiences	Laughter	Explore their environment
Good hygiene	Picture books	Value	
Sleep	Television		
Exercise	Role modelling		

Young children aged 3–9

Physical needs	Intellectual needs	Emotional needs	Social needs
Warmth	Play, role	Respect	Develop
Shelter	modelling	Love	routines
Balanced	Stimulation	Encouragement	Meet many
diet	Advanced	Laughter	people
Protection	toys	Value	Play and learn
Good	New	Dignity	with others
hygiene	experiences	Learning	Explore
Sleep	Books	independence	their own
Exercise	Television	Self-esteem	environment
Sleep	Education		Use social
			facilities

Try it out

When care workers went to Romania to help care for children who were orphaned or abandoned they found many of them lying in cots, unable to smile, play or respond to any stimulus. It took the workers many months of nurturing to improve the health of these children.

Discuss with others why you think these children were unable to respond.

Think it over

Anwar and Amina are twins aged eight years old. They both attend Pollam County Primary School. They really enjoy going there because they feel they are treated like young adults. Teachers are always polite to them when they ask for something and they are expected to be polite back.

Anwar remembers feeling really embarrassed at his last school, when his teacher asked him in front of everyone why he had been off sick. He had to tell her he had had diarrhoea, so he whispered his answer, but some of the class heard and burst out laughing!

Which of the children's health needs do you think are met by Pollam County Primary School? Why do you think these needs are important for the development of young children?

How do you think Anwar's teacher failed to meet his needs at his last school? What could the teacher have done differently?

Try it out

Gemima is nine months old. She spends most of her time lying in her cot staring at the ceiling. She has no toys and nothing to look at. She tends to be listless and uninterested in anything that happens in her room, because, she knows, even at such a young age, that it will not have much to do with her.

What do you think could be done to stimulate Gemima? What sort of activities would you arrange to make sure that her physical, intellectual, emotional and social health needs are met? It might be helpful to use PIES as headings to put your suggestions under.

Talk it over

Working in pairs discuss the different needs between an infant and a young child. You could use PIES as a starting point for your discussion. You can also discuss how a carer can make sure that the needs of a young child are fully met.

Make notes of your discussions and keep them.

Adolescents aged 10–18

This is often described as the most difficult age group. They are neither adults nor children! The health needs of adolescents are very similar to those of children, especially the physical needs. The major differences are in emotional and social health needs. Adolescence is also a time for increasing intellectual skills. It is important for adolescents to find out more about their environment and the skills and knowledge needed to survive as adults. It is almost a 'practice' time for adulthood. You could be working through the adolescent stage yourself.

Adolescents have many health needs, such as:

- learning to be independent – perhaps learning to drive

- respect from their peer group (friends)

- learning about work and work relationships

- developing new skills – both work and recreation

- developing working relationships

- making loving relationships

- keeping fit

- learning when to stand up for themselves and to say no to friends, partners

- taking responsibility for themselves and others

- keeping sexually healthy

- learning to budget.

Try it out

Working with another person make a large diagram of a pie and divide it into four parts using PIES. Then decide which part of the pie each of the adolescents needs in the list should go. Some of the items might go in more than one piece of the pie. If you come up with any other adolescent needs add them to your pie chart.

Adults aged 18–65

Many people really think that a person's health needs stop once they reach 18 years of age – i.e.

Try it out

Jenny and Priya are best friends. They have known each other for ten years. They go everywhere together and discuss all their problems and worries together. Every Monday evening they go to the athletics track to train with their coach. They are both cross-country runners and represent their local club at national events.

When they first started going to events their parents always took them, but now that they are 16 they want to go by themselves. They have been doing it for about three months.

At first their parents did not like them travelling alone, but both girls insisted that they did not want to be taken, as it made them look silly in front of the rest of the team.

They have now got used to the travelling. At first they worried about not finding their way to some of the events. They got on the wrong train more than once!

They used to argue with each other about the best way to travel, but now they are able to discuss things together and come up with a solution that they both agree with.

Working in pairs identify the emotional and social needs that Jenny and Priya support each other with. Make a list of the needs that you identify and file it in your portfolio.

Think it over

Nazir has just enrolled on a part-time health studies degree programme at his local college. He has spent the last two years studying in the evenings to gain the entry qualifications needed to be accepted on the course. He has now got his Advanced Level GNVQ in Health and Social Care and plans to follow a career in social work when he has completed his college studies.

His friends could not believe it when he returned to education, as it had been 30 years since he left school. However, Nazir is fed up with his dead-end job and wants to change his own and his family's lives by getting a better one.

He and his family live in rented accommodation and his job is the lowest paid among all his friends. His three children have all started talking about leaving school as soon as possible and getting jobs in the same place as him.

He really wants things to be different for them. He does not want them to experience the poverty that he and his wife have.

What changes do you think Nazir's family will experience when he becomes better qualified? You will need to think about the house they live in, their environment and the children's expectations.

How will the changes affect the family's health – physical, intellectual, emotional and social?

Learning is an important part of life, no matter what age

once they become an adult. This is not true! The government's initiative to stimulate intellectual health, called 'Lifelong Learning', has already been mentioned (page 40). This was set up because learning is a very important part of life, no matter what our age.

Health needs for adults are as varied as they are for younger people. In any age group the importance of different health needs changes with time. So health care workers need to be in tune with their clients' health needs at any time so that they can help to meet the changes as they arise.

Older people aged 65+

Older people also have the same health needs as younger adults, but sometimes as people get older they become ill and too frail to look after their health needs themselves. It may be that health needs will change to include more physical care needs. However their intellectual, emotional or social needs still need to be met. In many cases, health and

care workers can help older, frail or sick people to meet their every need in a variety of different ways.

Older people have the same needs as other age groups. Very few people choose to live on their own, yet many older people have to face this when they lose a beloved partner. Having social and emotional needs met can become harder as a person becomes older and as they lose family and friends through old age.

It is important to encourage older people to take part in activities that include meeting other people and making new friends as old ones are lost.

? Did you know?

That women usually outlive men.

This means there are more widows than widowers.

Talk it over

Hannah lives on her own in a small terraced house with three steps up to the front door. She is 83 years old and up until falling and breaking her hip she enjoyed a very active life, which included trips out with friends and visits to the library and theatre.

Now she cannot get out of the house because the steps are too much for her. She is waiting for a visit from the occupational therapist who will make recommendations for some alterations to her house so that she can get in and out more easily.

The occupational therapist has suggested that the steps are removed and a ramp with handrails is put in its place. Hannah is delighted.

Working with others identify which of Hannah's health and care needs are being met by the changes to her house. You will need to think about more than just physical needs. Include in your discussions other aspects of PIES.

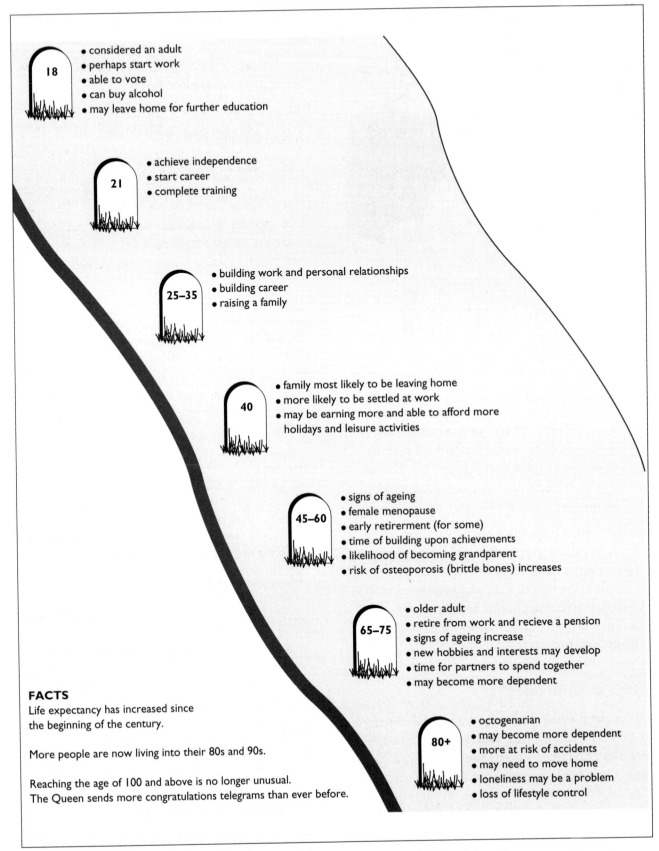

18
- considered an adult
- perhaps start work
- able to vote
- can buy alcohol
- may leave home for further education

21
- achieve independence
- start career
- complete training

25–35
- building work and personal relationships
- building career
- raising a family

40
- family most likely to be leaving home
- more likely to be settled at work
- may be earning more and able to afford more holidays and leisure activities

45–60
- signs of ageing
- female menopause
- early retirerment (for some)
- time of building upon achievements
- likelihood of becoming grandparent
- risk of osteoporosis (brittle bones) increases

65–75
- older adult
- retire from work and recieve a pension
- signs of ageing increase
- new hobbies and interests may develop
- time for partners to spend together
- may become more dependent

80+
- octogenarian
- may become more dependent
- more at risk of accidents
- may need to move home
- loneliness may be a problem
- loss of lifestyle control

FACTS

Life expectancy has increased since the beginning of the century.

More people are now living into their 80s and 90s.

Reaching the age of 100 and above is no longer unusual. The Queen sends more congratulations telegrams than ever before.

Milestones of a journey through adult life

Mrs Gronheim is a 75-year-old widow. She lives alone in a two-bedroomed house. Her relatives live some distance away and only visit occasionally. She is unable to walk because of rheumatism and swollen knee joints. This also prevents her standing to do the cooking, cleaning and shopping.

Besides the specific health needs of warmth and shelter, what other health needs do you think Mrs Gronheim has? How would you, as a health care worker, help to meet these needs? Make notes for your portfolio under the headings of PIES.

Try it out

Working in pairs try to arrange to talk to an older person about their life. Make notes of the things they tell you and then make a wall chart to explain their health needs. You will need to remember to be polite and respect their privacy if they do not want to talk to you. Using the care value base of 'confidentiality' will be very important. If you tell them you are studying to become a health and care worker, they may be very willing to help you.

2.2 Factors affecting health and well-being

There are some things that affect our health that we cannot control very easily. For example, a person buys an expensive house in a particular place and soon after a motorway is built nearby. That person may have to live there for the rest of their lives, if they cannot sell the home to someone else! However there are other things that can affect our health and well-being that we can control quite easily. For example:

- we can choose our diet and what we eat each day

- we can choose to exercise (or not!)

- we can make some time for recreational activities

- we can choose to use the health and care services available.

The things we have control over are often called 'lifestyle factors'. In other words, they are about the way we live and the things we choose to do. But we need to remember that not everyone knows how to eat a healthy diet or how much exercise to take. As a health and care worker you should have a basic knowledge that will help you to support others who may need your help and advice on such matters.

Diet

Diet is important to our health. In Western countries – such as Britain – not many people go hungry. It is more likely that people will not eat food in the correct amounts or in the right balance. In these cases diet may damage people's health.

Many people now eat 'fast foods'. These are often high in fat, sugar and salt. However they are quick to prepare, taste good (that's the fat!) and are easy to make or buy. If we eat too much of this kind of food we run the risk of becoming overweight or ill.

A balanced diet

No single food provides our bodies with all the nutrition needed to help it work to the best of its ability. Healthy eating messages tell us that we should be choosing our daily meals from the five main food groups shown here. The food groups are called nutrients.

Most of our food should come from the bread, cereal and potato group, with the next largest amount coming from the vegetable and fruit group. The milk groups should be the smallest amounts taken.

In a government health policy document, *Our Healthier Nation*, the Department of Health

A balanced diet

Did you know?

Fat is hidden in:

- chocolate
- cakes
- biscuits
- red meat
- dairy foods (milk, butter, cheese etc.)
- crisps and crackers
- fast foods.

recommends that people should eat less fat in their diet. Many people are eating as much as 30 per cent too much fat in their diet.

We need many different kinds of food to keep our bodies healthy. This is because the body can do a great many different things with the nutrients in food, as shown below.

Carbohydrate Provides the body with energy, helps to fill you up.

Fibre Absorbs water and helps to get rid of waste products. Food with fibre also makes you feel full for longer.

Protein Helps the body to grow and repair itself.

Fat Small amounts help the body to keep warm and protects some of the body's organs. Too much can increase your weight.

Even if you are busy it is possible to get the food balance right. If you need to buy pre-prepared food because of your busy lifestyle, you will find that frozen and tinned foods are prepared in a way that retains all the nutrients. As long as food is not over-cooked

(which removes the nutrients) it is still possible to get the balance right.

Hints and tips for getting the balance of diet right

- Try not to miss any meals (especially breakfast).
- Go easy on dairy products.
- Drink plenty of water.
- Eat plenty of fruit and vegetables.
- Check how much fibre you eat and increase it if necessary (increase slowly and drink more water).
- Choose white meats (chicken and poultry) more often than red meats.
- Eat more fish (it's good for you).

Think it over

Mike lives alone in his flat. He has a busy lifestyle and hardly ever has time to cook for himself. His mother says 'he lives off take-aways'.

He knows he should eat a more balanced diet but does not know how to change his meals so that he is eating more healthily.

What advice would you give Mike to help him change his habits so that he is eating a more healthy and balanced diet?

Vitamins and minerals

Vitamins are needed for health and growth. Minerals are needed in very small amounts to maintain health. They can be found in food along with the vitamins.

- Calcium = Keeps teeth and bones strong and healthy

- Iron = Carries oxygen around the body

- Sodium = Keeps the muscles working.

Foods containing vitamins and minerals	
Food source	*Vitamins and minerals*
Dairy products, cheese, milk, butter etc.	Vitamin A, B2, calcium
Red meat	Vitamin B3, B1, iron
Bread, flour, breakfast cereals	Vitamin B3, B1, sodium
Fish and fish oils	Vitamin D, sodium
Fruit and vegetables	Vitamin K, C, A, B1, B2, B3, iron, sodium

? Did you know?

Vitamin A = Keeps skin healthy, helps you to see in the dark

Vitamin B1 = Helps with energy supplies

Vitamin B2 = Helps skin stay healthy

Vitamin B3 = Helps the body with energy supplies

Vitamin C = Keeps the body tissues healthy

Vitamin D = Helps keep bones strong and healthy

Vitamin K = Helps the blood to clot.

Did you also know that the main source of Vitamin D is from sunlight!

Try it out Choose one of the minerals and find out more about its benefits to the body.

Exercise

As a health and care worker you should understand about the way physical exercise affects health and well-being. Have you ever exercised? If you have, think about how you felt after you had finished the exercise. Do you remember feeling:

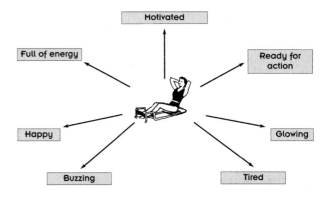

If you haven't look what you are missing!

Physical exercise is very important for good health and well-being. If you recall the case of Rob earlier in the unit (page 39), you will remember that his social health was affected because he could not properly join in his girlfriend's favourite pastime – walking. His physical health is also suffering because his muscles and bones never get a 'good work out'. We can also say that his emotional health is affected because he does not feel good about himself.

Regular exercise means carrying out an energetic activity at least three times a week. It should be something that makes you feel 'puffed' and hot and sweaty. Current medical experts tell us that if we do something energetic every day for a total of at least 30 minutes we can improve our health and well-being.

The kinds of activity that we can all easily do are:

- walking up stairs instead of using the lift

- walking to the shops instead of using the car

- putting more energy into house work

- washing the car ourselves instead of using a car wash

- weeding the garden.

For all-round fitness, the exercise should include:

- suppleness

- strength

- stamina.

Exercise	Strength	Stamina	Suppleness	Kcal/min
Badminton	**	**	***	5–7
Cycling (hard)	***	****	**	7–10
Golf	*	*	**	2–5
Dancing (disco)	*	***	****	5–7
Ballroom dancing	*	*	***	2–5
Swimming (hard)	****	****	****	7–10
Walking briskly	*	**	*	5–7
Climbing stairs	**	***	*	7–10

*Fair **Good ***Very good ****Excellent

Suppleness

Suppleness (or flexibility) is an individual's ability to move all his or her joints through a full range of movement. The body needs to be able to bend, turn and twist. Restricted suppleness can have an effect on everyday living. For example, some people are unable to bend down to tie their shoelaces. As we get older, suppleness may be lost, leading to dependency on others. An example of this would be an older person who has difficulty in dressing and in maintaining personal hygiene.

Regular exercise can help to prevent loss of suppleness. Effective suppleness exercises will take a joint through its full range of movement. The stretching should be gentle and controlled, as in yoga exercises where

muscles are gently stretched and held for varying amounts of time.

Suppleness exercises are often used by athletes and other sports people to prepare the body for more vigorous activity. They are also used to *cool* the body following energetic activity.

The illustration below shows a person's arms circling forwards to exercise (or 'mobilise') the shoulder joints.

Strength

Strength is the maximum force that a muscle is able to use when completing a task – such as lifting or pulling a heavy object. Strength is important because it helps to maintain good body posture, which in turn improves body shape.

Older people who have lost some muscle strength may find it difficult to get up from a chair or out of the bath, because muscles at the tops of their legs do not cope very well with the weight of their body. Strengthening exercises may lead to improved performance in this.

An example is an infant who is learning to stand. The infant will repeatedly pull itself

into the upright position by holding on to furniture. This becomes easier as leg strength improves.

Strength is maintained through regular exercise which leads to the fibres of the muscle becoming more developed, which in turn leads to an increase in muscle power.

Stamina

Stamina exercises are important for maintaining a healthy heart and lungs. People who have good health are able to carry out everyday activities much more easily and they are less likely to suffer from heart disease as they get older.

Exercises which improve stamina are known as aerobic because they involve a steady supply of oxygen to the body. Examples of this type of activity are jogging and swimming.

Physical activity like sprinting, which involves short, intensive action does not use up so much oxygen. This is known as anaerobic exercise and cannot be maintained for long periods of time. It is often combined with aerobic work. Football is an example of this type of activity as the participants may run to a maximum capacity for short periods, followed by a more leisurely pace, which allows them to 'get their breath back'.

Weight control

Exercise also plays an important part in weight control. Body weight can be maintained if there is equal food intake and exercise output.

For example, a person who weighs 60 kilos and eats 300 kilocalories (about the amount in a Mars bar or a moderate serving of chips) needs to run 5 kilometres in 30 minutes to use up the energy in what they have eaten.

Other benefits of exercise

Regular exercise has many other benefits. For example:

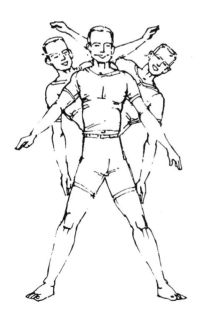

Suppleness – the ability to bend more freely, to stretch and turn through a full range of movement.

Strength – the ability to exert force for pushing, pulling and lifting. Strong muscles protect against strains and sprains.

Stamina – the ability to keep going – walking, swimming, running and so on – and to acquire the reserves to make sure that everyday tasks are well within the individual's ability.

- Exercise can help people to feel good in mind and body. It makes them feel more energetic and more relaxed.

- It is sociable. It helps people to make new friends and make the most of their leisure time.

- It helps people who are overweight to get slim, and slim people to stay that way.

Achieving fitness

Anyone can improve their fitness through suitable exercise. It is never too late to increase the amount of exercise you do, but there are some sensible precautions you should always keep in mind:

- Increase the amount of exercise you do gradually.

- Warm up your muscles by doing gentle stretches and bends before vigorous exercise.

- Cool down gradually afterwards in the same way, or by taking a gentle walk.

- If you are in doubt about whether you should exercise because of a medical condition, see your doctor first. It is unwise to exercise if you have a cold or a sore throat.

Four golden rules for exercise!

1 Get moving

2 Build up slowly

3 Exercise regularly

4 Keep it up!

Encouraging people to take up regular exercise is not easy, but you can suggest simple changes to everyday living that will include exercise as part of daily routines. For example, walking to the shops or getting off the bus one stop early.

Talk it over

In pairs discuss other ways you could increase the amount of exercise taken as part of daily routines.

Talk it over

Emily hates exercise. She cannot be bothered doing anything after a hard day working in the residential care home for people with learning disabilities. Last week her supervisor asked her to start taking Sidney out for a walk in the afternoon. She is dreading it!

She took Sidney out for his first walk yesterday. They visited the local park, following a nature trail that identified the different trees that they passed. As they walked, Emily told Sidney the name of any of the trees she knew.

When they got back home Emily could not believe that they had been out three hours. She felt full of life and glowing. She thought to herself 'Maybe this exercise lark isn't too bad after all!'

In pairs discuss the benefits to both Emily and Sidney of regular walks in the park. You might like to think about PIES as you do this activity.

Recreation

Using leisure time to improve health and well-being is another very important part of life. Imagine how you would feel if you never had time off from studying or work! Not only would you feel exhausted and fed up, you would probably feel as if life was not worth living!

Recreation is about taking the time to relax. It is a time to do something different and re-charge our batteries. This is the time for doing what pleases ourselves.

Recreation time is important because it:

- helps us to take a break from work

- can provide interesting activities
- keeps us interested in life
- can make us feel good
- gives us the chance to meet other people.

Talk it over

Discuss with a partner why leisure time is important to you. Then make a list of all the things that you like doing with your leisure time.

Recreation helps us cope with too much stress. Stress is when we feel overloaded with problems and feel that we cannot cope with our daily lives. As a health and care worker, it is likely that you will have contact with many people suffering from stress. If stress is left untreated it can lead to:

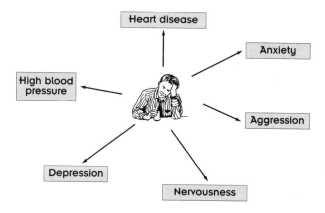

The people who need recreational activities the most are sometimes those who cannot face planning anything for themselves. This might be because they are:

- ill
- depressed
- too busy
- not aware they need to take a break.

In these cases it is important for the health and care worker to help people discover the pleasure and benefits of relaxation. A health care worker can explain benefits such as:

- improved health
- increased self-esteem
- better coping strategies in everyday life.

The kinds of recreational activities you can safely carry out yourself or recommend to clients are:

- joining clubs
- visiting people
- walking
- reading
- hobbies
- dancing
- cinema
- voluntary work.

Before telling people about the kinds of activities available find out what their interests are and what they are able to do. For example, there is no point advising a young child to

Talk it over

George is 45 and has been off work for three months with a stress-related illness. He is still suffering from depression and cannot be bothered going out or joining in anything that his family is doing.

He prefers to spend his time in front of the television.

Working with a partner discuss how recreational activities could help George cope with his depression more positively. How could his family help him join in with their activities?

take up reading – they have too much energy. Nor is there any point advising an older person to take up running if they have never done it before or are are not able to do it!

Try it out

Desmond and Ann live together in a small bungalow. Ann has recently been ill and has been told to stop swimming every day until she has recovered from her illness.

Ann is really upset about this because since she retired 14 years ago she has never missed a week without swimming.

Desmond still goes out on his bike twice a week but feels that he should find some sort of recreational activity that they can do together. He does not want Ann going off on her own until he is sure she can cope again.

What kind of recreational activity would you suggest for Ann and Desmond? You will need to think about their ages and their abilities. It might be a good idea to think back to PIES as well.

Monitoring and prevention

To monitor someone's health is to make regular checks to see if they are remaining healthy or becoming unhealthy or ill. Monitoring is also used to check on the progress of someone who is already ill or is in poor health. It is usually carried out to prevent someone from becoming ill or to stop an illness becoming worse. For example, a doctor can 'monitor' a client's high blood pressure by getting them to visit the surgery for a blood pressure check every week for a period of time.

By monitoring the client's blood pressure the doctor can take appropriate action if the client's condition gets worse. There are other forms of monitoring that also help to prevent illness.

Health screening

Health screening is a way of checking to make sure that certain parts of our body are working well. For example, a check-up at the dentist is called oral (mouth) health screening.

Currently, the major killer disease in the Western world is coronary heart disease (it often leads to people having a heart attack). To help prevent heart disease doctors now offer coronary heart disease screening to people who are at risk. This usually means a visit to the doctor or practice nurse for a series of checks and tests, such as:

- height and weight check

- diet check

- blood pressure and pulse check

- cholesterol test (to see how much 'fat' – cholesterol – is in the blood because fat blocks the blood vessels)

- alcohol check

- exercise test (to see how fit a person is).

After the checks and tests are complete the doctor or nurse lets the client know if they need to change their lifestyle to prevent them from developing heart disease. If they do have to change, the doctor or nurse will advise the client how best to do this. Screening does not mean that you have the disease. It is just a check to see if there is a problem beginning to build up.

Some health screening tests are for men only or for women only. For example, women are at risk of developing breast cancer and cancer of the cervix, so screening is carried out to prevent the disease or at least to catch it very early before it goes on to do too much damage.

Women aged between 50 and 65 can have a **mammography test** (which is like an X-ray)

Opticians provide a screening service

mumps, measles and rubella (German measles) – MMR.

Age	Disease
8 weeks 12 weeks 16 weeks	Diphtheria, whooping cough, tetanus – a combined injection Polio – taken by mouth Hib – injected *This is often called the 'triple'*
12–18 months	Measles, mumps and rubella – a combined injection. *Known as the MMR*
4–5 years	Whooping cough, tetanus – a combined injection Polio – taken by mouth

Vaccinations are also used to protect travellers to certain countries from diseases such as yellow fever.

to make sure the breast is clear of cancerous cells. Women can also have a **cervical smear test** every three to five years to make sure the cervix is also free from cancerous cells.

What about men? It is possible for a man to develop breast cancer, but because this is very rare there is no health screening available as a regular service. However, men are encouraged, and shown how, to examine their testicles for lumps, especially between the ages of 18 and 45 when they are most at risk of developing cancerous cells in the testicles.

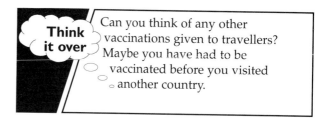

Think it over Can you think of any other vaccinations given to travellers? Maybe you have had to be vaccinated before you visited another country.

Meningitis is a disease often in the news. People at risk can be vaccinated to protect them against it. However, not all kinds of meningitis can be prevented by vaccination. Another vaccination we often hear about, especially for older people, is the 'flu vaccine'.

All these screening and preventative services, and many others, are free of charge or inexpensive. The pity is that not everyone has the sense to use them, often until it is too late.

Part of your role as a health and care worker is to encourage clients to make use of the screening and monitoring services available to help maintain their health and well-being.

If people use the screening and monitoring services available, they will be able to get

Try it out Working with another person, visit an optician to find out what kind of screening service they offer to their clients.

Vaccination

Another form of monitoring and prevention is vaccination. You may already know what vaccination is and why it is used. Babies are vaccinated against a range of diseases, such as

Talk it over

Discuss the kind of situations that might arise in which your client could need your support to visit a service.

Talk it over

There are many positive aspect to life in the country and city.

Discuss these as a group and make notes for your portfolio.

help as soon as they need it. For example, if Rob (see page 39) had visited his doctor he could have been referred to a dietician for advice to help him lose weight.

Environment

Where we live can affect our health and well-being in a major way. For example, if you lived in the middle of a war zone your health could be affected by physical injury (from bombs and gunfire), stress (worrying about the bombs), lack of services (no screening), and probably many more things.

Those of us who live in most Western countries are lucky not to be involved in warfare. However, there are other aspects of our environment that can affect our health. For example, suppose you did not have anywhere to live? Other problems in our environment include the following.

- **Living in the country.** There may not be regular public transport, the shops may not be easy to get to, health and care services may be a long distance away, there may not be ready access to jobs.

- **Living in a city.** There may be less space for children to play, motor vehicle fumes, and lots of noise (hard to find peace and quiet).

Compare your notes of things that could affect Michael's health with the list below. Did you think of the same things or did you come up with something different?

Talk it over

Michael lives in Manchester. He does not have a house or flat or even a room to live in. He spends most of his time on the streets trying to keep warm and dry. When he wakes up in the morning he is so stiff from being cold all night that it takes him ages before he can walk without pain in his joints.

The first thing he does in the morning is look to see if he has enough money to buy himself a cup of coffee so that he can get warm. It is not often that he has enough money to buy food as well. There are not many cafes open at six o'clock in the morning but he knows where the nearest one is.

Having a wash and shower is usually out of the question unless he is staying at one of the hostels for the homeless. He enjoys staying in the hostel because he always gets warm food and a comfortable bed for the night. The only problem with the hostel is that he is only allowed to stay there for a maximum of three nights in one month. He would love to have a house of his own but while he has no address he cannot claim benefits or even register with a doctor. He usually calls upon the accident and emergency service at the local hospital when he needs medical help.

The thing Michael hates the most about being homeless is the names people call him. When he is begging for money he already feels very guilty, but he feels there is nothing else he can do to survive. The last thing he needs is people telling him to get a job and get off the streets.

In pairs discuss how Michael's situation is likely to affect his health. You will need to think about PIES to make sure that you cover all aspects of his health needs. Make notes of your discussion for your class work.

Social class	The jobs people do
Social class I	Professional jobs: doctors, dentists, solicitors, accountants
Social class II	Teachers, managers, senior nurses
Social class III (N)	Secretaries, administrators, receptionists
Social class III (M)	Mechanics, cooks, plumbers, hairdressers, care assistants
Social class IV	Drivers, porters, security people
Social class V	Cleaners, labourers, refuse collectors

The government uses social class to compare the health and well-being of one group of the population with another group. By comparing groups of the population the government can plan how to spend the money it receives from our taxes – to decide on which groups to spend most of the money.

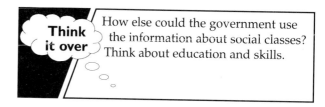

Think it over How else could the government use the information about social classes? Think about education and skills.

Because of research into the differences between social classes we know that:

- people in social classes IV and V are more likely to live in rented housing
- people in social classes IV and V are more likely to have accidents than people who are in social class I
- people in social class I are more likely to live longer than those in social class V
- people in social classes IV and V are more likely to develop coronary heart disease than people in higher social classes
- people in social classes I and II are more likely to have gardens than people in other social classes.

- Nowhere to cook or store food.
- Nowhere to wash or shower.
- No way to keep warm.
- Not having a good night's sleep.
- Not being able to keep himself safe from harm.
- Not being able to buy enough food.
- Stress from name-calling as well as everything else.

Social class

Social class is a major issue. Books are written about the subject. Some people would argue that there is no such thing as different social classes, and that all people are the same.

People are the same, however in many ways, they are also different. Social class is a way of measuring the differences between people. One way of measuring the differences in social class is by grouping people according to the job they do. You need to remember that a complete list of jobs is much longer than the examples given below.

Talk
it over

Nigel lives at home with his parents. They live in a large, detached house that is surrounded by large gardens. In fact there is so much land that Nigel's parents need to employ a gardener to help them care for it.

Nigel attended a private school where he learned to play cricket and became a member of the rugby team. He has continued with both hobbies.

His house has a swimming pool but he is usually so occupied with other hobbies that he does not get much chance to swim more than once a week.

Working in pairs discuss the likely health differences between Michael and Nigel. You could use PIES for your heading.

Employment

Health and well-being can be seriously affected by employment. For example, some jobs are very stressful, and this can lead to illness. Other jobs might involve using dangerous chemicals that could affect a worker's health. Some jobs in health and

Talk
it over

Working in pairs discuss why you think these jobs may be dangerous to health. Don't forget to use PIES to help you.

social care might involve a care worker working with people who are terminally ill (dying). This could affect the emotional health of the care worker.

Think
it over

Think of five jobs that could affect health and well-being. Write them down in a list. Now compare your list with our spidergram and identify a range of jobs that could be called dangerous to health.

In any job it is important to follow health and safety guidelines to keep yourself and other people as safe as possible. However, sometimes accidents will happen, even when safety guidelines are followed.

? Did you know?

That not having a job is bad for your health.

Talk
it over

Lisa has been looking for a job now for six months. It feels like a lifetime since she was made redundant when the textile factory closed down.

She has applied for seven jobs in the last month and hasn't even been offered an interview. She is beginning to feel really depressed and worried about the situation. Her redundancy money has all gone and she has two children to bring up on her own.

If she does not get a job soon she does not know how she is going to pay the bills, as well as feed and clothe the children.

In small groups discuss how this situation will affect Lisa's health. How might her children's health be affected? Again, it will be useful to start with PIES. Make notes of your discussions for your portfolio.

People who are unemployed are often sick and very depressed. Having a good job is important for the health of the individual, as well as their family. It is possible for people who are constantly worried about money and paying the bills to become:

- aggressive
- sick
- depressed
- suicidal.

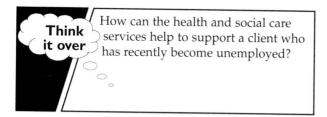

Think it over — How can the health and social care services help to support a client who has recently become unemployed?

2.3 Risks to health and well-being

Some people put their health (and their lives) at risk doing the things they do! As a health and social care worker it is helpful if you can understand why some people do unsafe things.

A good starting point may be to look at your own behaviour to see if you have any habits or behaviour that could put your health and safety at risk! If you have, try to understand why you behave in those ways.

There are various things that can put our own or others' health at risk. Other people can put you at risk. For example:

- people driving under the influence of drugs
- someone taking drugs that makes them aggressive and violent
- an employer asking an employee to work with unsafe machinery.

Physical, intellectual, social and emotional health can all depend on what we do to the

environment and ourselves. Some habits and activities are not helpful in maintaining health and well-being. For example:

- smoking tobacco
- drinking too much alcohol
- taking drugs
- being a couch potato (not taking any exercise)
- eating too much fatty food
- taking part in unsafe sexual practices
- working in an unsafe environment.

Recreational drugs

We need to be clear what recreational drugs are. The term can mean different things to different people!! A hard drug user, such as someone who takes heroin, might say they only take the drug during their recreation time. Does that make it a recreational drug? Some people argue that cannabis is a recreational drug that does no harm. But is this always the case?

Clearly there is no 'safe' way of using illegal drugs. All drugs have the potential to kill

Talk it over

Wendy had finally decided she was going to try cannabis with her friends. They had been encouraging her to join them for weeks and now she had finally given in.

She met her friends at Tony's flat. They seemed to be having plenty of fun. Everybody was totally relaxed and having a good laugh at a children's video. Sam passed Wendy some cannabis and soon she was laughing as much as the rest of them.

Later she got up to go home. She walked out of the house, across the pavement and straight into the path of an oncoming car.

Working in pairs discuss Wendy's situation. What made her finally 'give in' to her friends? Why do you think she walked straight into the road?

What advice would you have given Wendy before she visited her friend's flat?

their users. That is why only doctors are allowed to prescribe drugs and medication for treatment. All drugs need to be monitored and used under the supervision of a health professional.

Think it over

What recreational drugs might be freely available to the right age groups?

There are 'drugs' that can alter the way you feel, such as:

- alcohol
- tobacco.

Drinking alcohol

If used in moderation alcohol may benefit your health. Research has shown that one glass of wine (especially red wine) on two or three days a week, can reduce the risk of heart disease. The bad news is that drinking more than that will increase the chances of having a heart attack or developing liver disease. So the message must be:

- keep to the sensible drinking limits each week

- never drink all the weekly alcohol units in one go

- always have two or three alcohol-free days each week

- don't drink alcohol alone

- don't drink alcohol to cheer yourself up (it is a drug that makes you feel even more miserable!)

- never drink and drive or operate machinery.

How much you can drink and still stay healthy is measured by the number of units of drink. What a unit is however varies according to the kind of alcoholic drink, as shown below:

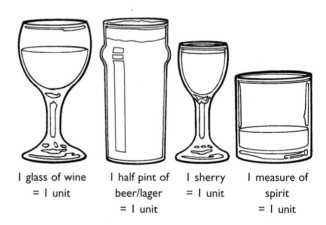

| 1 glass of wine = 1 unit | 1 half pint of beer/lager = 1 unit | 1 sherry = 1 unit | 1 measure of spirit = 1 unit |

The limits for men and women are:

- not more than 14 units of alcohol in a week if you are female

- not more than 21 units of alcohol in a week if you are male.

Too much alcohol can lead to:

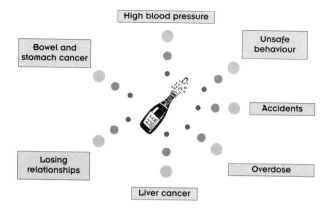

Another problem with smoking is that it can affect people who do not smoke.

Breathing other people's tobacco smoke is called passive smoking. Research has shown that this kind of smoking definitely causes problems such as lung cancer, asthma, coughing and sore eyes.

Smoking tobacco

Tobacco is another recreational drug. It can be more dangerous than alcohol. There is no safe limit for tobacco. You and your clients should definitely not smoke. For some people that is easier said than done. Many tobacco smokers become addicted.

The main health dangers from smoking are:

Smoking also affects the environment in other ways:

- homes need re-decorating more often
- creates litter
- smokers' homes are more likely to be set on fire by discarded cigarettes
- clothing and rooms smell of tobacco smoke

There are organisations dedicated to helping smokers quit the habit. One of these organisations is called QUIT! The kind of advice they provide is:

- if you don't smoke don't start
- choose a day to stop and then plan towards it

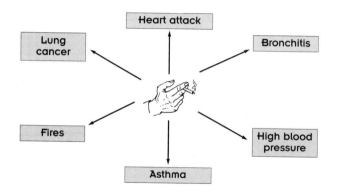

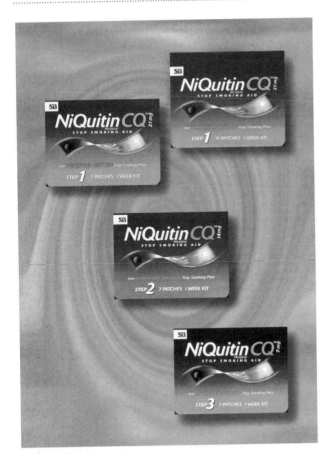

- when the day comes ... STOP!

- organise activities to keep your mind off smoking

- change routines so that you don't find yourself wanting a cigarette after meals

- drink plenty of water

- phone a friend for support when you get the 'craving'.

Diet

We have already explored the effects of diet on health and well-being, but it will do no harm to remind ourselves of just how important a balanced diet is for good health.

Some people's unusual eating habits put their health at risk. For example, those who only eat one kind of food are not getting enough vitamins and minerals in their diet. Some children suffer from this when they are growing up. Have you ever come across a mother who says her child will only eat breakfast cereal or bread and jam? This will do no harm if it only goes on for a short time. However it is important that children – and adults – are encouraged to eat a wide variety of different foods so that they have a balanced diet.

SNAPSHOT

Sharon starts a diet every Monday morning! She cuts her food down to the bare minimum for about three days and then finds herself so hungry that she eats huge amounts of the 'wrong foods' just to fill herself up.

Over the years she has gained three stones in weight and she despairs of ever getting back to her ideal weight.

She went to her doctor to talk it over and he has referred her to a dietician who has explained that Sharon will lose weight if she follows a balanced diet and does a little exercise.

People who go on 'crash' diets are in danger of becoming ill through developing eating disorders (such as anorexia nervosa). They are also likely to gain weight! It is true, 'dieting does make you fat'. A balanced diet will help to maintain a good body weight.

Talk it over

Discuss with another person how you would encourage a young child to try different kinds of food

Risks of a poor diet

There are many diseases and illnesses that are caused by a poor diet. For example:

- malnutrition

- having no energy

- developing brittle bones or rickets (which is due to a lack of vitamin D in the diet or not getting enough sunlight)

- not being able to concentrate properly

- developing heart disease

- developing some cancers, for example of the digestive system.

Personal hygiene

Poor personal hygiene is another risk to health. For example, not cleaning your teeth for days could put your health at risk. There are various reasons why a person may not clean their teeth.

It could be because they are too young and no else has done it for them; they are ill and cannot do it for themselves; they cannot be bothered; they do not have a toothbrush and toothpaste.

The effects of not cleaning your teeth can be:

- gum disease

- bad (decayed) teeth

- bad breath

- upset stomach (from swallowing all those germs!)

- green teeth

- no friends!

- poor diet, because you cannot *chew* certain foods.

Personal hygiene is not just about keeping our teeth clean. It is about keeping the whole body clean and in 'tip top' condition. Personal hygiene is about:

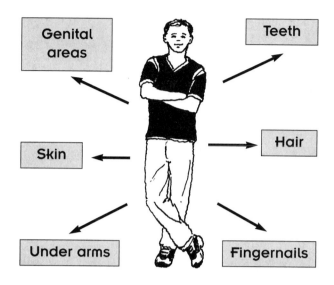

The best way to keep ourselves clean is to take a bath or shower every day.

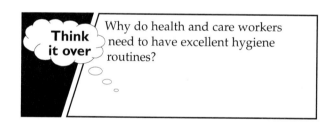

Think it over Why do health and care workers need to have excellent hygiene routines?

Talk it over

Gillian is a care worker and today she is taking Tommy to have a dental check-up. Tommy has learning disabilities and even though he is 17 he wants Gillian to come into the dental surgery with him.

The dentist asks Gillian to hold Tommy's hand but when she leans close to Tommy the dentist cannot help but notice that not only are her teeth dirty but there is a strong smell of body odour.

In pairs discuss the sort of example that Gillian is setting for Tommy. What would you have said to Gillian if you had been the dentist?

Besides maintaining our own personal hygiene, we will sometimes also need to help clients with their personal hygiene routines.

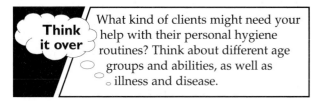

Think it over What kind of clients might need your help with their personal hygiene routines? Think about different age groups and abilities, as well as illness and disease.

Read the list and then identify ways of reducing the risk to your own health and your client's health from poor personal hygiene.

Good hygiene checklist

✓ Wash thoroughly every single day

✓ Keep nails short and clean

✓ Make sure hair is clean and not getting in the way of work

✓ Do not share your personal hygiene equipment (hair brush, tooth brush, comb etc.)

✓ Wash hands after using the toilet

✓ Wash hands before preparing any food

✓ Use handkerchiefs when coughing and sneezing

✓ Keep cuts covered with clean dressings

✓ Clean teeth every day

✓ Always wash or shower after exercise.

Exercise

Lack of exercise is a major risk to health. The human body was built to use energy.

When people lived in caves they had to run, hunt and work hard to survive. These days we don't have to do anything physical if we don't want to! Our food is easy to buy, we just go to the shops! Other exercise-saving devices are:

- remote controls

- cars/buses/trains

- washing machines

- electric lawn mowers

- escalators and lifts.

It is no wonder that the National Fitness Survey, carried out by the Health Education Authority and the Sports Council in 1992, showed that very few people in this country were physically fit.

If you are encouraging people to exercise you will need to think about the sort of physical activities they are able to do. Think about their health, age and their ability before you recommend any activity. The kinds of physical activity you could suggest are:

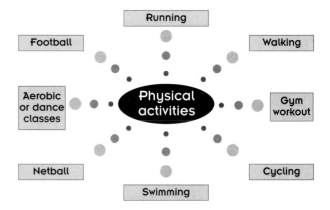

Looking at the list of activities that can be safely recommended, we can see that some activities involve other people and some we can do alone. It is important to choose an activity that involves mixing with others if that is what we want, or to choose one that gives us time alone if that is what we prefer.

Try it out Carry out a quick survey of the kinds of physical activity that your friends like doing. You could design a questionnaire to fill in. When you have collected their answers you could make a 'giant' bar chart to show the kinds of exercise people like doing.

Try it out

Adam is five years old and needs to follow an exercise programme that will help to build up the strength in his legs. Three months ago he was involved in a road traffic accident that resulted in both his legs being broken.

Now he is learning to walk and run again.

Working with another person identify a range of activities that will help Adam strengthen his legs. You will need to think of his age and his abilities as you discuss this.

Talk it over

Gail and Tim have been in a loving relationship for the last three years. They are planning to get engaged soon. However, Gail recently went abroad on holiday and one night she got very drunk in a disco.

When she woke up the following morning she was in bed with a man she had never met before the previous night. She is very worried about the consequences.

Discuss with another person the possible consequences of Gail's good night out. What advice would you give her?

It is important when choosing exercise to make sure we are doing something we like. If we do not like the exercise we will not do it again!

Remember! Exercise only becomes a regular habit if people:

- enjoy the activity
- feel good after the exercise
- want to do it again
- gain something from it.

? Did you know?

That a 30 minute, 5 kilometre run burns up 300 calories

Talk it over

In pairs make a list of physical activities that would be suitable for people over the age of 65, and another list suitable for adolescents.

Sexual behaviour

Sexual behaviour can be a major health risk. We have all heard about the health risks from HIV and AIDS. But these are not the only health risks from sexual behaviour. It is possible to catch a range of diseases or conditions from unprotected sexual activity, such as:

- gonorrhoea
- syphilis
- non-specific urethritis
- genital herpes
- lice
- chlamydia.

Most hospitals have special clinics – called genito-urinary medicine (GUM) clinics – dealing with sexual diseases. They give advice and treatment to those who have a sexually transmitted disease, or think they have. The consultation and treatment can be completely confidential – a person need not even give their name. Doctors and nurses working in the special clinic will not pass details of results or treatment to a client's own doctor.

? Did you know?

Signs are things you can see

Symptoms are things you can feel

Signs and symptoms of some sexually transmitted (passed on) diseases		
Sexual condition	*Signs*	*Symptoms*
Gonorrhoea	Discharge from the penis or vagina	Burning feeling when passing water
Syphilis	A small hard 'sore' called a chancre. This disappears after a few weeks. Rash and and swollen glands	Years later heart, brain and nervous system become infected leading to death
HIV/AIDS	No signs	No symptoms until years later when death is the result
Non-specific urethritis	Discharge from the urethra (the tube through which urine passes)	Burning feeling when passing water
Genital herpes	Blisters around the genital area	Pain and fever. There is no cure for this. The blisters and pain go away with treatment but can return at any time
Lice	Crab lice living in the genital area of the body. They can spread to other parts of the body as well	Severe itching and skin irritation
Chlamydia	There may be none or women might have vaginal bleeding	Women may have abdominal pain or pain during sex. Men might have stinging sensation when passing water

Try it out

William had his first sexual relationship three weeks ago. He has recently noticed that his penis burns when he passes urine. He is really worried in case he has caught something from the girl. After all he had only known her a few days when they slept together. He has not seen her since.

In pairs use the chart to identify which of the sexually transmitted diseases William has caught.

? Did you know?

Chlamydia is a sexually transmitted disease, sometimes called the 'silent sterilizer' because there may be no symptoms, but it can leave women unable to have children. It is caused by a bacteria.

It is the fastest growing STI (sexually transmitted infection) amongst young people.

Chlamydia is easily treated by taking antibiotics. For protection, use a condom.

Reducing the risks from sexual behaviour

It is important to protect our health and well-being from unsafe sexual behaviour. We can do this by:

*   not having sex in a relationship until you are sure it is the right thing to do

*   not having many sexual partners

*   always using a condom and knowing how to use it (even if the girl is using other contraceptive methods)

*   keeping yourself safe from the influence of drugs and alcohol. (People are more likely to have unsafe sex when they are drunk or on drugs. This is because we lose control over our decision-making skills.)

If you know the risks of unsafe sexual behaviour you can make sure that people in your care who need to know about the risks are made aware of them as well.

Unsafe practices in the home and workplace

? Did you know?

There are more accidents in the home than anywhere else?

Why do you think this is?

The people most at risk from accidents in the home are young children and older people. This is not because they are careless, but for a variety of reasons. For example:

- loss of eyesight
- loss of hearing
- loss of mobility (twisting and stretching)
- lack of strength (for lifting pans and kettles)
- illness that affects short-term memory.

But there are other things that can be hazardous around the home, as you can see in the case of Sarah.

Try it out

Milly is almost three years old. She has gone with her mother to visit a good friend who has a small swimming pool in the garden.

There is a flight of concrete steps leading to the patio where the barbecue is being held later on and a sand pit close to the garden rubbish heap.

Milly's mother tells her to go and play with the other children, but not to go too close to the pool.

Discuss with another person the dangers to Milly in this garden.

Think it over

Where do you think the most dangerous places are inside a house? Make a list and then compare your answers with the ones in the spidergram.

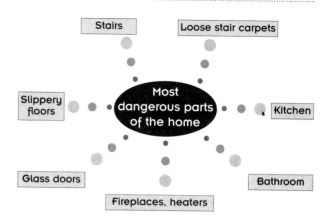

Most dangerous parts of the home — Stairs, Loose stair carpets, Slippery floors, Kitchen, Glass doors, Fireplaces, heaters, Bathroom

Accident prevention

It is easy to prevent most accidents happening. This means thinking ahead. If we know where the most dangerous places are and we know the people most at risk of having an accident, we can usually do something about it.

Many things around us are potential risks to our health. To keep ourselves and our clients safe we need to think 'prevention' at all times.

Accident prevention checklist

- ✓ Keep plug sockets covered (so that little fingers cannot be poked into them)
- ✓ Keep hot liquids in a kitchen away from the edge of work surfaces
- ✓ Keep stairs well lit
- ✓ Never polish floors to the point that they are slippery
- ✓ Fasten carpets and mats down if they are likely to move under someone's feet
- ✓ Fit fire alarms
- ✓ Make sure there are no trailing flexes or wires
- ✓ Keep the house tidy and put things away.

Think it over

What other things could be done to make a house safe? Make a list and then compare it with another person's. Is your home safe?

Too much of anything – even exercise – is not good for physical health. You should try to have a balanced lifestyle that includes some of the things that give you pleasure. The only habits you should completely avoid are smoking and the use of illegal drugs. Neither will benefit your health in any way.

2.4 Indicators of good physical health

When people are trying to improve their health and well-being they need some kind of measure to monitor their progress against. We all like to know 'how we are doing'. We can use several different measures of health and fitness to show our clients (or even ourselves) how they are progressing towards any targets they may have set. For example:

- height and weight charts
- peak flow monitor
- body mass index.

The kinds of health targets that people set for themselves, or have set for them by a health

professional, could include any (or even all) of the following in the spidergram:

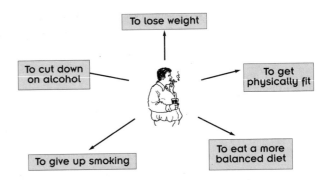

Using measures of progress can strongly motivate people, particularly if they show how well a person is doing. This can help them to stick to the changes they are making to their lifestyle. The hardest part about making change is sticking to it!

Height and weight charts

These charts show ideal height and weight ratios – i.e. is a person the right weight for their height. For example, given that Rob is 173 cm tall and weighs 100 kilos, you can see from the chart that he is in the very overweight band. By losing weight he can get himself into the ideal weight for height band.

It is important to be realistic about these charts. They are only a guide. The case of Lynda shows this.

Ideally we should be in one of the ranges shown on the chart – if not, there has to be a good reason why not!

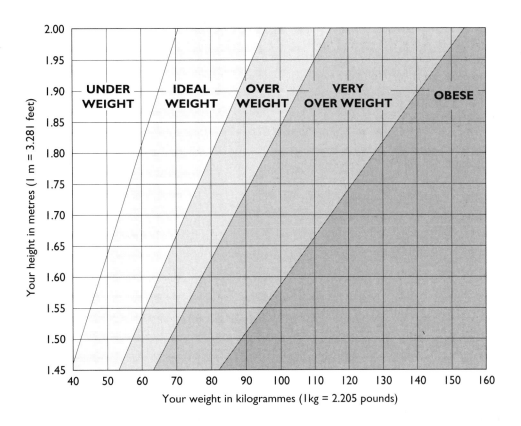

Your height in metres (1 m = 3.281 feet)

UNDER WEIGHT · IDEAL WEIGHT · OVER WEIGHT · VERY OVER WEIGHT · OBESE

Your weight in kilogrammes (1 kg = 2.205 pounds)

SNAPSHOT

Lynda is 155 cm tall. She weighs 62 kilos. She takes size 12 clothes.

Though she is small Lynda is a fell runner and has very powerful muscles. This means that she will weigh more than an unfit person who is carrying a lot of fat because lean muscle weighs more than fat!

Weighing scales can also help to motivate people into losing weight, or maintaining their weight once they have got it down. However they should only be used once a week to monitor progress. Once a person has reached their goal weight they can use the fitting of their clothes as a guide to whether they are putting weight back on.

Weight can be a serious issue. Make sure that people do not become so obsessed with their weight that they develop serious eating disorders such as anorexia nervosa or bulimia nervosa.

Look it up

Look up anorexia nervosa and bulimia nervosa in a dictionary. You might need a medical dictionary to help you find out what they are.

Peak flow

Another way of checking on your health is by using a peak flow monitor. These have many different uses, but basically they are used to see how effective (strong) a person's lungs are. A peak flow monitor can be used to monitor the health of people with asthma.

To use a peak flow monitor the person has to blow as hard as they can into a cardboard tube. This then moves the score counter along the tube to a certain point, at which you can read off the number it has reached. The best score out of three blows is usually used.

> ## ! Find it out!
>
> Ask a nurse or other health professional about how peak flow monitors are used to measure the health of people with asthma.

Regular physical exercise can make a difference to the score you reach on a peak flow monitor. Exercise makes the lungs more powerful and improves their ability to take in oxygen.

A peak flow monitor can be used at the start of an exercise programme, then again in the middle of the programme to show how the person's lungs are improving, and again at the end of the exercise to show the client how well they have done.

Try it out 	Karan Thompson is a health and fitness consultant. Her job is to advise people on how they can get fitter. She regularly uses the body mass index to explain to a client how much fat they are carrying. She is advising Rob at the moment. She has measured his height and weighed him. Now comes the maths.

Sometimes it takes at least six weeks before any noticeable improvement occurs in a client's lungs. So you should be careful not to monitor again too close to the first one!

Body mass index

This an indicator of good health that measures the amount of fat in a person's body in relation to their height. it is not the same as a height:weight chart! The body mass index measure needs some maths to help you carry out the test.

The formula to calculate the body mass index (BMI) is:

$$\frac{\text{weight kg}}{\text{height metres}^2} = \text{BMI}$$

Ranges are different for males and females:

Female less than 18   underweight
18–20   lean
20–22   average
26–28   plump
30–36   moderately obese
40+   severely obese

Male   18–19   lean
21–22   average
24–25   ideal
32–33   obese
40+   severely obese

The body mass index helps to indicate if weight loss is needed.

Unit 2 Assessment

For this unit you are going to create a plan for health which will assist you in helping a chosen person (which could be you!) to improve or maintain their physical health and well-being. You will use the information gained from this unit, and also from Unit 5, to help you.

You will have the opportunity to work towards a pass, merit or distinction grade.

The activities are ordered in such a way as to guide you through this assessment. The levels of assessment are clearly indicated as:

- P for Pass
- M for Merit
- D for Distinction.

You may wish to discuss with your tutor the level of activities you do.

Working towards a pass grade

All students must complete the first four P activities to achieve the minimum for Unit 2.

The scenario below is used as an explanation, but if you cannot find someone to use for the plan, and you do not want to use yourself, you may use this case study.

Activity 1P

In order to create a plan for the person, you must show some understanding of their life and what they do.

- Write a profile or even a little story like the one we have given you about Moira, relating to those factors in the person's life which affect his or her physical health and well-being. You might outline what they eat, what they do in the day, what kind of environment they live in, and any other

CASE STUDY

Moira's week

Moira is 18. She is 168 cm tall and weighs 83 kilos. She is at college, has lots of friends and gets good grades in her assignments. After college, she has a job four evenings a week at the local supermarket. She thinks she is lucky: college and home and work are only about 200 metres from each other. She hardly ever has to walk anywhere and she gets up much later than the others. The supermarket has a lovely staff canteen, with staff discount, and great cakes and eclairs, her favourites. She is always hungry after college, so she pops in there and has a couple of eclairs and a coke before starting work. She is a cashier: sitting down from 5.00 to 8.15 with a 15-minute break. She practically falls into bed when she gets home, she is so tired.

Although Moira has lots of friends at college, she doesn't go out a lot because she knows she is overweight and doesn't like to be reminded of it when all her friends are wearing smart clothes and short skirts. She often says she is too tired when they ask her to go into town with them on Saturday.

But last week was her best friend Sophie's birthday and she had said she would go and have a pizza with everyone and maybe go to a club. They were all going into town on the bus and were late setting out, so they had to run to the bus stop. They nearly went without her: she couldn't keep up with everyone and the bus had to wait. She practically passed out when she finally made it to her seat because she felt so ill. She felt angry and embarrassed too, because the bus driver was a bit rude and called her tubby!

factors you believe are important. Age and gender may also be important.

You could illustrate this with photos, create the story through an interview, or even draw it as a cartoon. Be as original as you like!

- Discuss in a couple of sentences whether the person is healthy or not, and why you believe this to be the case.

Activity 2P

- From what you have described in 1P, identify any risk factors in the person's lifestyle which may affect their health and well-being. They may be overweight, like Moira, or may smoke or not care about their personal hygiene.

- Why would you describe these as risk factors? You must identify at least one risk, but you may wish to list more.

- If the chosen person has a perfectly healthy life, with no risk factors, describe what risk factors he or she has managed to avoid or do something about.

Activity 3P

- You are now going to decide (in discussion with your chosen person, if this is appropriate) one factor to work on to improve. You will use your understanding of measures of health to work out which factor to improve. If your chosen person does not need to improve his/her health, decide which risk factor he or she is going to maintain. This will be your health target.

For example, in the scenario about Moira you could look at height:weight measurements as a basis for your suggestion.

- Write a short explanation of the factor you have chosen and why.

Activity 4P

- You are now going to create a plan for your chosen person, which shows how you will go about achieving the health target. Create a plan for, say, a week, which could be repeated until the target is achieved. Using the Moira scenario, the plan could be that she starts to cut down on the cakes she eats, and begins to take exercise.

You could set it out on a grid pattern, with Monday–Sunday as references. You can illustrate this if you like.

	Diet	Recreation	Exercise
Mon			
Tues			
Wed			
Thurs			
Fri			
Sat			
Sun			

- Include some explanations, after you have written out the plan, about why you think it might work, but also about what some of the problems might be for the chosen person. For example, dieting is always a good idea at the time, but keeping it up can be difficult.

If you are going to do this with another person, you will be able to discuss this with them to ensure it is realistic!

Working towards a merit grade

To achieve a merit grade you must carry out the activities for the pass grade, plus the additional steps to Activities 3, 4 and 5 below.

Activity 3M

You must identify two measures of health to work into your targets for the individual. For example, in the case of Moira you could use peak flow measurements as well as height:weight measurements. You must be able to show that you can interpret the results of these health measures, so you will need to include the measurements and what they mean.

Activity 4M

As well as working out a plan, you are going to identify:

* at least two *short* term and

* two *long* term targets with your chosen person, or for yourself, and

* clearly indicate on the plan what they are and when they should be achieved.

These should be realistic. You should be aware that sometimes plans do not always work out quite as expected. Moira, for example, might have as one long-term goal that she will lose weight over six months by exercising for 20 minutes three times a week. However she might have flu for ten days and get behind in her schedule.

Activity 5M

When you have completed these four activities, you must provide a list of where your information came from and how you used those sources. You might have used text books, healthy eating pamphlets, information from your doctor's surgery or health centre, or even from the supermarket! Give the titles of the books and who wrote them. If possible, you can include the leaflets in your assignment.

Put this as a separate section at the end of the assignment.

Working towards a distinction grade

To achieve a distinction grade, you must carry out the activities for the pass and merit grades, plus the additional steps for Activities 4 and 6 below.

Activity 4D

* When you set out your plan, explain why you think this particular way is best for your chosen person. You must explain why the language and illustrations you use are appropriate for him or her (or you!).

Activity 6D

* This relates to the targets that have been set for your chosen person. Explain in your own words what the effects will be on him or her, once they have achieved them. It is not enough to say 'Moira will feel better'. You should relate them to:

  ° physical benefits

  ° emotional benefits

  ° social benefits.

For example, in Moira's case she will feel and look healthier if she takes more exercise, and her heart will be healthier too. This is a physical effect.

Your assessor will also take into account your ability to provide good quality work which is clearly presented in well-constructed language. A higher grade may also depend on you working independently, as much as you are able to, while still creating the required evidence.

UNIT 2 ASSESSMENT

Check your knowledge

Questions 1–10 require short answers.

Questions 11–20 are multiple choice questions. There is only one correct answer.

Short answer questions

1 What do the initials PIES stand for when talking about health and well-being?

2 Using yourself as an example, state one way that you look after your health in terms of PIES.

3 What do you understand by the term 'a balanced diet'?

4 Give two reasons why an older person should take daily exercise.

5 What do you understand by the word 'screening' as it relates to health, and give two examples of preventative health-screening programmes in this country?

6 How could the following affect health and well-being:
   a air quality
   b housing
   c noise levels?

7 Give two health risks attached to each of the following recreational activities:
   a drinking excessive alcohol
   b smoking tobacco
   c smoking cannabis
   d taking ecstasy tablets.

8 List four ways exercise can improve and maintain health and well-being.

9 What is body mass index and how can it be used as an indicator of health?

10 Give the signs and symptoms of two sexually transmitted diseases.

Multiple choice questions

11 Carbohydrates are divided into sugars and starches. A good example of a carbohydrate is:
   a bread
   b zinc
   c fish oil
   d chicken nuggets.

12 Protein is needed by the body for:
   a energy
   b protection against disease
   c to build healthy bones
   d growth and repair.

13 Vitamin D is necessary for:
   a energy
   b healthy bones
   c keeping the brain active
   d an additional supply of protein in times of need.

14 Exercise is essential for health and well-being. Exercises for stamina include:
   a stretching and bending
   b jogging and swimming
   c deep breathing before diving underwater
   d carpet bowls.

15 Recreational pastimes are good for health and well-being because:
   a they help get rid of unwanted body fat
   b they provide ways of meeting people, learning new skills and relieving stress
   c they are part of our cultural heritage
   d they describe the kind of parties and clubs you go to.

16 Social class is defined by:
   a how clever you are at intellectual activities

b the kinds of work or employment you do

c whether you live in England, Scotland, Wales or Northern Ireland

d beong included as part of the national curriculum.

17 You can protect yourself from sexually transmitted infections by:

a taking antibiotics

b only taking part in sexual activity if you haven't drunk any alcohol

c always practising safer sex

d only having one partner.

18 Chlamydia is:

a the name of a well-known band

b a girl's name

c a highly infectious sexually transmitted disease

d a Greek island.

19 Examples of good personal hygiene include:

a keeping the fridge door closed so flies cannot contaminate food

b bathing or showering every day

c visiting the doctor if you suspect you have flu

d being the right weight for height.

20 Heroin is an example of:

a an illegal 'soft' drug

b someone who is very brave

c an illegal 'hard' drug

d someone who is a drug addict.

Understanding Personal Development and Relationships

This unit explores the different stages of human growth and development. You will find out about the five main life stages from birth to old age. You will have the opportunity to explore the different things that happen to the human body as it grows and develops – for example, the way the body becomes older.

You will also be able to find out about the way work, money and other social factors can affect the development of human beings. There are many things that can help or hinder human development. It is not just chance!

The unit also gives you the opportunity to explore human relationships. You will find out how relationships can change and develop over time and the effects this can have on the people we know and care for.

You need to learn about:

*   the stages of human growth and development
*   the factors that affect growth and development
*   the effects of relationships on personal development.

3.1 Human growth and development

Human beings don't just 'get born and then die!', they go through several stages on the way 'from cradle to grave'. There are actually five different stages between birth and death. Each stage has a purpose. It prepares the body for the next stage to come by helping the person develop new skills and understanding and acquire the information they will need to cope with the changes and responsibilities that being older brings.

During each stage of development our skills knowledge and body grow and develop. This enables us to carry out more physical tasks, such as lifting, pulling and pushing things, and enables us to take part in more activities, such as education and recreation. It is all part of growing up and then growing older.

These are the five stages of life:

*   Infancy (0-3 years)

*   Childhood (3-9 years)
*   Adolescence (10 –18 years)
*   Adulthood (19 –65)
*   Old age (65 +).

During each of the five stages, every person develops special characteristics that make them unique in the world (there is no other human being who shares all the same characteristics as you – not even identical twins share all the same characteristics).

Look it up

Use a dictionary to look up the word 'characteristic'. Write your definition down and then compare it to someone else's definition.

Human characteristics can be classified into separate categories. For example:

Physical   ⇒   The size and shape of your body. The strength it has and the things it can do

Intellectual   ⇒   The learning ability that you have. How fast you learn new information and the way you prefer to learn

Emotional   ⇒   The way you think and feel about yourself and others

Social   ⇒   The way you get on with other people and the way they get on with you

You have come across these characteristics before in Unit 2 when we explored basic health needs. In that unit we called them PIES and we used them to look at the health needs of different client groups. We are going to use them again now to explore the typical growth and development features of each life stage.

A person's features or characteristics are very important. They help to make the person special and different from everyone else. Your characteristics are features of you that help other people decide whether they are attracted to you or not!

Examples of characteristics:

kind	clever
aggressive	creative
unsociable	bad-tempered
sociable	broad-shouldered
over friendly	strong
talkative	disruptive
tall	rude

Characteristics can be almost anything to do with the way people look, think, feel and behave.

Talk it over

Working with another person, decide which category (physical, social, emotional and intellectual) the characteristics in the list above should go into. For example, is being rude a social characteristic or a physical one?

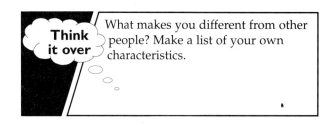

Think it over   What makes you different from other people? Make a list of your own characteristics.

Many psychology researchers think that some (if not all) of a person's characteristics can be inherited from their parents. Others think that characteristics are learned from the people we live with. This argument is called Nature (inherited characteristics) versus Nurture (learned characteristics).

Try it out

Ben is nearly three years old. He attends play school three afternoons each week. Unfortunately, Ben is not very popular with the other children.

He fights with any child that tries to take a toy off him and is regularly found having a temper tantrum. This is when he throws anything that comes to hand, usually at his carers.

Molly is 75 years old and has arthritis in her hips. This means that she cannot get out of the house very much.

She is never lonely because the children in the street where she lives love to visit her. She has a parrot that can talk and a biscuit tin that is never empty.

Identify the characteristics you think Ben and Molly have. Write them down in two separate lists and then compare your list with another person's.

Now that we have a better understanding of characteristics we can explore the five different stages of human growth and development. It is interesting to note the kind of characteristics that we find at each stage. For example, three-year-old children like Ben are often selfish towards other people. However when Ben grows up he may turn out to be a very sharing kind of person. On the other hand, Molly might have always been kind, sharing and fun to be with. We cannot always tell what kind of adult a child will make!

Infancy

In its first three years of life a baby is called an 'infant'. Once it starts crawling, pulling itself up and walking the baby is often called a 'toddler'. This stage of life is very fast, with the body growing and changing quickly. Many parents remember how fast their babies grew at this stage – and how it seemed that they 'had not been babies for two minutes'. This speed of growth and change occurs because of the body's need for physical strength and independence – to enable it to survive.

Physical development

Each infant grows and develops at its own rate. Usually there is not a great deal of difference between the development of infants. For example, most infants will 'cut' their first teeth at about six months of age. Others might be a little earlier or a little later, but there will not be a great deal of difference.

When a baby is born it has no control over its body or the movements its body makes. This all changes within a few weeks of birth. First, the baby begins to gain control over its head, and then the rest of the body from head to toe. At one month the baby can only raise its head slightly, however by six months it can guide its foot into its mouth quite easily.

Other developments of a child in the first year of life are:

- at 8 to 9 months the infant will be able to sit up and pull themselves up

Talk it over

Dan is looking after Melanie today because his partner, Trish, has gone to work. It is the first time he has spent all day with her since she was born three months ago. He is exhausted! He thought babies of this age just slept all day.

He has had no time for anything else except feeding and changing her, comforting her when she cries and playing with her to keep her happy. In fact, he has only just realised how much work there is with a new baby in the house.

Working in pairs discuss the basic needs of Melanie. You might like to think about PIES to help you decide what her needs are.

During the first years of life the human infant is completely dependent on its carers. All its basic needs have to be met by someone else, if it is to survive.

Talk it over

Ahmed is eight months old and he just loves meal times, especially now that he can have his own spoon.

His favourite meal of the day is porridge for breakfast. He beams a big smile of delight when he is given his plate in the morning.

His mother usually starts the feeding by spooning the food into his mouth but he gets so excited that he takes the spoon and 'does it himself'.

What a mess! More on the floor and his head than in his mouth.

Working with another person discuss the different parts of Ahmed's development that are progressing by learning to feed himself. You will need to think about PIES – for example, Ahmed's big smile attracts mother's attention as well as indicating his pleasure in the food.

Think it over

Shaheen is 12 months old and she has been walking for about five weeks. She has become quite confident on her feet. She can turn around now without falling over although she still wobbles a bit. She is also able to run without falling forwards but she sometimes puts her hands out in front of her. She has also discovered how to get back on her feet without using other people's hands to support her.

Walking is a very complicated skill made up of balance and movement. What sort of movements does Shaheen use to help her walk?

- at 10 –12 months the infant will be standing and walking (maybe with help).

Intellectual development

When the walking stage starts, so does the 'fun'. Many child carers say that this part of an infant's development is exhausting … for them! There is no stopping the infant. They are born naturally curious, with a need to explore their whole world and everything in it. They will want to do this any way they can – especially using their hands and mouth.

They can easily recognise their carer and other important people in their lives.

Talk it over

Kai is 18 months old and has just discovered the kitchen cupboards will open if he pulls them from the bottom.

He got a real shock the first time all the plates fell from the plate stand when he dragged it towards himself, but now he thinks it is a good game.

Working with another person discuss the dangers that Kai might face in the rest of the house now that he can walk and open things. Make a list of them. Which parts of his development have increased to allow him to do these things?

Emotional development

As the infant becomes older so its confidence increases. In the first two years of life the infant does not usually want to be parted from its carer. This close relationship between the infant and carer is called bonding and is very important for the infant's sense of security and belonging.

A toddler will explore its surroundings but only if the carer is present. Even when a toddler is ready to explore the surroundings a little, it needs to keep checking that the carer is still close by and within sight. As the child gets older, it becomes more adventurous and will explore further, especially as it realises the carer will still be there. It is important at this stage of a child's development not to let them down by disappearing!

Key developments in the infant stage

- Recognising carers
- Learning to eat solids
- Learning to walk
- Learning language
- Beginning to recognise letters and numbers
- Learning bladder and bowel control
- Knowing the difference between boy and girl.

Think it over

Victoria has started play school. This is her first week there. She really wants to have a go on the slide but this means leaving her carer's side.

She decides that she will be adventurous, so she runs across to the slide, quickly climbs the steps, smiles at her carer before coming down the slide and then runs straight back to her carer's side for a hug.

Why do you think Victoria was so quick to get back to her carer and have a hug?

Social development: the importance of play

Play is an important part of infant development. Games and toys help the child to find out about the 'real' world. For example, playing with soft toys and dolls helps a child develop caring emotions. Talking to dolls and teddies allows the infant to develop language skills and imagination.

It is quite easy to provide play opportunities that are stimulating. For example, allowing a child to play with cardboard boxes gives it the chance to use its imagination – the box can be a house, car, train, or anything else the child wants it to be!

Play starts off as a solitary activity (playing alone). Gradually children learn to play alongside others, but not with them. From around three years of age children start to play with others. In other words they are learning to be sociable.

Try it out
Find the time to watch an infant playing. You could use a real life situation or children's television. Make notes about the way the children are playing and the kinds of toys and objects they are playing with. Discuss your findings with your group.

Childhood

This is the stage of development, between three and nine years of age, that many carers love the best. It is often a time when carers will say the infant has 'become a little person with all their own characteristics'.

Children do not have to rely on their carers for all their needs. Between three and five they can dress and feed themselves with some help, but as they head towards nine and 10, they can do these things independently, even

preparing simple foods for themselves if necessary.

Key developments in the childhood stage
• Making relationships
• Developing physical skills
• Learning to read, write and do maths
• Developing some independence
• Learning right from wrong
• Developing attitudes to people and situations.

Older children can:

• go to some places on their own

• tidy up

• wash themselves

• play team games

• cook a basic meal

• read and write

• understand rules.

Physical characteristics

The physical appearance of a child begins to change as they get older. They lose their baby shape and begin to look like small adults.

Infant

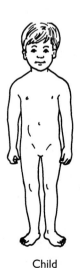

Child

The infant's fast rate of growth begins to slow down during childhood. Physical, intellectual, emotional and social development is still taking place but the child is now really beginning to learn some very complicated skills.

As the child grows and develops its balance becomes very good. This means they can run, climb and jump (and of course get into all sorts of danger as a result!).

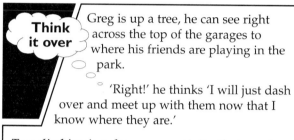

Think it over

Greg is up a tree, he can see right across the top of the garages to where his friends are playing in the park.

'Right!' he thinks 'I will just dash over and meet up with them now that I know where they are.'

Tree climbing is a dangerous activity that requires certain developments to take place before a child can do it. What do you think they are?

At four years old a child can usually fasten the buttons on the front of a coat. It can also make itself more comfortable by making choices about a range of things.

Talk it over

Jane is four years old. She has just started nursery school. It is her second day there.

Today she is playing in the sand pit but the weather is very warm and she is wearing her cardigan.

She decides to unbutton the cardigan and take it off whilst she is playing.

Working with another person discuss the fact that Jane has clearly made herself more comfortable in the hot weather. How else do children of four and five years of age make themselves more comfortable?

As children become older still they learn even more complicated skills as their development continues to progress.

Intellectual characteristics

The development of the brain and the mind is all part of childhood intellectual development. The features of intellectual development include:

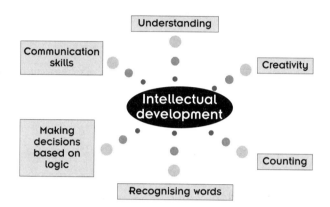

Children are interested in everything. They usually ask questions until the 'carer is dizzy'. However it is only by asking questions (and getting answers) that the child will learn about their environment and the culture (customs and practices) of the society they live in.

As a child's intellectual development continues it can begin to carry out a range of more complex (difficult) activities, such as:

- reading and sums
- making and keeping relationships
- cleaning teeth
- table manners

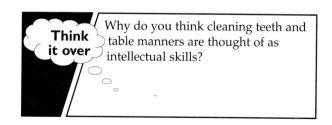

Think it over

Why do you think cleaning teeth and table manners are thought of as intellectual skills?

- writing their own name

- understanding the rules of team games.

The child begins to mix different skills to complete a complicated task. For example, playing a team sport like football requires the child to understand the rules (intellectual development), be able to kick the ball in the right direction (physical development) and talk to their team mates about the strategy to follow (social development). They also have to cope with negative (or positive) feelings when the game has been won or lost (emotional development).

Children learn to do things by watching others. This is called 'modelling'. It is often amusing to see a small child copying something their parents have said or done. On the other hand, some children learn from poor behaviour that can lead to difficulties as they get older.

Did you know?

Twenty years ago it was possible for children to buy sweet cigarettes at the local sweet shop. They cannot do this now.

Think it over

Why do you think you cannot buy sweet cigarettes now? Discuss with another person other ways adults might influence a child's development.

Emotional characteristics

Children have to learn to cope with their feelings and the feelings of others in the same way that they have to learn a new skill, such as table manners. Children learn to cope with their emotions through playing with other children. Some emotional characteristics are:

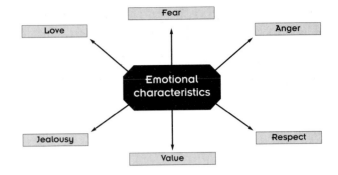

Infants may have temper tantrums, however as they become older these become less frequent. By the time a child is five years old it usually wants to be in the company of

Think it over

Khadija is so upset. Her rabbit died during the night. When she got to school the next day she told her friend Thomas. She was still in tears.

After school Thomas asked his mother if he could give 'Billy Rabbit' to Khadija because he had two rabbits and Khadija had none!

What emotions are Thomas and Khadija showing here?

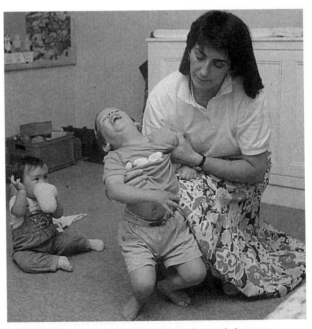

Infants may express their feelings through temper tantrums

other children. At this age they are able to play together and join in team games.

By the time a child is 10 years old it has begun to learn how to cope with its feelings. They will have discovered jealousy and anger and ways of appropriate coping.

Talk it over

Sonia and Daisy are best friends. One day Sonia was taken to see a famous 'boyband'. She even got to meet them backstage after the performance.

Daisy was so upset at not being included she cried for three days. She refused to speak to Sonia until Sonia said she was sorry for going without her.

Discuss with another person the ways in which Daisy coped with her feelings of anger and jealousy. Do you think she could have coped differently?

Children are very sensitive to criticism and do not react well to 'a telling off', especially in front of other people.

Try it out

Debbie had done it again! She had invited her best friend to her home for an evening meal without asking her parents first.

Her mother was furious because she had already explained to Debbie that she must not do this without asking permission first.

Her mother shouted at her in front of her friend, so Debbie ran upstairs shouting to her mother, 'I hate you, I hate you'.

Discuss with another person why Debbie has behaved in this way. Include thoughts about emotional and social development in your discussions.

Social characteristics

Developing good relationships with other people is a skill we begin to develop from birth onwards. The way we learn and the kind of skills we learn will depend on the culture we are born into. For example, a person from a culture that does not approve of males and females mixing together outside the home may choose to become friendly with someone of their own sex. On the other hand, some societies allow mixing between all age groups and all sexes.

Some children are good at developing lots of social relationships, others are better at keeping a few special friends for a long time. We are all different!

Think it over

Think about the friends you have at the moment. Have they been friends for a long time? Or are you just getting to know them? Do you have a best friend?

Talk it over

Peter is nine years old and has become a member of the scouts. He wants to go to the next scout meeting with another boy. He does not want his mother to take him. His mother thinks it is too far for him to walk by himself. It will take him at least 15 minutes.

It is important that Peter is allowed to develop socially as much as possible, however it is understandable that his mother worries about his safety. Working with another person discuss the benefits to Peter of joining the scouts. Then discuss the benefits of walking to the scout meeting with his new friend.

Developing social networks

During childhood, a child learns to make friends with others. They learn the importance of good relationships in a variety of settings, for example:

- in the home
- at school
- in clubs and groups (sports, drama, music etc.)
- where they live
- in religious settings.

Adolescence

Adolescence starts at around 10 years of age and continues until about 18. This stage is often called 'puberty'. Many young people in this stage of life call themselves 'teenagers'.

During this stage of life new roles and responsibilities are developed. Young people are:

- developing more understanding relationships with people of all ages
- accepting themself as they are
- learning, ready for work
- achieving independence
- developing a set of values and morals
- developing socially responsible behaviour
- preparing for a lasting relationship.

Physical characteristics

This stage of life is very interesting because so many changes are taking place. The male and female body begins to prepare itself for reproduction (giving birth). It becomes possible for males and females to become parents.

Body size and shape continues to change. More hair begins to grow on the body and boys experience a change in their voice and girls begin to menstruate. These changes are signs that the body is 'maturing' (getting close to full development). Some young people begin to develop skin and weight problems (due to hormones) during this time, but these are usually only temporary whilst the body is going through its changes.

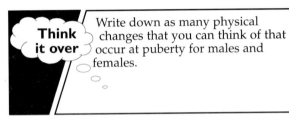

Think it over Write down as many physical changes that you can think of that occur at puberty for males and females.

Major female physical changes are:

- gains weight
- grows body hair
- periods start
- breasts develop
- shape changes
- skin and hair changes
- becomes taller.

Major male physical changes are:

- gains weight
- grows body hair
- penis and testicles develop
- voice 'breaks'
- shoulders broaden
- skin and hair changes
- shape changes
- becomes taller.

Think it over

How have you changed over the last ten years? What changes have you liked and not liked?

Emotional and social characteristics

Emotions are often very important during the teenage years. Hormones may be out of balance and in some cases this can lead to mood swings or aggressive behaviour. These kinds of emotions usually settle down as the teenager becomes older. However while moods last they can make caring for someone in this age group very difficult.

During this time of development and change it is important for the adolescent to be able to talk to someone who can help them understand the variety of feelings and strong emotions they are having.

Think it over

Tina is 15 and really fed up! She can't wait until she is 16 and allowed to go to her local disco for the under-18s. She thinks her present life is boring – it's all school and homework!

It's a good thing she has her best friend Shanaz to share her problems with. They spend hours together, usually in Tina's bedroom. They have some personal space there, away from their parents, who are always going on about the importance of homework!

Tina and Shanaz love to talk about everything and anything, but especially about the time when they will both be 16.

They are anxious about the way their bodies are changing and developing, but they don't want anyone else to know, so they keep their discussions to themselves. They spend quite a lot of money on magazines that tell them which clothes to buy and the best way to get a well exercised and fit body.

What is important about the relationship between Tina and Shanaz? How are they supporting each other physically, intellectually, emotionally and socially?

Talk it over

As she is about to go out with her friends Jo has this conversation with her mum.

'Where do you think you are going dressed like that?'

'I told you before it is Rachel's birthday. And what is wrong with me?'

'That skirt! Look at it! And you've got far too much make-up on for a girl of your age.'

'Mum don't get so stressed, I am 16 nearly 17 remember!'

'I suppose you have not tidied your room?'

'No why should I? I am the one who has got to live in it and how do you know what my room is like? I did not give anyone permission to go into my room. Anyway mum it is Saturday and I want to go out.'

'Your father and I would like to think that just for once you might want to stay in with the family.'

'What with him snoring in front of the telly and you waiting for the lottery results …You have got to be joking. Anyway I am off mum … Bye!'

'How are you getting there and what time will you be home …'

'Will is picking me up, don't worry I won't be late … here he is now in the car!'

Discuss with another person the kinds of growth and development that Jo is demonstrating in this conversation with her mum. You will have to think about PIES to help you with this activity.

Lack of confidence and low self-esteem are problems faced by many teenagers. Some teenagers will even become very depressed about their lives. They may need to talk to understanding friends and relatives. It is not always easy for them to talk to their parents or carers about these problems.

We need to remember, though, that adolescence is also an exciting time. It is a time in our lives when we begin to have relationships with other people. These could be:

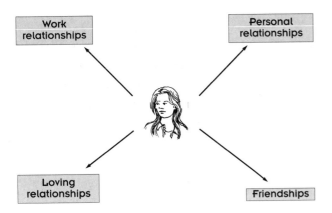

Work relationships

Personal relationships

Loving relationships

Friendships

It is also a time for learning new skills and learning more about the world. For example, many teenagers:

- learn to drive
- get a job
- study for university
- study for careers
- travel abroad.

There is so much to do during the teenage years and all of it is leading in some way to the next stage of our life – adulthood.

Adulthood

Adulthood is the longest stage of our development and is often a time of 'stability' (we begin to settle down). Many new skills and a great deal of knowledge have been learned. We never stop learning, however the speed at which we need to learn can slow down. Problem solving becomes a major part of life – in our jobs as well as in the rest of our lives. We have to solve problems about:

- where to live
- who to live with
- what job to do
- how to find the money needed to live
- how to keep healthy and fit.

During adulthood, which lasts from 18 to about 65, the body does not change very much. However the way we live and the things we might choose to do can be very different from when we were teenagers. Some people choose to go and live in a different country, some choose to travel the world, others may choose to develop a relationship and settle down to raising a family. Everyone chooses what is right for them at the time. Whatever an adult chooses to do with their life they will have certain needs that are basic to helping them grow and develop, such as:

- security (safe from harm, warmth and shelter)
- companionship (from others)
- love (from another and for self)
- interest (to keep motivated)
- approval (from others)

- value and respect (to feel good about themselves)
- a place in society.

The sort of things adults make decisions about as they develop are:

- civic responsibility
- starting a family
- buying/renting a house
- work
- bringing up a family
- travel.

Physical changes to adults

Women aged about 50 years usually 'go through the change of life'. This is called the menopause. It is the time when a woman's periods stop and she is no longer able to have children. It is a normal part of growing older, however some women may experience unpleasant symptoms such as hot sweats, depression and tiredness. Many other women do not experience any symptoms at all.

Many men and women go grey. In other words, their hair loses its original colour. Some men go through other changes. For example, losing the hair on their head and going 'bald'. This sometimes happens when the man is quite young! The skin loses some of its elasticity and wrinkles and lines begin to appear. As they get older men and women are more likely to suffer from health problems, such as heart disease. It is important to keep physically healthy by eating a healthy diet and being as active as possible.

Intellectual development

Many adults make changes to their lives, one of which may be to change their job or return to study to get more qualifications.

In Unit 2 we dealt with the government's plans for 'Lifelong Learning' (see page 40).

Talk it over

What do you think are the benefits of lifelong learning?

Talk it over

Ray and Eileen are both in their late 50s and have a very full and active life. They are members of a local climbing club and enjoy walking and climbing in the Scottish mountains. In fact, Ray collects 'Munroes'. This means he is trying to climb every mountain over 900 metres (3,000 feet) in Scotland.

He has noticed that these days it is taking him a bit longer to get up and down a mountain and sometimes his knees ache after a long day on the fells.

What benefits do Ray and Eileen get from their lifestyle? Compare them with Jo's parents (see page 85). Remember to use PIES to help you.

Think it over

Siobhan is 55 and has been working in care for 20 years. Two years ago she heard about the NVQ Level 2 in Care qualification that her local college was offering with the support of the hospital.

She decided to enrol on the NVQ course. Every Tuesday night she comes to college to learn about the knowledge and skills she needs in addition to her practical care skills.

She has nearly completed her NVQ and is very proud of her work. The hospital has now said that it will pay for her to do the Level 3 NVQ that will give her more responsibility and better pay at work.

How has Siobhan grown and developed intellectually by taking up the opportunity for studying? Has she developed in any other ways?

Emotional development

During adulthood most people look for steady and satisfying relationships. Some form couples in order to satisfy the need for love, security and companionship. Often couples have children, which arouses feelings of protectiveness, love and togetherness.

Adult relationships can also involve a variety of other emotions, such as anger, resentment and jealousy.

Talk it over

Lesley is so angry that Kirsty has been given the job that she wanted and felt it should have been hers. After all, she had worked very hard for it.

She has not spoken to Kirsty since the interviews and now Kirsty is feeling very guilty and wonders whether she should turn the job down.

Discuss with another person the feelings that Lesley and Kirsty have.

Coping with emotional changes can be difficult at times, so it is important that adults learn to communicate with each other openly and honestly. Sometimes relationships fail and this can result in anxiety, stress and bitterness.

Having children affects all four characteristics of human growth and development, especially the emotional development of adults. During the early years of adulthood, many people form relationships that lead to marriage or living together and have children of their own to raise.

Adults show love and affection for each other and their children. Some adults demonstrate love and affection more openly than others, for example by hugging and kissing in front of others. Other adults are more restrained, but this does not mean they love each other or their children any less.

Talk it over

Pen and Anthony have been married for 20 years and have three children. They both work hard, but try to do lots of things together at the weekend when there is more time. They enjoy going to the cinema together and having friends for dinner. They also enjoy cycling in the country.

They do not mind holding hands in public or giving each other a kiss goodbye. Anthony phones Pen once a day, usually before he is about to come home from work to see how her day has been.

Their children are also affectionate towards their parents and each other. They do not think it is strange to show how much they care for each other.

Compare Pen and Anthony's relationship with another couple from a television programme of your choice. Working with another person discuss the differences and similarities.

As adults reach their older years, they may find that their own parents need help and support as they become elderly or frail. In some cases adults become informal carers as they begin to take on the care of elderly relatives.

Social development

Many things can bring about a change in the social life of adults, such as having children. For example, it may not be possible to go out and have a meal with friends at a restaurant, if children have to be cared for. Instead, many adults maintain their social relationships with friends in their own homes and own environments.

Look it up

Ask a parent of a small child what changes have occurred in their life since the child was born. Make a note of all the changes and put them under the headings of PIES.

Some of the changes could include:

- watching videos together instead of going to the cinema

- having meals in one another's homes

- meeting friends and their children to play games (board, card, or others)

- visiting the local leisure centre

- day trips.

Having children of their own should not mean an adult having to give up all the things they like to do! Sometimes it can be an excuse for an adult to do 'childish' things, like going to the cinema to watch a cartoon, playing with their child's toys (lots of parents do this!), as well as visiting fun fairs and going on all the rides!

Old age

Many people think that becoming older is a negative thing to happen. But there are some advantages, such as being able to retire from work and do more of the things that they

want to do. The ageing process however does involve some changes to the body.

As people become older the changes that occur to them are varied. For example, they might experience some or all of the following:

- adjusting to having less physical strength

- getting used to retirement

- accepting the loss of friends and partners

- changing accommodation (to supported housing or residential care)

- living on more or less money

- teaching grandchildren

- adjusting to poor quality eyesight or hearing

- enjoying more leisure time.

 Think it over Some of these changes are physical, others fit more into emotional or social changes. Make a list and put them under PIES.

Many older people keep busy

It is important not to stereotype older people. That is, we should not think of older people as being all the same! After all, old age spans a long time. Someone who has just retired at 65 will not be the same physically as someone who is 95. Some people do not regard older people as being useful to society. How wrong can they be!

Talk it over

Working in pairs discuss the kind of roles older people often take on in society. Make a list of the roles as you discuss them.

? Did you know?

In some societies, as in China, the older a person becomes the more they are respected and valued.

Physical development

The physical part of ageing is usually quite slow. However this is different for different people. You might not always notice the changes because they 'creep up' slowly. Usually the physical changes are:

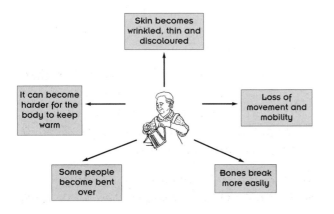

Skin becomes wrinkled, thin and discoloured

It can become harder for the body to keep warm

Loss of movement and mobility

Some people become bent over

Bones break more easily

Other parts of the body may not work as well as they did. Older people may also have problems with their hearing and their eyesight. It would be very unusual to find an older person who did not need glasses for either reading or seeing things in the distance.

It is important for older people to take care of their health by eating a good diet with extra iron, calcium and vitamins, if necessary. Exercise is also important in helping an older person keep healthy. Just because people are becoming older does not mean that they have to spend all their time sitting down!

Read about how Desmond keeps himself fit and healthy.

Think it over

Desmond is 74 years of age. He has cycled for most of his life. When he was a young adult he joined a local cycling club to make friends with people who shared the same hobby as himself.

His wife died three years ago and he now lives alone. However every Thursday and Sunday, Desmond gets his bike out and meets with friends from his club. He enjoys a good diet because he tells his friends that just because his wife is no longer there any more does not mean he cannot cook himself a good meal.

He has seen many people come and go (some have died) from the club over the years, but he still knows everyone because he goes out with them so regularly.

These days he sometimes feels a 'hand' on his back when he's cycling up steep hills. It's usually a younger member giving him a 'hand up'. Something they have a laugh about, but Desmond really appreciates the support.

How has Desmond's life physically changed as a result of him becoming older? How is he keeping himself physically healthy?

Desmond is a good example of an older person keeping himself fit and well in several different ways. He is keeping physically healthy (through cycling and good cooking), he is keeping socially healthy (through meeting his friends) and he is helping his emotional health by keeping himself busy. He must miss his wife very much and the cycling and friendship can help him cope in a positive way.

Intellectual development

People do not become less intelligent as they become older! However older people might need support with their confidence, especially if it is a long time since they acquired new skills and knowledge.

Some local colleges run courses for people in retirement. These can range from learning about computers to learning new languages.

Look it up

Find out the age of the oldest student in your place of study. You might be surprised at the answer.

Talk it over

Merris and Pat are really good friends. They have decided to study at their local college. They want to go together to share transport and support each other.

The only trouble is they want to study different things. Merris has decided that she wants to do 'Navigation by the stars', which is taught on a Wednesday night, and Pat wants to do health studies, which is taught on a Monday afternoon.

The deal is, they both go on a Monday and Wednesday, and while one is in class the other is doing assignments in the learning centre.

Discuss with another person the intellectual benefits to Merris and Pat of their decision to study at college together.

Emotional development

A change in life such as retirement can have many effects on an older person. For example they may have:

* more time to spend with others

* more time to do the things they want to do

* a loss of self-esteem (feeling less useful).

Some older people do lose their self-esteem when they finish work – as if they see themselves as useless to society.

Try it out

Robin is so depressed. He finished work three months ago and now he cannot be bothered to do anything.

He went to his doctor because he felt so useless and ill with it all. His doctor has suggested that he goes out to meet people. He even suggested Robin should consider doing some voluntary work to help others less able than himself.

Robin cannot decide what to do. It feels like too much hard work!

Working with another person decide what the emotional benefits would be to Robin if he was to get out and about more.

Social development

It is generally accepted that without older people, society could not work as well as it does. They have so much experience and learning to pass on.

One benefit of growing older is that often there is more time for older people to spend with grandchildren or other young family members. Older people are able to help younger people to develop and learn new skills.

For some older people physical disability, such as not being able to get around so easily,

Older people can help younger ones to learn new skills

Look it up

Working with another person find out about the roles of older people in a culture that is different to yours.

might limit their opportunities for social activity. They may need support and help to visit the places of their choice. Hilda is a good example of this.

SNAPSHOT

Mike is Hilda's grandson. He takes her to the horse races once a month because she cannot use public transport anymore.

She loves travelling to all the different race meetings across the country. She enjoys a little bet now and then. She also enjoys meeting up with the people she knows and making new friends.

She can certainly teach Mike a thing or two about horses!

3.2 Factors that affect growth and development

If all things were equal we could expect everybody to grow up and develop in the same way. Everyone would have the same levels of health and fitness. We would expect everyone to have the same intellectual ability and the same social skills. This is obviously not the case! There are so many factors that can affect our health and personal development it is almost impossible to name them all. In this section we are going to explore a few of them. These factors are:

- physical and genetic
- diet
- environmental
- social
- economic.

These are the main factors that make us different from each other. Each of them can be sub-divided further. Let's make a start by exploring the physical and genetic factors that affect growth and development.

Physical factors

The way our body is made can be described as a physical factor that will affect our health and personal development. For example, being tall or short, big-boned or small-boned will all have an effect on how you feel about yourself and how others see you. These are physical factors that we inherit from our parents and cannot do anything about.

Genetic factors

These are the factors that can be passed from one generation to the next – for example, from mother to son. This means that you are born with certain conditions or tendencies –

that is, with genetic 'traits' passed on to you from your parents. Things like:

- hair and eye colour
- body size and shape
- skin colour
- looks
- personality traits.

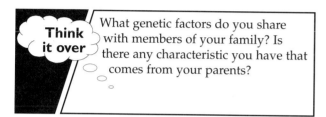

Think it over What genetic factors do you share with members of your family? Is there any characteristic you have that comes from your parents?

We can also have genetic conditions that affect our personal development as well as our health and well-being. In some families there may be a history of heart disease. This usually means that other family members have had heart problems. If this is the case then it is important for new family members to eat a healthy diet and get plenty of exercise.

Twins have similar characteristics

Other genetic conditions could be:

Down's syndrome

Children who are born with this condition suffer from a range of disabilities. Some are physical – many children born with Down's syndrome have enlarged heart muscles, very large tongues and sometimes small skull bones. It is usual for these children to have learning difficulties as well – some of them never learn to read and write. However some of the children are able to attend school and do very well with their learning. It is important not to stereotype these children. All children are different!

 **SNAPSHOT**

Maria is ten years of age. She is the eldest daughter of Ted and Milly who have two other younger children.

Maria was born with Down's syndrome. Because this is a genetic condition, which can be passed on, Milly was tested for the condition when she was expecting her other two children. None of them had the condition.

Maria is a happy, energetic girl who loves helping her mother and father with the two younger children. She has taught her younger sister to dress and feed herself.

Maria attends the local primary school where she is learning to read. She is given extra help with her speech and extra help with writing her name.

Maria enjoys going to school where she has many friends to play with. She is always being invited to friends' parties, which she loves to go to, especially when they are held at the local swimming pool.

It is clear that Maria has a healthy approach to her life. She enjoys being with people and swimming for exercise, and she is getting extra help with her intellectual development. When she is older she might attend a school that will support her in developing the skills and knowledge required to live independently of her parents and family.

Sickle cell trait

This is another genetic condition that can be passed from parent to child. It is a condition of the red blood cells. The shape of the blood cell is 'sickle' (like a half moon).

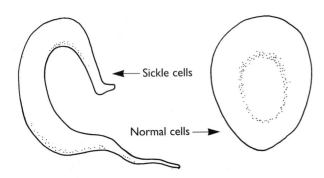

This condition can cause a great deal of pain because the blood cannot pass easily through the blood vessels. The red blood cells can even get stuck in various places in the blood vessels so that the person has a 'crisis' and needs hospital treatment.

Another problem with sickle cell trait is that the blood cells are very fragile and cause a

kind of anaemia that makes the person feel unwell and very tired.

The sickle cell trait condition however only affects certain population groups. These are people from Africa, parts of Asia and some European countries, such as Greece and Turkey.

Diet

Diet is a major factor affecting our health and personal development. When we talk about diet we mean all the food we eat and drink! You can read more about a balanced diet in Units 2 and 5, pages 47 and 146.

People who do not eat enough of the right kind of foods can be affected physically, mentally and socially. The lack of a balanced diet can make people:

- very tired all the time
- unable to concentrate on their work
- anaemic (short of iron in the blood)
- malnourished (not getting the right nutrients)
- ill with bone disease.

Talk it over

Hanif has sickle cell trait. He was planning to play football with his friends. Suddenly he had an awful pain in his stomach, and he began sweating and feeling very sick. His mother decided to call the doctor, and insisted that Hanif stay in.

Discuss with another person how having sickle cell trait might affect Hanif's growth and development.

The effects of a poor diet	
Lack of carbohydrate	No energy, no stamina, cannot concentrate
Lack of protein	Body does not grow properly, cells do not repair themselves
Lack of fat	Damage to nerves, lack of energy, hard to keep warm
Lack of vitamins	More likely to develop illness and not recover, body does not grow properly
Lack of minerals	Body does not grow properly
Lack of fibre	Constipation, bowel disease and cancers
Lack of water	Dehydration and kidney disease

Think it over

Gordon is 14 and thinks he is overweight. He has decided he needs to lose some weight. He is going on a diet by cutting out breakfast, having diet drinks and low-fat yoghurt for lunch and only having a small supper, sometimes only an apple or bar of chocolate. He is certainly loosing weight, but gradually he is finding that he has no energy and cannot concentrate on his studies.

He has recently had a bad case of flu' that he cannot shake off.

Gordon is not being very sensible. How is his poor diet affecting his growth and development?

Environmental factors

When we talk about our environment we mean the area we live and the kind of house that we live in. Where you live can have a major effect on the way you grow and develop.

? Did you know?

People who live in damp houses are more likely to have asthma and other chest illnesses.

People who live in houses with old, faulty electric wiring are more likely to have house fires. Other ways housing can affect a person's growth and personal development are:

- overcrowded housing (no space for privacy, or studying)

- no gardens (nowhere safe for small children to play)

- high rise flats (no playing areas for children)

- housing without bathrooms and toilets (poor hygiene conditions)

- homelessness (people living on the streets suffer from poor health).

The area you live in can also affect growth and personal development. Read about Abdul to discover how his life is affected.

Talk it over

Abdul is 19 years old. He lives in an industrial town in the north of England.

His family comes from northern Pakistan but he was born and brought up in England.

There have been many violent racial problems in Abdul's town over the last six months and now he is scared to go out in case he is attacked. He feels ill with worry and depression because he feels he cannot do anything about the situation.

He has to rely on his father driving him to college because he does not want to be on the streets.

His friends do not visit him as often as they used to because they all prefer to stay indoors.

Working with another person decide how Abdul's environment is affecting his growth and development. Use PIES to help you with your discussions.

It is clear that Abdul's personal development is being affected. He is not going out as much as he should and this is affecting his social development. The situation is also making him depressed, which is affecting his physical and emotional health.

Social factors

Growth and personal development can also be affected by social factors. These are:

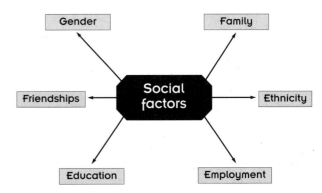

Family

Family affects personal development in a variety of ways. Much of what you learn and the way you learn comes from your family. This learning process is called socialisation. For example:

- we learn to eat and cook the same foods as our parents

- we usually like to do the same things as our families – if exercise is a regular family activity then we will probably do the same!

- we may get the same kind of job or follow the same kind of career as others in the family – for example, if your mother is a doctor you may be influenced to become one!

- when we leave home to live by ourselves or get married, we often live in housing fairly close to our families.

Friends support one another

the same activities because they are doing them. If our friends are drug users, it is possible that we could be influenced to try them ourselves! Refusing friends can be very difficult.

Our friends often have the power to make us happy or sad. Friends will often support us when we are in trouble, often without questioning why it happened. We can also learn new skills and information from our friends.

If we are not allowed to have friends when we are growing up, we will not develop our social and emotional skills fully. We will also lose the chance to have someone special to share our problems and worries with.

> **Think it over**
>
> When David was seven years old he went with his father to fish in the canal. He had his own rod and net and was often found in the garden practising to 'cast' his rod just like dad.
>
> Now he is 19, and still goes fishing. The only difference is he likes to fish in the sea with his friends whenever possible.
>
> *How had David's father influenced the social and intellectual activities that David does as a young adult?*

> **Think it over**
>
> How do your friends influence your development. Think about PIES as you make notes for your portfolio.

Friendship

Our friends can also affect our growth and personal development. This happens through us wanting to do the same things as they are doing. This is called peer group influence.

Even if our friends have dangerous hobbies, such as rock climbing, we might choose to do

Education

Education has a major influence on our growth and personal development. It can play an important part in us having a satisfying and healthy life. It can make a difference to the kind of job we get, and therefore the income we earn and how much satisfaction we get from doing the job. A person who is well-educated and well-qualified usually has a better quality of life than someone with little education and no qualifications.

Education can be different for different people. Not everyone wants to go to university to acquire the knowledge for some future career. Many people are more interested in developing the skills as well as the knowledge required for a vocational career. These people usually look for qualifications that are related to the kind of job they want to do, such as NVQs and GNVQs in Health and Social Care.

Read about Steven below.

Talk it over

Steven left school without any qualifications. He was just happy to leave!

He got a job working in the local factory, making cardboard boxes. He earned a reasonable wage and could afford to run a car. If ever he was ill or had to have a day off work his pay was cut. At first that did not matter to him.

Then he got married three years ago and had two small children. His wage packet mattered very much then. He was always worried about being ill and having to take time off work. He sold his car to make sure there was enough money for the family.

Last year he decided he had had enough of worrying. He went back to college to study at night to gain some more qualifications. He is now a qualified computer technician and about to start work with a major computer manufacturer.

He will be earning an extra £60 per week and will have a company car. But the best thing is that he will be paid (up to 6 months) for any time off from work through sickness.

Discuss with another person how Steven's actions have affected his own growth and development. Include discussions about how his actions might affect the rest of his family's growth and development. Make notes for your portfolio.

It is clear that Steven's decision to improve his education will help him to a better standard of living. This means that his family will also have a better start in life.

Employment

The kind of work we do will affect the growth and development of ourselves and our families. The following are some examples.

- Teaching can be a rewarding job to do, and a teacher also has the opportunity to increase their intellectual and social development.

- Women radiographers who are pregnant are exposed to X-rays that may affect the physical development of their unborn baby.

- People who work with children and animals may find that their emotional development is affected – they might become more caring.

- People who work with dangerous substances may find their physical development being affected.

- People who work with other people, such as carers, might find that their social development is affected by making new friends.

Think it over

Glenis is a nursery nurse. She has been doing the job for three years. Tim has been in her daily care for over 12 months now, and she has become very attached to him.

She has just been told that he developed meningitis two days ago and has just died. His mother is calling in later to collect his personal belongings. Glenis is dreading meeting with her as she does not know what to say.

How is Glenis' job affecting her social and emotional development? Think about the skills she is going to develop, as well as her feelings.

Talk it over

Brian works for himself. He spends all day in his small workshop making plastic moulds.

Sometimes the phone rings and he can have a conversation with a customer or the supplier of his materials, but other than that he does not usually speak to anyone else all day.

Working with another person discuss how the sort of situation below would make you feel. How is Brian's social development likely to be affected? Make notes for your portfolio.

Gender

There are basic physical differences between males and females that affect their growth and development, such as:

- males are usually taller than females

- males are usually stronger than females.

But there are other differences that can affect males and females. There are differences in the way boys and girls are brought up. In some families, girls are encouraged to do 'girly' things, such as playing with dolls or helping with the housework and cooking, whilst boys are discouraged from doing 'girly' things, such as cooking or sewing.

It is important that children and adults are encouraged to do the activities or work that interests them the most. There should be no such thing as girl's work and boy's work. If a person is able and wants to develop the skills and knowledge for doing a particular job then they should be encouraged to do that.

Think it over

How many jobs can you think of that are gender specific for one reason or another? Make a list and then compare it with another person's.

Sometimes there are difficulties with certain jobs which have traditionally been for one gender or another, as in the case of Liam.

Talk it over

Liam wants to be a dancer. Whenever he hears music his feet start tapping and he just wants to dance.

He is worried about telling his parents that he wants to study dance and drama at the local college because his father thinks that he should be a fireman, or at least get a job with a local building company.

Working with another person, discuss how Liam's father might react to the news. What effect could his reaction have on Liam's development?

Derek is a male nurse. He has been qualified for 10 years. He really enjoys his job but has decided that he is ready for a change.

He is applying for midwifery training. He is not sure how the admissions tutor for midwifery will react to his application.

Discuss with another person the difficulties that Derek might experience as a midwife. Do you think he should be allowed to train and then deliver babies?

Ethnicity

The population group you belong to will affect personal growth and development. In some groups of the population, such as people from the Indian sub-continent, there is a tendency for people to develop diabetes. This is a physical factor affecting development.

People from different countries can grow to different heights. For example, people from Denmark and Sweden are known for being very tall and blonde. In contrast people from Far Eastern countries, such as Japan, tend to be smaller. Remember however that we must not stereotype people. Many of the physical differences between people are in fact due to the availability of food. If a child lives in a country where there is a shortage of food, then they are likely to grow up to be smaller adults than those children living in a country where food is plentiful.

Personal development can be affected if you are living in a country where the main population is socially different to you. We have already seen what happened to Abdul, in an earlier case (page 95). If people feel threatened or different from everyone else around them, their personal development can be affected.

The beliefs and customs of the racial group that we live with will also affect personal growth and development in some ways.

Economic factors

Money is essential to make sure that you, your family and your clients are able to develop to your full potential.

Income

A person's income (how much money they have coming in) is going to affect:

- where they live
- what they eat
- holidays
- recreation time
- clothes
- how they feel about themselves.

Talk it over

Rachael is from an orthodox Jewish community. She does not go out on a Friday night or Saturday as these two days are special to her religion and her family.

Her mother prepares a big meal on Friday night for all the family to get together to celebrate their holy day on Saturday.

Discuss with another person how Rachael's development will be affected socially and intellectually by her family's religious celebrations. You will need to think about the benefits offered by belonging to a close-knit community.

Think it over

A person with plenty of money often feels good about themselves and other people.

Why do you think this is?

How much a person earns will affect every part of their life.

Compare the cases of Gina and Sarah below.

Talk it over

> Gina lives in a pleasant neighbourhood in a big house with a lovely garden. She has three rabbits, a hamster and a puppy. The school she goes to is quite close by, and all her friends go there too. They are very lucky at the school. The parents have raised lots of money for books and equipment and they even have a small swimming pool. They are now raising money for a minibus. The children are looking forward to that because it means they will be able to go on extra trips.
>
> Sarah's experience is quite the opposite. She lives in a flat with no garden, and although she would love a pet, her mother has said they could not afford it. Her school is shabby, and poorly furnished. Although the classrooms are bright and cheerful, in Sarah's room one of the posters they made for a display was ruined by water coming in through a leak in the roof. The parents would like to raise money for the school, but find it quite difficult. Some are out of work or are in low paid work and simply cannot afford any money for the school.

Discuss with another person how income may affect Gina's development. What might be the benefits for Gina of the school she goes to? What effects might low income and her school have on Sarah?

Cost of things needed

It is important to recognise that we need money for the essential things in life, such as housing, warmth and food. If we are to help our children and families to grow and develop we need to make sure that we have enough money to cover 'the bare necessities'.

Availability of money for other things

Many of us would also like to have some money for those things that are not essential

Talk it over

> Malcolm has lost his job through illness. He is very worried because his savings have all gone and he has a big gas bill to pay. He has just received a final demand from the gas people saying they are coming to cut his gas off.
>
> Malcolm does not know how he will keep his family warm through the winter.

How has the cost of the gas affected Malcolm? How will his family be affected by a lack of warmth in winter?

to survival. It would be nice to have holidays in hot countries – or even any holiday at all – or to be able to buy fashionable clothes.

Sometimes not having money can affect personal development. For example, if you wanted to learn a new skill, but were short of the money you needed to join a club or buy special equipment to learn that skill, then you could not develop that part of you.

? Did you know?

Money that you spend on the things you do not need is called 'disposable income'.

It is clear from what has been said in this unit that a person's health, employment prospects, level of education and self-esteem can affect their growth and development in a variety of ways.

Try it out | Use the cases in this unit and discuss with another person the ways in which health, employment prospects, level of education and self-esteem can affect a person's growth and development. Make notes of your discussions for your portfolio work.

Richard and Samina have gone shopping together. Samina has just bought a complete outfit, including shoes. She is looking for a new winter coat as well.

Richard is doing what he calls 'window shopping', in other words he cannot afford to buy anything today.

He is beginning to feel embarrassed now because every time he says he likes something, Samina says 'well buy it then'.

How is the additional income affecting Samina's development? How do you think Richard will feel after being in Samina's company all day? How is his growth and development being affected?

The effects on growth and personal development

Health

You may have found from your discussions that growth and development are affected by health in many ways. For example poor health can:

- affect physical growth and development – through illness-related disease or other conditions

- affect intellectual development – through not being able to go to school or work

- prevent positive social development – through not being able to meet with other people easily

- affect how we feel about ourselves – we might feel inadequate because we cannot do the same things as everyone else. This is part of having low self-esteem.

Employment prospects

Our work opportunities and the jobs we do can affect our health and well-being. For example:

- good jobs usually pay well – we gain from better housing, more money, better quality food, more holidays

- unemployment – we suffer from less money, poorer housing, depression and other illnesses.

Level of education

The better educated we are the better chance we have of getting a well-paid job.

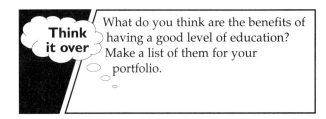

Think it over
What do you think are the benefits of having a good level of education? Make a list of them for your portfolio.

Self-esteem

The way we feel about ourselves is called self-esteem. If self-esteem is high we think well of ourselves. We are usually happy with how we look and the things we can do. On the other hand, if our self-esteem is low, we are often unhappy with ourselves.

Working with another person discuss how low self-esteem might affect growth and personal development. Remember to use PIES to help you.

3.3 Effects of relationships on personal development

People can have many different kinds of relationships. These are usually with other people in a variety of different settings (places), such as:

- close friends – in and out of work
- family – immediate and distant relatives
- sexual relationships
- working friendships.

Some people, especially if they live alone, may develop a caring relationship with their animals and pets.

Friendships

Most people find relationships with friends very satisfying and maintain the friendships for a long time. After all, we can choose our friends! On the other hand, some people change their friends regularly. As we become older we often hold on to our friends because we feel the most comfortable with them. In other words, they know us and we know them!

Have you ever noticed how important friends are whenever we want to learn something new or visit a new place? Read about Daniel to find out how important friends are to him.

Talk it over

Daniel is bored, bored! He is 17 years old and has no interesting hobbies or things to do when he gets home from his boring job in a warehouse.

He has decided to go to his local snooker hall to practice his snooker skills. He has heard that the town snooker team needs new members. The only thing is … He does not want to go alone!

He thinks he will look daft going into the place himself, when he does not know what to do. He has decided to ask Damon to go with him.

The problem is, Damon hates snooker! Still he rings him and uses all his persuasive skills to talk him into going, just once, to help him.

It works! Daniel and Damon are going to the snooker hall together!

Working with another person discuss what the benefits are for Daniel having a friend like Damon. How do you think Damon will feel helping Daniel?

We can see that Damon is very supportive of his friend, even to the point of doing something he does not want to do! At the same time, Daniel is dependent on Damon. He will not go to the snooker hall without him. We also rely on friends for other kinds of support. For example, smaller, younger people sometimes 'hang around' with older, bigger people for physical protection.

People often become friends with one another because there are things that they especially like about each other. This is called attraction. Sometimes they are drawn to each other because they have the same interests and values (things they believe in).

Friends may provide one another with mutual support – that is help each other in various ways. This may involve having someone:

- to share problems with
- to go out with
- for protection
- you can trust
- to take an interest in
- to take an interest in you.

? Did you know?

Most friendships are between people of the same sex. Friendships between people of different sexes usually involve mixed sex couples.

Friends are very important to our personal growth and development for various reasons.

We often make new friends as we get older and change. This is because we need different things from our friends at different times in our lives. This does not always mean that we lose our old friends – sometimes we stay friends with the same person for ever!

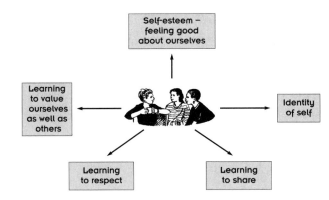

acceptable and unacceptable behaviour. In other words, they tell us what we are doing wrong! Families are there to support us when we are growing up. Remember, young children are dependent on their carers, who usually make sure that all their needs are met. Older family members are especially helpful for supplying information or giving advice – older people tend to have 'seen it all before'.

If we develop close, loving relationships with our family members, the chances are that we will be able to tell each other anything. It is important to be honest and open with each other.

Talk it over

Working with another person discuss how each of the things in the spidergram can be learned or developed through our friendships.

Family relationships

Have you ever heard the saying 'blood is thicker than water'? This means that families stick together, no matter what the problems. We ask our family members for support or advice whenever we need it. Sometimes we get it when we don't want it!

Families help with our personal growth and development by guiding us in what is

Think it over

Lisa is ready to go to her first disco. Her mother has offered to buy her a new outfit. When they reach the shops Lisa's mother wants her to buy a 'nice dress', but Lisa would rather have trousers and a top.

Lisa does not want to upset her mother, but she does need her to understand that she would like to be grown up and make her own choices.

How do you think this relationship between Lisa and her mother will affect Lisa's personal development? Do you think her mother's personal development will be affected?

Talk it over

When Mick decided to move in with Nancy his parents decided not to tell his grandfather. They said it would 'kill' him if he ever found out. So Mick pretended that he still lived at home whenever he saw his grandfather. It helped to keep the peace.

After about three months Mick was visiting his grandfather when the old man suddenly asked Mick if he was still living with that nice girl.

He had known all along and it did not bother him at all!

Discuss with another person Mick's situation. How do you think keeping secrets affects him and his grandfather? Were his parents right to stay quiet? How was the whole family's development affected?

Think it over

Are there any circumstances when you would not tell a family member something no matter how close you are to them?

Families are essential to us developing a **sense of identity**. In other words, they help us to 'find out who we are' (the kind of person we are).

Families also teach us about the importance of sharing. Brothers and sisters often share clothes, CDs and other things. Sometimes they share bedrooms, which is one way of learning to respect another person's personal space! On the other hand, brothers and sisters often fall out – usually over personal space!

Sexual relationships

Developing a good sexual relationship is an important part of human development and growth. A sexual relationship with a suitable partner (usually through physical attraction) can be a very loving and special experience. Knowing we are loved makes us feel special and good about ourselves. Our self-esteem is raised and this helps to make us feel happy and confident about ourselves.

A loving sexual relationship is important to our development

Most people find that their sexual relationship changes as they become older. As people get older they may not be as sexually active as they were when they were younger. However, we need to remember that every relationship is different. The important part of a sexual relationship is making certain that both partners are happy with their situation. We should never use the power of love and attraction to make partners do things they may not want to do.

Working relationships

Most people enjoy positive working relationships with work colleagues. A good working relationship involves:

- being professional (getting the work done)
- being helpful (to all the people involved)
- valuing the work of others
- having your own work valued
- being respectful (to all levels of workers)
- being well-organised (not causing confusion for others)
- being on time (not making other people late through your actions).

Talk it over

Catherine has just started a new job as an administrator. She is feeling nervous about the new work because she does not know anyone in the company.

When she gets to work, her new manager meets her at the door and takes her to her work room.

She introduces her to the person she will be working with and explains where to keep her personal belongings and how to make the coffee.

Working with another person discuss how you think Catherine's manager has made her feel?

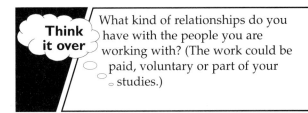

We need to develop good working relationships to help our personal growth because we can learn so much from experienced work colleagues. Sometimes the people we work with will be the ones recommending whether we should be given more responsibility, and maybe even promotion!

Some people enjoy socialising with work colleagues outside of work. This is acceptable, as long as the relationship does not affect performance at work.

Working relationships often involve power. People in authority (the boss or supervisor) usually have the power to ask you to do certain jobs. Other people may have power because they have the information or the skills that you need to do a particular job. In a working relationship it is important that power is not used to disrupt the work that has to be done.

Barriers to effective relationships

People themselves are the major barriers to effective relationships. This can be because they:

- don't like the person
- don't have time for the relationship
- are not allowed to have the relationship

- are too young for the relationship
- have other friends or family interfering in the relationship
- have no patience
- have no understanding and sympathy.

Other barriers are to do with the environment, such as:

- too far to travel to meet friends
- an unsafe environment – remember the case of Abdul
- no transport available.

Developing good personal relationships takes time and effort on everybody's part. If a friendship, of any kind, is worth having, it is worth taking care about.

Unit 3 Assessment

You will be externally assessed (tested) for this unit. You will need to produce evidence which shows your understanding of the main stages of human growth and development, the factors that affect growth and development and the effects of relationships. You will have the opportunity to work towards a pass, merit or distinction grade.

The activities based on the case study of Charmaine and Stephen below are ordered in such a way as to guide you through this assessment. The case study is also an indication of a study that you may have to work with for an external assessment. The levels of assessment are clearly indicated as:

- P for Pass
- M for Merit
- D for Distinction.

CASE STUDY — Charmaine and Stephen: a tale of two lives

Charmaine O'Mara and Stephen Males have known each other all their lives. They grew up in a small village on the edge of the Berkshire Downs. Stephen's father said their family had been there since the time of King Alfred the Great! Their families are still involved in local farming and agriculture, including working in some of the big horse stables (it's great country for training race horses).

They went to playgroup together, with all the other children in the village, and then to the local primary school and finally to the nearest big town to secondary school.

It was a peaceful life, but neither Charmaine nor Stephen wanted to stay in the village and work on their family farms, although both of them had brothers and sisters who would. Stephen had always wanted to be a paramedic, and Charmaine had always imagined setting up a mobile hair and beauty salon, like her cousin Tina did in Oxford.

After their GCSEs they went to college. They had always gone out together, and even at college they saw each other nearly every day, and always over the weekend. But their paths started to separate.

Stephen was determined to study hard to get a merit in his GNVQ, but Charmaine found that the freedom of being at college was getting in the way of her studying. She made lots of new friends and began to go out more than ever, even giving up her job on Friday evening in Top to Toe, the local beauty salon. She began to fall behind with her assignments and then failed one of her important tests. Her tutor said she would probably have to repeat the year.

Stephen didn't like Charmaine's new friends, and tried to discuss things with her: he even said he would help her with her work, but she said she couldn't be bothered. She started going to the pub a lot and drinking with people much older than her. Stephen meanwhile was just about to complete his course. He felt sad and depressed about Charmaine. He was very fond of her, after all they had known each other 'for ever' and he felt she was the only girl he would ever really want to marry.

After college, Stephen got a job in the Blood Transfusion Service, which he needed to do for two years before he could begin his paramedic training. Charmaine had left college, was working in the kitchen of a local racing horse trainer and before she knew it, found herself getting married and having a baby. Not to Stephen but to someone, she later said, she hardly knew and didn't really like. It was just a way of

CASE STUDY – Charmaine and Stephen: a tale of two lives (continued)

getting out of the job. All her ambitions to set up her own business had long gone.

Three years later, her husband left her, and she had to leave the tied accommodation where they were living and move into a council house in town with the two children – Zoe, who was nearly four, and Jason, who was only 5 months old. She began to drink, and refused help from her parents and grandparents. She said she wanted to be independent.

But Charmaine was miserable, and when Stephen came to see her, he couldn't believe how she had changed. The children seemed hungry and were poorly dressed. Although it was summer, the house seemed damp and not well-ventilated. Zoe had asthma, Charmaine said, and Jason just cried all the time.

Stephen was now practically qualified and about to start work with the ambulance service in Reading. Everything was going well for him.

Things got so bad for Charmaine that she realised if she didn't get help she might lose her two children to the social services who had already checked up on her.

The family got together to discuss what to do. Charmaine broke down in tears, but her grandmother, fit and active and really wanting to help, said she would have the children for three days a week while Charmaine found a job.

Charmaine is now back working at Top to Toe and doing her NVQ Level 2 in Beauty Therapy. The children love being with Gran, and there is even a suggestion that Charmaine might be able to move back to the village if she can afford a car.

Stephen popped in the other day. He looked great in his ambulance uniform. Charmaine gave him a cup of tea.

Who knows what may be around the corner.

All students must complete the first four P activities to achieve the minimum for Unit 3.

Activities to achieve a pass

Activity 1P

* Identify the five life stages in the case study by listing them with the characters' names and approximate ages.

Activity 2P

* Identify in the case study at least five factors which affect growth and development and explain how these relate to the characters in the study. You could do this as a table if

you like. See if you can identify at least one from each of the PIES factors.

Activity 3P

* There are many relationships described in the case study above. Can you identify three different relationships between some of the characters described? You can draw these as cartoons or stick figures to vary the presentation, if you like.

Activity 4P

* Each of the relationships you have identified is different. In your own words, identify the important features of the three relationships you have chosen to describe.

Working towards a merit grade

To achieve a merit grade, you must carry out the activities for the pass grade, plus the additional steps to Activities described below. You must list the books, journal articles, websites and other *sources* of information to show where your work information has come from. Your work must be in your own words, not copied directly.

Activity 2M

You have identified at least five different factors that affect growth and development.

- For each factor you identified describe how it may affect human growth and development at different life stages. Again, you could put this in a table, to make the presentation clearer. You could illustrate the table, if you like.

Activity 4M

- Having described the relationships, now extend this to say what effect these relationships have on personal development. You may possibly think of some of your own relationships which are similar to those described in the case study, to help you complete this activity.

Working towards a distinction grade

To achieve a distinction grade, you must carry out the activities for the pass and merit grades, plus the additional steps to Activities 2 and 4 below.

Activity 2D

- You have identified factors relating to growth and development and how they affect different life stages. For this activity, you have to compare how each factor may affect growth and development in a positive and negative way. For example, you may have said that education is a factor affecting growth and development. Stephen had a good education and was able to get a good job with increasing employment prospects. However, Charmaine did not take up her educational opportunities, and the effect of this was that she could not get a good job.

This is quite a difficult task, and you may need to think carefully about it.

Activity 4D

- Extending your discussion of the relationships in Activity 4M, you can now write about how these relationships may change over time, and how these changes can affect personal development. Again, you might like to refer to your own experiences to help you show an understanding of what happened to the characters in the case study.

These activities are all quite challenging for you, and in assessing your work your assessor will be looking at the quality of your work, the originality of presentation and your ability to work independently.

Check your knowledge

Questions 1–11 require short answers.

Questions 12–21 are multiple choice questions. There is only one correct answer.

Short answer questions

1 Between one and three years, an infant will learn to smile, pull itself up, walk, feed itself, recognise its mother's voice, play with simple toys and achieve bladder and some bowel control.

Arrange these developments alongside the PIES headings:

P

I

E

S

There may be more than one under each heading.

2 In childhood, language skills are a very important part of social development.

Describe, in two lines, how language can also be part of:

- emotional development

- intellectual development

- physical development.

3 Why is play important for a child's development?

4 Give three examples of genetic factors that could be transferred from one individual to another.

5 In adolescence, peer influences are thought to be important factors in growth and development. What does this mean?

6 List four physical changes which adolescents undergo during puberty.

7 Bob is 25 and just about to become a father. List four changes in his life which may occur as a result of being a parent.

8 During adulthood most people become employed. How does employment relate to the intellectual and social development of the individual?

9 List four advantages of being an adult in comparison to being an adolescent.

10 Describe three ways in which older people can maintain their intellectual development.

11 Describe two ways in which retirement can benefit older people, and two ways in which it could hinder an older person's personal development.

Multiple choice questions

12 In infancy, bonding is important to growth and development. Bonding means:

a eating independently

b learning to read

c toilet training

d developing a strong relationship with a carer.

13 Infants learn to respond to sounds and voices, so it is important that carers:

a ignore them

b talk to them

c give them lots of healthy snack food

d take them to the park to play.

14 At school, children learn to mix with others, play together and share. This is part of:

a social development

b physical development

c attention-seeking behaviour

d financial independence.

15 Adolescents can undergo a variety of mood changes and 'highs and lows' as they move through their teen years. Coping with these moods is part of:

a club culture

b emotional development

c taking part in a range of social activities

d physical development.

16 Down's syndrome is an example of:

a a place in England where you can ramble across open countryside

b a school for emotionally disturbed children

c a viral infection

d a genetic condition affecting both males and females.

17 Low self-esteem in adulthood would most likely be caused by:

a owning your own house

b moving to a new part of the country

c losing your job

d becoming a parent.

18 Having an adequate income is an:

a intellectual factor in growth and development

b   economic factor in growth and development

c   factor in the adult's past experiences

d   important physical factor in growth and development.

19 Sharon lives in a high-rise block of flats with nowhere to play. Amira lives in a detached house with a big garden. The differences in their housing is an example of:

a   the food they eat

b   a loving relationship with their carers

c   environmental factors in growth and development

d   whether they have pets to play with.

20 Going to a day centre or club can help older people:

a   remain socially active

b   prevent the physical ageing process

c   look after their grandchildren

d   draw the pension.

21 A social factor affecting personal development is:

a   exercise

b   the ageing process

c   adequate nutrition

d   family.

Investigating Common Hazards and Health Emergencies

This unit explores the health and safety laws and rules that apply to health and social care work settings. You will be able to find out how to recognise health emergency situations and how you can help to deal with them safely. You will also investigate some of the common work-related hazards that can occur in health and social care settings and find out about ways of reducing the risks to yourself, your clients and your colleagues.

The information in this unit will help you to become a more effective health and social care worker. You will be able to offer your employer a range of useful skills and knowledge that will contribute to a safer working environment for all.

The unit will also give you the opportunity to practice your skills and knowledge of providing emergency care. You will be able to demonstrate your ability to help a client during a potentially life-threatening event, such as choking or suffering from a heart attack.

You need to learn:

- about the hazards and risks associated with care settings

- about dealing with emergencies

- about basic first-aid procedures.

WARNING!

Although you will read about first aid procedures in this unit, you should never carry out any procedures on a casualty without recognised first-aid training.

4.1 Hazards and risks in health and social care settings

Health and safety is very important in all health and social care settings, not only for the safety of our clients but also for our colleagues and ourselves. Every year thousands of people are injured in their workplaces. Sometimes it is because they have been careless or because they have not followed the health and safety rules that apply to their care setting. On the other hand, it can also be because the equipment they are using is broken or faulty and not suitable for the job they are carrying out.

Health and social care settings have the potential to be dangerous places to live or work in. This is due to a variety of reasons, such as:

- many people living together (e.g. residential care)

- sick and infectious people in the same place (e.g. hospitals)

- storage of medicines, drugs and other hazardous substances

- the use of complicated equipment for moving, handling and treating people

- possibility of fire.

When accidents or hazardous situations occur we usually find it is because of a combination of one or two things. These are:

- human factors (actions caused or carried out by people)

- environmental factors (caused by buildings, equipment, materials and substances).

Human factors

Hazards are sometimes caused by human error, in other words, the way we work can be hazardous, often without us knowing it. For example:

- handling and moving people without training

- forgetting to check the battery in a fire alarm

- leaving dangerous substances, such as bleach, within reach of a child.

Not knowing how to use equipment safely can lead to another form of human error. It is essential that health and care workers know how to keep themselves and their clients safe by using equipment properly.

Environmental factors

The environmental factors are all the physical conditions surrounding us, such as the place you live or the building you are working in. You have to ask yourself if the environment is:

- well lit, or very dark?

- full of furniture so that there is no room to move?

- full of narrow corridors?

- full of people and equipment?

Or has it got:

- broken, unsafe equipment?

- slippery floor coverings?

- steep, narrow stairs?

- beds laid too close together?

It is important for carers to recognise the environmental factors that can cause accidents or injuries so that something can be done to prevent the accidents happening.

> ### Hints and tips to avoid human error
>
> - Always follow the rules and regulations of your workplace.
>
> - Never take 'short cuts' with your work.
>
> - When doing a job see it through to the finish if possible (never leave it to someone else).
>
> - If you are not sure what to do, ASK your supervisor or manager.

A steep flight of stairs can be dangerous

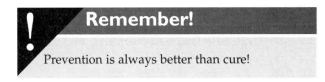

Remember!

Prevention is always better than cure!

Environmental factors can be:

- static (there is nothing we can do about them, for example a busy main road outside the care setting)

- dynamic (we can change the risk factor, for example making sure stairs and passageways are well lit).

Hints and tips for a safe environment

- Use bright lights in dark places.

- Never block corridors and doorways with furniture or boxes.

- Make sure there is enough space in a room to be able to move easily.

- Never have slippery floors.

- Make sure carpets and rugs do not trip anyone up.

- Secure handrails on stairs, toilets, baths etc.

- Check fire alarms and equipment regularly.

- Have electrical equipment checked by a qualified person regularly.

- Check all fire exits are accessible.

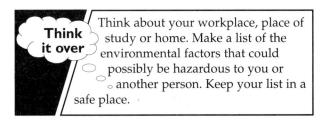

Think it over Think about your workplace, place of study or home. Make a list of the environmental factors that could possibly be hazardous to you or another person. Keep your list in a safe place.

The spidergram highlights the kind of situations or equipment faults that can lead to hazardous situations in health and social care settings.

Let's take each one of these and see what kinds of hazards and risks to health and safety each one carries.

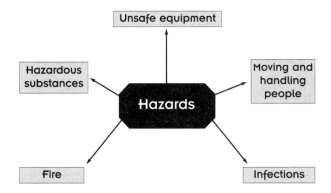

Unsafe equipment

Broken or unsuitable equipment causes a huge number of work-related accidents. However these accidents are generally avoidable (they do not have to happen).

In a health and care setting you will usually find a wide range of different kinds of equipment being used. These can range from the same kinds of things you would find in your own home, such as:

- kitchen equipment (cookers, knives, kettles etc.)

- electrical equipment (televisions, computers, fridges, washers etc.)

through to specialised equipment, such as:

- lifting equipment (hoists, stair lifts)

- mobility equipment (wheelchairs, walking frames, sticks)

- equipment for treatment (catheters, feeding aids etc.).

Commonsense tells us that equipment that is broken should never, ever be used but unfortunately it still happens. The following are just a few of the mistakes people make:

Talk it over

Working with another person discuss the kinds of equipment you have seen or used in a health, social or early years care setting. If you have not been involved in a health and social care setting yet, think about the equipment you have seen in your college or home. Make notes of the items you have come across.

- Use broken chairs and ladders to stand on.

- Use machinery without guards (a meat slicer, for example).

- Use rickety walking aids that are at risk of breaking.

- Use electrical equipment with broken plugs or cracked wiring.

- Use cooking equipment with broken handles.

We could go on and on! It is likely that you could add to this list the kinds of 'dangerous' things you have seen people do in the workplace.

Think it over

Think about your own home or workplace. Is there any broken equipment being used, is there a piece of equipment in need of repair? If there is, make a note to tell someone about it.

Talk it over

In pairs discuss what might happen if the following pieces of equipment were used: a walking stick with a crack in it and a pan with a loose handle. Make notes for your portfolio of evidence.

Broken or unsafe equipment can lead to a wide range of accidents and injuries, as occurred in the case of Walter.

SNAPSHOT

Gregore is a care assistant at Hamley Manor retirement home for old soldiers. He cares for Walter who is 84 years of age. Gregore enjoys providing care for Walter because they chat together about times long since past, which Gregore finds really interesting.

Today, Gregore is depressed and upset because Walter is in hospital with a broken hip. Whilst he was lifting him into the bath yesterday the strapping on the hoist broke and Walter fell heavily into the side of the bath.

'If only I'd seen the frayed strap', thought Gregore.

Hazardous substances

Substances come in many different forms, some of which are chemicals. It is very likely that some of the substances you are using regularly are capable of burning the skin, or causing breathing difficulties if inhaled (breathing in the fumes).

Many substances are only harmful if used wrongly. If you follow the manufacturer's instructions you will keep yourself, your work colleagues and your clients safe from accidental harm. The kinds of substances you are most likely to come across in health and social care settings are:

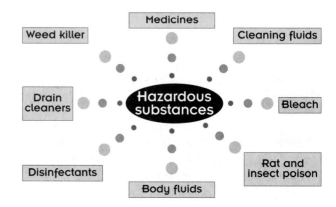

When you look at the wide range of different substances in a care setting you can see why it is so important that all care workers know how to treat and store each one.

Look it up

From the spidergram choose one of the substances that you do not know very much about. Find out all you can about how it should be used and stored. Share your findings with another person who has looked up a different one to yourself.

Hints and tips for the safe use of substances

To keep substances safe, always:

- follow the manufacturer's instructions
- follow the rules and regulations of your workplace
- fully label bottles and containers
- store substances in a locked cupboard
- put substances away as soon as you are finished with them
- keep substances away from people and animals
- if a substance is unknown and unlabelled do not use it.

Look it up

If you would like to know more about the laws relating to dangerous substances find out about COSHH (Control of Substances Hazardous to Health).

Talk it over

Miriam works in a residential care home for young children. She has only been there one week and she is trying to be as helpful as possible to her employers.

She has been asked to clean the kitchen cupboards, which are in a dreadful state. When she looked in the unlocked sink cupboard she found bottles of all sorts of substances. Some of the bottles were dirty and the labels had fallen off them, others had no tops. Miriam knew these were dangerous, but as she did not know what to do about it she just gave them a good clean and put them all back again.

Working in small groups discuss what should have been done about the situation in this care home. Include in your discussions what the dangers are to the carers and the clients from a situation like this. Make notes of your discussions.

Infections

You will almost certainly already know, or have heard about disease and infections in some way or another. It is likely that you know that some diseases and infections are more dangerous than others. Here we are going to concentrate on those diseases that can be passed from one person to another.

? Did you know?

Infection is the process by which a disease is passed from one person to another.

A major part of a carer's job role is to keep their clients safe from all kinds of hazards, including the hazard of infectious diseases that can be passed on in a variety of health and social care settings.

Infectious diseases are caused by organisms (microbes) that are so small we cannot see them without the help of a microscope.

Each type of microbe can cause a different disease, for example fungi can cause thrush, which babies sometimes pick up from their feeding bottle.

Think it over

Find out about thrush (also known as Candida albicans) and the different parts of the body it can affect. You could also try and find out how it can be treated. Make notes of your findings and share them with your colleagues.

A virus can also cause infection in children and adults, such as the one that causes measles, or the one that causes the common cold and which can be passed from one person to another.

Infectious disease can be spread in many different ways. For example:

- coughing and sneezing spreads microbes through the air

- microbes on clothing or bedding can be passed by touch

- microbes passed from one person to another by unwashed hands

- microbes from hands or dirty cooking utensils passed to food.

Think it over

Shanaz works in a large hospital. Her job means that she has to take her clients from the ward where they are staying to the other departments for treatment. Today she is taking Annie for an X-ray.

When they got in the lift a visitor to the hospital was sneezing and coughing the whole time. He did use a handkerchief, but Shanaz thought to herself, 'I hope Annie does not catch his cold, she is too old and frail to be catching them now.'

Should a carer or visitor who has a cough or cold go to a place where there are sick or frail people?

Sneezing spreads infection

Talk it over

Discuss with another person other ways in which microbes can be passed from one person to another. Make a list for your portfolio.

Talk it over

Marcus is very worried. Last night he had unprotected sex with a partner he has not known very long. Now he is really concerned in case he has caught some kind of sexually transmitted disease.

His best friend Bashir has advised him to go to the genito-urinary medicine clinic based at his local hospital. The service is totally confidential and does not cost anything.

Bashir has said that if there is anything wrong at least he will be able to get it treated quickly.

Discuss with another person the way sexually transmitted infections are passed from one person to another. What kind of infectious diseases are likely to be passed on? Make notes of your discussion for your portfolio.

In certain conditions, such as warm, moist atmospheres, microbes can multiply very quickly. Within a few hours one or two can become thousands, or even millions! Just imagine the illness and disease they can spread in a care setting.

In a care setting, the microbes typically live in kitchens, bathrooms, toilets, showers and bedrooms (in fact, just about anywhere!). Unless very strict cleanliness routines are followed, they will get onto food, food containers, towels, face cloths, sponges, dish cloths, cleaning equipment, such as mops and floor cloths, and bedding.

It is extremely important that all these items and places where microbes are found are cleaned regularly and thoroughly. Those most at risk of catching infectious diseases are the:

- very young
- old
- frail
- already ill.

For any of these people catching an infectious disease the result could be disastrous, someone might die!

Hints and tips for preventing infection

- Wash your hands after handling any soiled item.
- Always wear gloves and apron for cleaning any body fluids.
- Always wear gloves and apron for cleaning floors or surfaces.
- Clean up spillages immediately.
- Clean rooms regularly (don't forget the corners!).
- Dispose of soiled nappies immediately.
- Keep fridges and freezers at the correct temperature.
- Keep cooked and raw meats separate in the fridge.
- Store food separately from cleaning equipment.
- Make sure all personal toiletries (face cloths etc.) are washed regularly.
- Keep bedding well-aired and clean.
- Make sure you wash your hands after handling food, clients, medication, cleaning equipment.

Moving and handling people and equipment

Moving people and equipment is definitely a hazard in the workplace. It is important for carers to make sure that they have had appropriate training before they try to move or handle anything. This includes people as well as equipment. It is far too easy to try and move something heavy and damage your back because you do not know how to move and handle people and equipment safely.

Factors which can make carers more likely to injure their backs are:

- lifting patients

- working in an awkward, unstable or crouched position, including bending forward, sideways or twisting the body

- lifting loads at arms length

- lifting with a standing and finishing position near the floor, or overhead or at arms length

- lifting an uneven load with the weight on the side

- handling an uncooperative or falling patient.

Moving or handling a client or an object is not an easy task. There are many risks associated with lifting and handling things, such as:

- injury to the carer

- injury to the client

- dropping expensive equipment (and breaking it!)

- injury to people around us

- loss of job and income

- loss of confidence.

Moving and handling should never be carried out until you have had the proper, recognised training. Carers often find themselves being asked to assist a client with a movement. In these cases, it is important that you are trained to move the person safely. If you have never had any training, ask your employer or supervisor to show you how it can be done safely.

In working with babies and small children it might be difficult to eliminate all manual handling in these cases. But it is still important to avoid or reduce the risk of injury. Take the same precautions to move and handle children and babies as you would with any other client.

Fire

Fire is a major danger in all health, social care and early years settings. Can you imagine how difficult it would be to safely evacuate all the clients from a busy hospital if a large fire was to break out at night! Nurses and other staff have to have special training to help them evacuate bed-bound patients safely and efficiently.

Most health care settings now operate a 'no smoking policy'. This is intended to:

- improve the health of clients

- reduce the amount of passive smoking (breathing in other people's tobacco smoke)

- cut down the cost of redecorating (nicotine stains walls and furniture!)

- and most especially to cut down the risk of fire.

? Did you know?

When fires do happen more people die from breathing in the poisonous smoke fumes than from the flames themselves!

We have to trust people to obey the rules of a workplace. Unfortunately, those rules are often broken and hazardous situations then develop.

Keeping your clients, colleagues, workplace and of course yourself safe from fire is not an easy task. You would need to think about all the situations that could lead to fire breaking out in your workplace. These include:

- naked lights
- cooking methods
- electrical wiring
- clients who smoke
- natural heating fires
- electrical equipment
- gas or oxygen cylinders.

Talk it over

Working in pairs identify those causes of fire that could apply in your own place of work or the centre where you are studying. Make notes of your discussions for your portfolio.

Knowing what to do in the event of a fire is the very first stage of keeping everyone safe from harm. If you, or your colleagues, do not know what to do in your workplace, then everyone is at risk from serious injury or even death!

Identifying and reducing risks in the workplace

There are many ways we can contribute to the overall safety of a health, social care and early years workplace. For example, we can carry out safety checks, we can learn what to do in case of fire and we can certainly learn about codes of good practice for maintaining a safe working environment.

Environmental safety surveys and audits

One of the ways you can help to reduce the risk of accidents in your workplace is through safety surveys and audits. Read the case study to see how Debbie carried out a safety audit in her place of work.

CASE STUDY – Doing a safety audit

Debbie works part-time in a day care centre for people who have been ill but are now recovering. All the clients are trying to regain their health and mobility.

Debbie's line manager has asked her to carry out a safety audit of the premises. This means that Debbie will have to carry out a survey. The first thing Debbie did was to make a list of all the rooms in the building. She divided them into 'upstairs and downstairs'.

Next she visited every room to see what kind of furniture and equipment was stored there. Once she had done this she returned to the staff room to think about what to do next.

She made a list of all the things she thought could affect the health and safety of clients or staff. Her list had headings like:

- Electrical equipment
- Furniture
- Windows and doors
- Floor coverings
- Cleaning equipment and materials
- The placement of fire-fighting equipment and alarms
- Client aids.

She then went back to each room and checked everything on her list. During her survey she found that:

- the plug on the television in the sitting room was broken
- the carpet on the third tread of the stairs was loose

CASE STUDY (continued)

- Mrs Smith's walking frame had lost a rubber foot

- the window lock in the bathroom was hanging loose

- the lifting strap on the hoist was fraying

- the smoke alarm at the top of the stairs was beeping.

She made a list of all these things and passed it immediately to her manager, who arranged for maintenance staff to make all the necessary repairs.

Debbie's line manager was very impressed with her approach and professional manner. She especially liked the speed with which Debbie told her of the faults.

Questions

1   What sort of safety audit would you make for either your workplace or home? Work with another person. If you prefer you could choose another place that is used by many people or has many rooms.

2   Think about Debbie's approach. Do you want to follow her method or have you another idea for carrying out a safety survey?

Talk it over

Lynne works on reception in a busy early years school. When parents and other people come to visit, she has to ask them to sign in on the visitors book.

She then gives each person a sticky name badge to wear and a copy of the health and safety procedures just in case they should need them.

When the visitor is leaving, Lynne asks them to sign out of the building by making a note of the time they leave.

Discuss in small groups the reason why you think Lynne keeps her register. Make a list of the benefits to the organisation and the visitor.

It is likely that you have found many reasons for Lynne keeping her register, apart from the fact that it is part of her job to do so! Compare your list with ours. Is it the same or are there some differences? The register is important because it is:

- a record of who is in the building in case of fire

- a record of contact names should they be needed

- a record of visitors to staff members

- a record of where to contact a visitor if someone else needs them

- a record of how many times a person visits the centre and how long they stay.

Look it up

Working with another person find out if visitors to your workplace sign a register and are informed about the health and safety procedures in place. Make a note of the requirements of your workplace and keep them in your portfolio of evidence.

Staff training

Staff training is an important part of working in a caring environment. Most employers provide regular staff training that covers a wide range of work-related activities, such as:

- safe moving and handling

- emergency evacuation procedures

- fire drills

- completing accident notification procedures.

Staff training that can help to identify and reduce risk could be:

- regular fire practice

- learning how your workplace is kept secure

- regular updating about rules and regulations in your workplace

- attending classes (inside or outside the workplace) to learn new skills

- first-aid training

- being shown by a health professional how to care for clients (e.g. bathing someone safely).

Talk it over

Discuss with another person the benefits of staff training being carried out by an experienced member of staff in the workplace. Make a list of the benefits that you have discussed.

Regular checking and servicing of equipment

Another way to identify and reduce risks in care settings is by making sure that equipment

is regularly serviced and checked for faults. All hospitals and health centres have to have their electrical appliances checked once a year (in some cases more often) by a qualified person. This is sometimes called a PAT test (Portable Appliance Testing).

Think it over

Have you ever noticed a small sticker attached to a plug or piece of equipment that shows the date it was last tested and the date of the next test? If not, have a look in either your place of work, your college or some other large organisation that regularly checks their equipment.

Talk it over

Lynda works in a small health centre and shares an office with two other people.

The 12-month electrical appliance test is due to be carried out today. Alban, the electrician, has arranged to do the testing.

He checks the kettle, the wall heater and the computer. He places a sticky label on each item with the date he called and the next date they are due to be tested again.

Working with another person discuss the benefits of having electrical equipment checked regularly. Make a list of the benefits and keep them in your portfolio.

Equipment that is used for the treatment of clients must be checked frequently to make sure that it is still functioning correctly, especially if it is not used regularly.

Try it out Working with another person ask 10 other people to give you one advantage of having equipment checked and regularly serviced. Make a list of advantages from their answers.

Talk it over

> It is 7.00pm and the alarm bell is going off in the bathroom of number 9 of the sheltered housing complex. Mrs Dugdale rushes off to see what has happened to Agnes who lives there.
>
> When she arrives she finds Agnes on the floor of the shower. She had tried to sit on the shower stool while she had a wash. Unfortunately, it collapsed beneath her and now she cannot move.
>
> 'If only I had checked the stool before she moved in', thought Mrs Dugdale.

Working in pairs discuss how checking the contents of Agnes' shower room might have helped to reduce the risk of this accident. What action could Mrs Dugdale have taken?

There are many advantages to having equipment checked and regularly serviced, such as:

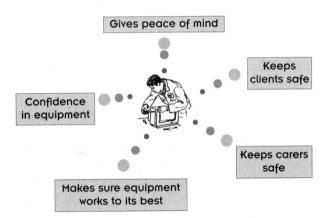

Gives peace of mind

Keeps clients safe

Confidence in equipment

Keeps carers safe

Makes sure equipment works to its best

Putting in place rules and regulations relating to health and safety and fire

There are laws to help us reduce hazards and keep a safe environment for ourselves and our clients when we are working. The main law is the Health and Safety at Work Act of 1974. Under this Act employers and workers both have a duty and a responsibility to protect and care for the health of themselves and their clients.

Talk it over

> 'What is that racket', thought Surrinder as he woke up. He looked at the clock, it was only three o'clock in the morning. Suddenly it dawned on him that it was the fire alarm.
>
> He leapt out of bed and rushed down the corridor shouting 'Fire! Fire!'
>
> He saw that the fire was in the store cupboard. So he grabbed a fire extinguisher and tried to use it to contain the fire. It just wouldn't work!

Discuss with another person what would happen if this situation arose in:

a   a hospital
b   a residential home for older people
c   a nursery school for 40 children.

Make a note of your discussions for your portfolio.

Hints and tips for safe practice when using specialist equipment

- Always follow the manufacturer's guidelines.

- Never leave equipment lying around.

- Always store the equipment in the correct way.

- Never 'play games' with it.

- Only use the equipment with the client who should be using it.

Responsibilities of the employer

- An employer must provide a safe environment for all employees. This means taking action to assess and reduce risks. This is so that dangers in the workplace can be kept to a minimum.

- The employer must also develop a health and safety policy. It is not enough to simply try to avoid accidents. The employer must provide written guidelines on what to do in an emergency. There must be company rules and regulations to help keep staff and clients safe from harm and injury.

- The employer must also make sure that all staff have proper training and instruction on health and safety. Training should always be carried out when a person starts a new job. Training should be updated regularly.

- An employer must provide a clean workplace with enough space (to prevent accidents).

- The employer must make sure that all equipment is safe to use. This includes any equipment that will be used by the client, such as hoists and stair lifts.

But it isn't just the employer who must take action to keep the working environment safe and free from hazards.

Think it over

Milly is a nursery nurse. She has responsibility for six children in her care. Today a young trainee, Samantha, is coming in to do her one week placement with her.

Milly is looking forward to working with Samantha for the week. On the second day Milly noticed Samantha was using a chair to reach the top of a high cupboard to lift down some heavy boxes.

What do you think is likely to happen in this situation? What action should Milly take?

The Health and Safety at Work Act says that employees have certain responsibilities. These are:

- If you know that an action will be dangerous, don't do it!

- Always take reasonable care about the safety of others (Milly should have told Samantha to come down and then found assistance and the right equipment).

- Always follow the correct procedures and safety rules in your workplace.

- Report anything that you think might be a risk to health and safety.

- Always wear the correct protective clothing.

- Immediately report any accidents to your employer.

- Never play with equipment and machinery that you are not qualified to handle.

Rules and regulations relating to fire

Most workplaces have rules and regulations that explain what an employee must do if there is a fire. In all cases a carer is expected to act in a sensible and professional manner.

Look it up

Working in pairs find out what the fire regulations are for a care organisation near you. Include an investigation into who is responsible for maintaining a safe environment in that care organisation. Make notes for your portfolio of evidence.

What you can do if fire breaks out

- **Call the emergency services.**
- Tell the **operator** your **name** and your **telephone number.**
- Tell the **operator** the **location** of the **fire** or **accident.**

Action to take on hearing the alarm.

- Help your clients to leave the area safely
- Follow escape routes
- Do not use lifts

- Remain calm
- Meet at assembly point
- Do not re-enter the building.

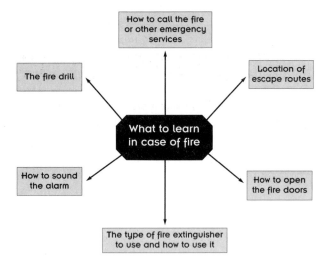

Personal and general hygiene

Care workers are expected to have excellent personal hygiene routines. It is therefore unlikely that you will come across a policy that explains in great detail how you should be keeping yourself clean and tidy for work. However, there may be a written policy to tell staff about what is expected of them in terms of a dress code in the care setting. For example:

- In many places care workers have to wear a uniform. This is not for looking good, it is to protect you and your client from infection and hazardous substances. The same applies to wearing gloves and aprons.

- Many care settings also have policies about who can go into the kitchen area.

Look it up

Find out about each of the points listed in the spidergram. Make a note of different fire extinguishers and what kind of fires they are used for. Write down your nearest fire escape.

Think it over

Does your workplace or place of study have any rules and regulations about the kind of clothes you should be wearing? If so, write them down.

Talk it over

Mario has worked in the residential care home for six months. He enjoys his job but does not like having to do 'sleep overs'. He feels very responsible for the people in his care during the night. He is always frightened in case something happens.

Last week fire broke out in the sitting room downstairs. Fortunately Mario heard the fire alarm but then he panicked and ran along the corridors shouting 'Help, Help!' but did not know what else to do until a senior nurse told him to calm down and gave him instructions to follow.

Working with another person discuss what Mario should have done. How can he gain more confidence in himself?

Talk it over

Working with another person write a policy (as to expected behaviour, rules and regulations) on a suitable dress code for a nurse working on a busy ward in the local hospital. You will have to think about uniforms, personal hygiene and footwear.

It is important for a care worker to keep themselves clean and tidy at all times. We have already explored the importance of not passing infectious diseases from one person to another. Clean clothes helps us contribute to the prevention of infectious disease.

A clean and tidy appearance also helps to inspire confidence in those for whom we are caring.

For example, if you work in a hospital you cannot go into the food preparation area unless you are dressed suitably.

Provision of safety and warning notices

Have you ever looked around a care setting and seen the number of notices that are on show? We have, and there are many different ones. Look at the list for the different kinds of signs you can find.

- Fire exit
- No smoking
- What to do in case of fire
- Emergency exit
- No naked flames
- Duty rosters
- Staff on duty
- Keep clear
- Directions to services.

Think it over
What do you think is the purpose of each of these signs. Make a note for your portfolio. Thinking about safety might help you with this task.

Think it over
Jack is a resident at the Woodlands home for people with disabilities. He smokes about 20 cigarettes a day and has no intention of giving up.

He was just going to light a cigarette when he noticed the no smoking sign next to his room mate's bed.

'Probably because of the oxygen', he thought. 'I will go downstairs to have a cigarette.'

How has this warning sign helped to prevent an accident?

Thinking about visitors and new members of staff, you can easily see the importance of having signs and notices to help people find their way in and out of a building quickly if necessary.

Look it up

Find out what the warning and safety signs are in your place of work or study. Make a list of them. Compare them with the list collected by another person.

4.2 Dealing with emergencies

An important part of keeping clients safe from harm is knowing what to do in a personal health emergency. This is different to helping keep the environment safe. This is about knowing what to do if there was an emergency situation with a client's health.

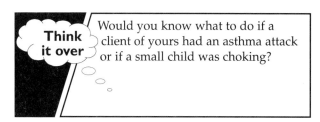

Think it over
Would you know what to do if a client of yours had an asthma attack or if a small child was choking?

It is not usual for health emergencies to be happening all the time in a care setting. However, it is likely that at some time or another you will have to deal with one. Therefore, it is important that you have a good understanding of what to do if something should happen. Common health emergencies are:

- fits
- electric shock
- broken bones
- asthma attack

- choking

- head injury

- burn and scald injuries.

Talk it over

Some emergencies are more likely to happen in certain settings than others. Working with another person discuss which of the care settings you are most likely to find broken bones and choking in. List your reasons for this.

It is likely you have identified those settings involving children or older people as those where broken bones and choking are most likely to occur. Did you list the following reasons?

- Children take risks (e.g. more likely to fall out of trees).

- Small children don't always chew their food properly.

- Very small children might put objects in their mouth.

- Older people develop brittle bones which break easily.

- Older people who have had a stroke may be unbalanced and unable to chew their food properly.

There are lots of reasons why older people and small children are at risk of health emergencies, but they are not the only groups at risk.

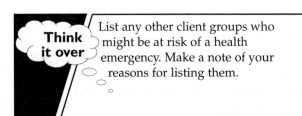

Think it over

List any other client groups who might be at risk of a health emergency. Make a note of your reasons for listing them.

Asthma attack

This can be very upsetting for the person having the attack. The muscles in the airways (trachea and bronchus) go into spasm so that it becomes very difficult for the client to breathe. It is especially difficult for the client to get their breath out. A long attack can make the person feel very tired and weak.

In a very severe attack it is possible for the patient to become unconscious and stop breathing.

Look it up

Alice is staying in a Younger Persons Disabled Unit for an assessment of her needs. She is enjoying her time there, but cannot wait to get home to her family again.

She is feeling unwell at the moment, her chest feels tight and she is having great difficulty in breathing. She calls for a care worker to help her.

By the time the care worker arrives Alice is wheezing and her skin has a blue tinge to it. She is very distressed and could only speak in a whisper.

The carer reassures her and tells her to stay calm. She calls for assistance and then gets Alice's inhaler so that Alice can use her medication. Next she helps Alice to lean forward slightly to help ease the breathing. The attack starts wearing off, but the carer knows that if it had been severe or lasted a long time then an ambulance would have been needed to take Alice to hospital.

Using the case of Alice and working with another person, make a list of the signs and symptoms of asthma. Make short notes on how to treat the condition.

Choking

Choking happens when a person's airway becomes blocked with something such as food or an object. Slippery boiled sweets can be a real danger to both children and adults.

A person who is choking will:

- not be able to breathe properly

- have difficulty speaking

- possibly develop bluish looking skin

- probably panic.

In most cases the cough reflex will move the object causing the blockage. In some cases however the client needs help to remove the blockage. In this case quick action is needed to save a life!

Helping an adult who is choking

- Bend the client forwards and give four or five sharp slaps between the shoulder blades.

- If this does not work try abdominal thrusts. This requires the carer to put their arms around the client, link the hands together in front of them, and give a sharp, sudden pull upwards against the diaphragm.

In very severe cases it may be necessary to send for additional help. If the client loses consciousness and stops breathing, resuscitation and the emergency services will be required.

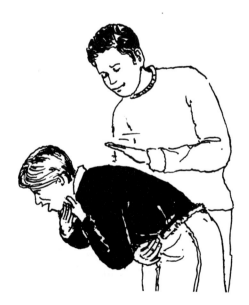

Helping a small child who is choking

- Put the child face down across your knee and give four or five sharp slaps in between the shoulder blades

- If this does not work turn the child over and give five sharp thrusts to the bottom of the breastbone. Use just one hand to do this.

Do not try to feel for the object unless you can easily reach and remove it. Otherwise the blockage could be pushed further down and make the situation worse. If the child loses consciousness, send for the emergency services and begin resuscitation if the child stops breathing (see page 133).

Head injury

If clients have a head injury we should not take any chances if it looks serious. If a person loses consciousness we should always call the emergency services. It is possible for a person to develop concussion (bruising part of the brain), usually after a hard blow to the skull. The problem is that sometimes it might be a few hours after the client has hit their head before they begin to show signs that something is wrong. If a person suffers a blow to the head we should watch for:

- severe headaches

- dizziness

- irritability

- not liking bright lights

- sleepy and difficult to waken up.

Some head injuries lead to bleeding. If the bleeding is severe the client might need treatment. Any bleeding that occurs from the mouth, nose or ears because of a head injury should result in the emergency services being called at once.

Burn and scald injuries

A burn is an injury to the skin (and sometimes the muscle underneath) caused by extreme heat or cold. Burns can also be caused by chemicals, electricity or radiated heat.

- Dry burns come from flames, hot objects, electrical equipment or friction.

- Electrical burns are caused by contact with electricity (overhead cables, plug sockets).

- Chemical burns are caused by acid or alkaline substances found in cleaning products or products used in manufacturing.

- Radiation burns can be caused by spending too much time in the sun, or, in exceptional cases, being exposed to radioactive substances.

- Scalds are caused by steam or hot fat and other liquids coming into contact with the skin.

- Cold injury is caused by frostbite or freezing metals and vapour.

Burns can be superficial, which means they are mainly on the surface and have been caused by short contact with the flame. Intermediate level burns usually show signs of blistering and are painful. Full thickness burns require immediate help from the emergency services. The person may not feel much pain, as it is likely the nerves will have been damaged.

Action for burns

Your research should have shown the treatment for burns is:

- cold water for at least ten minutes

- do not burst any blisters that appear (they are protecting the damaged skin)

- remove any jewellery (before swelling causes problems)

- cover the burn with a non-fluffy dressing to keep it clean

- do not use any creams or ointments

- if clothing is sticking to the burned area, leave it – do not try to remove it as more damage could be caused

- if clothing is on fire, roll person in blanket.

Fits

Epilepsy is a brain disorder which can occur at any time, at any age and to any sex. Abnormal electrical activity on the surface of the brain causes a person to have a fit or seizure. There are a variety of different causes of epileptic fits, such as:

- inherited disease

- head injury

Talk it over

Khalid is looking after Sajid whilst his mother has gone to the dentist.

Sajid has been playing quietly in the kitchen whilst Khalid is having a cup of coffee that he has made for himself.

Suddenly there is a loud scream from the kitchen. When Khalid rushes in to the kitchen he finds Sajid with water from the kettle dripping off his arm.

Khalid picks Sajid up immediately and puts his arm under cold running water from the kitchen tap.

After several minutes he checks Sajid's arm. It is very red but is blister-free. Luckily the water in the kettle had cooled down from boiling point.

Working with anther person discuss Khalid's treatment of Sajid. Why do you think the water helped? Find out if this is a useful way to treat all levels of burn. Make notes for your portfolio of the correct way to treat an intermediate level burn.

- flashing lights
- over-tiredness
- extreme stress
- not taking prescribed medication if you have the illness.

It is important to know how to help a client who is having a fit because they will not be able to help themselves.

It is not always the case that a person will lose consciousness with an epileptic fit. Some fits are so small that they are hardly noticeable. Signs and symptoms might include:

- staring ahead blankly
- movement of the head and lips

- strange behaviour or strange sayings
- loss of memory.

The main aim of emergency treatment is to reassure the client and protect them from any danger. Talk quietly and stay calm. Remain with the person until you are sure that they have fully recovered.

Electric shock

A small electric shock might cause no harm or injury (other than to give the person a fright!). On the other hand, a shock from a high voltage or high current source can be

Talk it over

Eunice, who worked at the children's residential home, had just popped out to the chip shop for her lunch. She was in the queue when she noticed Sylvia, a resident of the home, at the front of the queue. 'What is she doing here', she thought, 'she should be at school.'

Suddenly Sylvia fell to the ground and became quite rigid before arching her back and starting to make jerking movements. Her lips began to look blue and she stopped breathing for a short time.

Eunice recognised the epileptic fit and asked people to move away from Sylvia so that there was a clear space around her. She loosened Sylvia's clothing and when the spasms had stopped put her in the recovery position (see page 137) until she came round.

Eunice stayed with Sylvia until she felt better. When they got back to the care home, Eunice reported the fit to her supervisor who rang Sylvia's doctor to inform her.

Working with another person make a list of the signs and symptoms of an epileptic fit. Research ways of treating the client whilst they are having the fit and afterwards when the fit has passed. You may use an up-to-date first-aid manual for this. Make notes for your portfolio.

Talk it over

Eileen is a key worker for Manjit who lives in a small community home for people with learning difficulties.

He usually manages to look after himself very well. He is good at cooking and enjoys being in the kitchen. Today he decided to give the house a good 'spring clean'. This included cleaning inside the electric wall socket with a damp cloth. He pushed the cloth into the socket with a screwdriver and immediately received a massive electric shock.

Eileen heard the bang and dashed into him. Once she realised what had happened she took action.

1   She first turned off the electricity at the mains switch under the stairs.

2   Next she checked to see if Manjit was still breathing.

3   When she established he was she put him into the recovery position.

4   Then she called the emergency services immediately.

Working in pairs discuss how this situation could have been avoided in the first place. Find out what to do if the electricity supply could not be switched off at the mains. You could use the library to help with this research.

fatal. The electricity interferes with the normal beat of the heart. This could cause the heart to stop working altogether. If this happens, then treatment to restart the heart is required immediately.

It is important to make sure that you are safe from danger whenever you are dealing with someone who has been injured by electricity. If the person is still connected to the live current do not touch them or you too could receive a shock. Turn off the electric supply, or if this is not possible move the client away from the supply using something wooden. If you use metal, the electric current will travel up to you!

Broken bones

In an accident bones may be broken (fractured) or wrenched out of their socket (dislocated).

It is important to recognise when a bone is damaged so that treatment can be obtained quickly. Look for:

- unusual position of the limb (arms and legs)
- swelling or bruising
- bones sticking through the skin

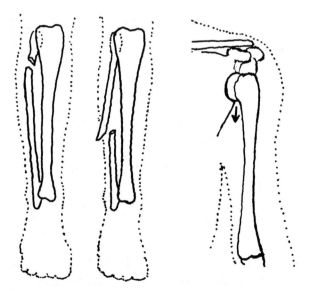

Open and closed fractures and disclocation

- listen for grating sounds (or even snapping) if you are there at the time of injury
- the kind and amount of pain caused.

Look it up

Cathy and Phillip had taken a small party of young adults out for the day walking in the Lake District. It was very windy and everyone was hanging on to each other, in case they were blown over.

Suddenly Cathy fell, she put her arms out to save herself and dislocated her shoulder. She was in a great deal of pain and had to walk back down the mountain.

Phillip tried to help Cathy by tying his scarf around her arm to provide some support and stop it from swinging loose.

Find out about the way a dislocation should be cared for until a doctor can be found. Make notes of your findings for your portfolio.

4.3 Basic first-aid procedures

It is likely that you can now recognise a wide range of health emergencies. You can probably tell when a bone has been broken and when someone is having an asthma attack. The signs and symptoms for both these conditions are fairly obvious. It is also likely that you will now understand how to cope with a health emergency when someone is choking or has a burn.

Think it over

What would you do if a work colleague burned their arm in the steam from a pressure cooker? Do you know what immediate action to take? If not, go back and read the section on burns again.

Do you know what to do if a small child has a plastic object stuck in their airway and they are choking? Do you know what immediate action to take? If not, go back and read the section on choking again.

There are other health emergencies that can occur in a health and care setting that do not have any obvious outward signs, such as:

* when breathing stops, or
* there is no pulse or heartbeat.

Other conditions that can occur are when:

* a person loses consciousness, or
* injures themselves causing bleeding.

It is important for you to learn how to cope with each of these situations, just in case they ever happen when you are on duty.

When breathing stops

Talk it over

Alan is on night duty in the residential care home for older people. He saw Mary go into the kitchen ten minutes ago to make a cup of tea but she has not come out yet.

Alan decides he had better go and check that she is OK.

When he gets there he finds Mary slumped on the kitchen floor.

Alan quickly bends down to see if she is still breathing.

Working with another person discuss how you could check if a person is still breathing or not. Make a note of the ways you might use and then compare them to the ways Alan does it.

Alan looked at Mary's chest and abdomen to see if they were moving as a sign of breathing in or out. They were not. He used his cheek to see if he could feel any air gently blowing on his skin from Mary's mouth or nose. He couldn't feel anything there either.

He knew he had to do something quickly or Mary might die.

Did you have these ideas on your list? Another way is to use a mirror, if there is one close by. The mirror is held in front of the patient's mouth to see if it steams up, a sign that the person is breathing!

Read about it

Take time to read the next section carefully. You will be asked to practice some first-aid techniques as part of your final assessment.

The ABC procedure

If an individual has collapsed and appears not to be breathing, it is essential to apply the ABC rule straight away:

A = **A**irway opened

B = **B**reathing restarted

C = **C**irculation of blood established

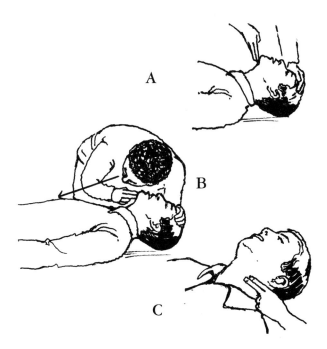

Alan decided to follow the ABC procedure to try and help Mary.

1   He checked her airway (A) for any blockages.

2   Then he checked to see if she was breathing (B).

3   Finally he checked her heart to make sure it was pumping blood around her body for circulation (C).

Dealing with blockage of windpipe

It may be impossible for the person to breathe at all, because there is a blockage in the windpipe (the airway). In order to survive the person needs to get oxygen in to their lungs through the nose or mouth. If an airway is blocked and breathing has stopped the signs will be:

- the skin of the face pale but with bluish colour

- no movement of the chest and abdomen.

The blockage could be caused by food, false teeth that have slipped, or even the person's own tongue that has been partly swallowed. Another common cause is vomit.

Whatever the reason for the blockage, it will be important to open the airway by using the correct technique. This is as follows:

- Kneel beside the person.

- Lift the individual's chin forward with your index and middle fingers of one hand.

- Press the individual's forehead back gently with the heel of the other hand.

If you need to clear an object from the airway:

- Turn the person's head carefully to one side.

- Use one finger and remove any blockage.

- Check the breathing again.

Mouth-to-mouth resuscitation

To check breathing, look at the chest and abdomen to make sure they are rising and falling. If the person is not breathing it will be necessary to start mouth-to-mouth resuscitation.

What is resuscitation?

Resuscitation is carried out on a person who may appear to be dead or collapsed or in

Talk it over

Working with another person try to find out where you could get training on how to carry out resuscitation procedures. You might need to think about voluntary organisations, your place of work or your place of study. Make a note of the places where resuscitation training might be offered.

shock. It can be given in the form of mouth-to-mouth ventilation or external cardiac massage. The resuscitation given will depend on the type of injury, the place of the injury and the age of the person. Children may require different procedures. It is important to follow the procedures given during first-aid training when performing any kind of resuscitation.

If you are employed as a care worker in a hospital, residential establishment or day care setting, your employer may provide resuscitation training for you. You might also

Action steps for giving mouth-to-mouth ventilation to an adult

Step 1 With the casualty lying flat on his or her back, place yourself at the side of the head.

Step 2 Open the person's airway by tilting the head and lifting the chin. Take a deep breath to fill your lungs with air.

Step 3 Pinch the person's nostrils together so that the air will go straight into the lungs.

Step 4 Seal your lips around the person's mouth and blow air into his or her lungs for about two seconds. Watch for the chest to rise. Remove your lips and allow the chest to fall. Aim for 10–15 breaths per minute.

Step 5 Give four breaths in this way and then check to see whether the person has started breathing naturally again. Also check the person's pulse (carotid).

Step 6 If the person's breathing is still missing, repeat the steps again until breathing restarts or help arrives.

be able to obtain one-way mouth coverings for use when giving mouth-to-mouth ventilation. These are intended to prevent infections (viruses or other micro-organisms) passing from one person to another.

Resuscitating children

The procedures used for resuscitating children are similar to those used for adults, but should be done faster and with lighter pressure.

When giving mouth-to-mouth ventilation to a child you do not need to breathe out (exhale) the complete air content of your lungs, because the child's lungs are smaller than yours. It is important that when you see the child's chest rise, you remove your mouth from his or hers and wait for the chest to fall before breathing into the mouth again. It is advised that 20 breaths per minute should be sufficient. Check for a pulse after your first four breaths.

A baby would only require a small amount of air to raise the chest when giving mouth-to-mouth ventilation. Placing your mouth over the baby's mouth and nose will probably prove easier than trying to pinch the nostrils together.

No pulse or heartbeat

It is the job of the heart to pump blood around the body. In order to check that the heart is doing this, a pulse can be felt for. A pulse is a wave of blood that is passing through an artery.

A pulse can be felt at many points, but the most commonly used ones are:

- the neck pulse, felt over the carotid artery

- the wrist pulse, felt over the radial artery

- the groin pulse, felt over the femoral artery.

In an emergency it is often easiest to feel the pulse in the neck, over the carotid artery.

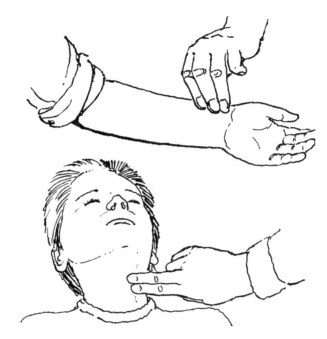

Feeling for a pulse at different points

- You will need to have the client lying on the floor, face up, with their head tilted back.

- Place your index and middle finger at the side of the person's Adam's apple.

- Slide your fingers towards you into the gap between the Adam's apple and the strap muscle that runs down from behind the ear.

Think it over

Alan had used his ABC technique on Mary and found that her airway was clear, but her breathing had stopped. When he checked the pulse in her neck he could not find any trace of a heart beat.

He knew he had to start resuscitation techniques straight away if she was going to have any chance of life.

He ran to a telephone and called the emergency services and then went straight back to Mary to start helping her.

Why do you think Alan rang the emergency services before he started mouth-to-mouth resuscitation?

The emergency services should always be sent for as soon as possible. Expert help increases the chance of survival. If another person is with you, then they can be sent to telephone whilst you start the resuscitation procedure.

Cardio-pulmonary resuscitation (CPR)

A qualified first-aider must teach you before using this technique yourself. However, it is important to have some knowledge now of how to carry out external cardiac massage, and about the situations in which it would be used, in case you are the only one available to give assistance. External chest compression (if needed) always follows mouth-to-mouth ventilation.

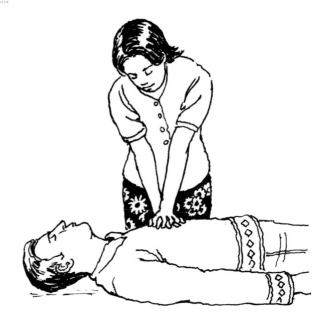

Action steps for giving external cardiac massage
Step 1 Kneel at the side of the person, keeping your back as straight as possible and getting as close as you can.
Step 2 Find the base of the breast bone, where the ribs meet. Place the heel of your hand two fingers' width up along the line of the breast bone – this is the point at which to apply pressure.
Step 3 Cover your first hand with your other hand and interlock your fingers together (make sure you keep them off the ribs).
Step 4 Keep your arms straight and press down on the breast bone so as to press it about 4–5 cm downwards. Release the pressure without removing your hands from the person's chest. Repeat the movement, aiming for approximately 80 compressions per minute. This is quite a fast movement.

Giving chest compressions is physically demanding work, so the recommendation is to give 15 chest compressions and then two breaths. This is again followed by another 15 chest compressions and another two breaths. This should be continued without stopping until help arrives. It is unlikely that the heart will start beating again without expert treatment, but you should keep checking to see if a pulse returns.

Try it out Place your hands one on top of the other (like the diagram demonstrates) and imagine you are pressing on someone's chest. How quickly do you have to repeat each movement to get 80 in one minute?

Cardiac massage to babies and small children

When giving external cardiac massage, only one hand is necessary for a small child, and two fingers for a baby. Use a lighter pressure and a faster rate of compression – 100 compressions per minute is recommended. Pressing down should only be 2.5–3.5 cm for a small child and only 2 cm for a baby.

It is important to monitor the client's condition over a period of time, as the situation might change.

Loss of consciousness

If you find a client who is unconscious, you will find that they will not respond to:

*   calling their name

*   pain

*   shaking.

Your main task is to provide immediate care for them. You will first need to check whether he or she is still breathing. This will mean opening the airway and looking, listening and feeling for any signs that respiration (breathing) is taking place.

Next you will need to check to see if they have a heartbeat. If one or both are missing you will need to start giving emergency resuscitation.

Causes of unconsciousness include:

- asphyxia (choking)

- epilepsy (fit)

- injury (especially of the head)

- overdose

- heart attack.

Bleeding

As we have already examined the procedures to follow if someone is choking or has been burned we will now examine what to do if someone is bleeding.

It is possible in some care settings that people will fall and injure themselves. For example, cuts and grazes are very common in an early years care setting. This kind of bleeding is not usually very serious and as long as the wound is cleaned and dressed no further action is required. However, it is important to assess all kinds of bleeding. This should be done as quickly as possible. The things that are important to consider are:

- what is causing the bleeding

- the type of bleeding (artery, vein, capillary)

- if there is an object in the wound such as glass or dirt

- how long has there been blood loss.

The sight of blood often causes people to panic, but sometimes a wound will look worse than it actually is. It is important for everyone involved to remain calm.

> **Think it over**
>
> Barney had fallen off the slide in the play area outside and hurt his elbow. As he ran to his carer he was screaming his loudest. And that was very loud!
>
> Victoria, his carer, lifted Barney onto her knee so that she could look at his elbow. She saw a large graze that was beginning to bleed. There was some dirt stuck to the wound.
>
> She calmed Barney down and then took him inside to wash and have a dressing applied to the wound.
>
> *Is this situation dangerous? How would you calm Barney down?*

Barney's situation is clearly not life-threatening, however there are other occasions when bleeding can be a threat to life, such as:

- bleeding from an artery (arteries are connected to the heart, which means that blood squirts out with every heartbeat)

- bleeding in a major organ (such as the brain or kidneys).

Controlling bleeding

The sight of blood can cause people to panic. It can be very alarming to both client and care worker. It is necessary to remain calm as time is important when assessing blood loss. It is also important to work quickly. Applying pressure to a bleeding part is a simple and effective way to control bleeding.

Types of bleeding

There are three main types of bleeding.

- Arterial blood (from an artery) is normally bright red and appears to spurt from the wound.

- Venous blood (from a vein) is generally darker in colour and may flow without spurting from the wound.

135

- Capillary blood is from very small vessels that may contain arterial or venous blood. In this case the blood will appear to 'ooze' from the wound.

Bleeding can also be named according to its location or site.

- External bleeding is on the outside, so it is very easy to see and assess the amount of blood loss.

- Internal bleeding is on the inside of the body and so is more difficult to check.

Points to consider

Before trying to control bleeding it is important to make your assessment of the situation.

When you have made this assessment you must decide whether it is necessary to seek expert help. If only a sticking plaster is required, no other help may be needed. If the wound is deep, and there is a lot of bleeding, help should be obtained immediately.

It is also important to find out the cause of the injury when assessing the need for expert help. The wound may have been caused by a dirty object that has penetrated deep inside the skin, with possible damage to nerves. This is also likely to cause an infection.

If there is a 'foreign body' in the wound, then it is best to let an expert deal with the problem, because it will be important not to press the object further into the wound by covering or putting pressure on it.

External bleeding

With external bleeding, the action to be taken is:

- apply pressure to the wound

- elevate the affected area if possible (i.e. lift an arm or a leg)

- use ice packs if possible and where necessary.

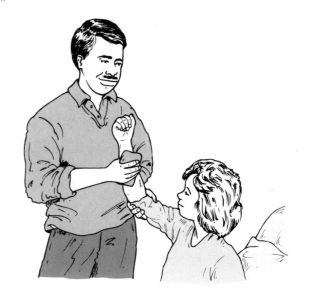

Applying direct pressure is a simple way of controlling bleeding. To do this, first cover the wound with a sterile dressing and apply direct pressure using the thumb and/or fingers or palm. Lay the individual down in a comfortable position and raise the injured part and support it. When the bleeding is controlled, put on a sterile dressing with padding to go beyond the edges of the wound. Press the padding down and fasten it with a bandage, tied firmly, but not so tight as to stop circulation.

Applying indirect pressure is a technique used when direct pressure cannot be given because of the type of injury. It is a method that can only be used to control arterial bleeding from a limb. Indirect pressure may be applied to a pressure point where a main artery runs close to a bone.

There are two pressure points used to control bleeding by indirect methods. These involve:

- the brachial artery which runs along the inner side of the upper arm

- the femoral artery which is in the groin and which passes into the lower limb.

Pressure is applied where the artery can be squeezed on to an underlying bone to flatten it and stop the flow of blood beyond that point.

Coping with internal bleeding

The causes of internal bleeding can be injury or disease. An example of an accident that might cause internal bleeding would be if a person fell hard on to his or her stomach. Alternatively a client might have felt unwell for several days, as the result of an ulcer that had been bleeding internally for some time.

The signs and symptoms of internal bleeding can include:

* bleeding from ears, nose, mouth etc.

* pain and discomfort

* a pulse which is both fast and weak

* confusion, perhaps collapse into unconsciousness

* a shortness of breath which is caused through oxygen not reaching the tissues

* pale skin colour, or cold, clammy skin

* swelling in the injured area

* thirst.

In such situations it is important to look for the signs given above. Check a pulse and help the person to lie down. Ask questions which may give other clues. Do not give anything to eat or drink. Loosen any clothing around

Talk it over

Eileen had fallen from her wheelchair trying to get into the front seat of her car. As she fell, she caught her leg on the pointed end of the car door. It caused a very deep gash in her ankle. Bright red blood was spurting all over her leg.

Working with another person identify the kind of bleeding that Eileen is suffering from. Make notes on how you would treat her injury. Keep your notes for your portfolio of evidence.

the suspected damaged area, and call for expert help immediately.

The recovery position

Monitoring a casualty includes making sure that he or she is not left in an unsafe position. An unconscious casualty should be placed in the recovery position if breathing and circulation are satisfactory. This is a safe position, keeping the airway open and with the head lower than the body, so that any liquids can drain from the mouth. It also keeps the head, neck and back in a straight line. If you have to leave an unconscious casualty alone while you go for help, the recovery position is the safest way to leave him or her.

The recovery position

Techniques for turning a casualty into the recovery position can be practised on a first-aid course.

Summoning the emergency services

Several times we have mentioned calling for the emergency services. You should be aware of how to do this in case you ever need to call for help. Do you remember the instructions for calling the fire brigade given earlier in the unit? Calling an ambulance is really no different.

Whenever we need to call the emergency services we must:

- remain calm

- give our name

- tell the operator which service we require

- tell the operator details of the emergency, such as who is involved, where they are, how long they have been there.

It is important not to become impatient. The questions are asked for a reason and that is to get help to both the caller and the injured person as soon as possible.

Talk it over

Working with another person discuss how you would call for an ambulance to take Eileen to the hospital. You might need to think about asking for help from a passer-by (remember Eileen is bleeding badly). Make a list of the information you would need to give to the operator.

Make notes on why the operator requires each piece of information from you.

Unit 4 Assessment

You need to produce a demonstration of your understanding of common hazards and health emergencies, which includes:

*   a workplace safety survey (audit)

*   an explanation of what may happen if you fail to follow correct health and safety practice

*   a demonstration of some first-aid procedures.

For this unit you will have the opportunity to work towards a pass, merit or distinction grade.

The activities are ordered in such a way as to guide you through this assessment. The levels of assessment are clearly indicated as:

*   P for Pass

*   M for Merit

*   D for Distinction.

You may wish to discuss with your tutor the level of activities you do.

All students must complete the first three activities to achieve the minimum for Unit 4.

Activity 1P

You are going to carry out a **health and safety survey (or audit)** of one workplace that you are familiar with. This could possibly be your own college or school. It may also be where you work, if you have part-time employment or if you are doing work experience. However, you would need to discuss this first with your workplace supervisor and explain that it is part of your college work.

*   Describe in a few lines the workplace you are going to survey. Include the client group/student group in your description.

*   You are now going to carry out the survey.

The case study on page 119 might give you some ideas about an audit of this kind.

*   Correctly identify any **basic hazards** in the workplace. These may be part of the normal working environment. For example, if you were working in a nursery, one hazard might be the cleaning materials used in the bathroom. Remember that hazards and risks might include such things as: unsafe equipment, infections, fire, moving and handling people and/or equipment, wet floors, blocked emergency exits, poor lighting.

*   Correctly identify any **health and safety features**. For example, if you are working in a nursery, you could identify safe storage of cleaning materials, safety gates, visitors books, window locks.

Both can be identified in a list, but you must clearly state which work environment you are referring to.

Activity 2P

Identify the consequences both to staff and clients of failure to follow procedures to maintain a safe environment. For example, a wet floor with no 'wet floor' sign could result in injury from slipping over.

Activity 3P

You must safely demonstrate the procedures for cardio-pulmonary resuscitation (CPR).

If you are unable to do this, you should be able to talk another person through the correct procedures.

The demonstration (or instruction) of CPR should not contain any major errors.

If you have a current first-aid certificate which includes demonstration of CPR, this is an acceptable substitute for Activity 3P.

Working towards a merit grade

To achieve a merit grade you must complete all the activities in the pass section. In addition you must complete the steps to Activities 1 and 3 below.

Activity 1M

*   While carrying out your audit, you must not only identify the hazards but also describe their location. You could possibly do this by using a floor plan of the workplace environment or by describing where they are in relation to key parts of the building. Drawings, illustrations or photos could be included to make this an interesting activity.

*   As part of this survey, accurately identify and describe the location of the health and safety features of the workplace. For example, you could include fire equipment, smoke detectors, emergency exits, first-aid boxes, childproof locks, location of the workplace health and safety policies.

Activity 3M

*   You must be able to show an understanding and give clear explanation of procedures for dealing with three of the health emergencies listed in the unit, *as well as CPR*. For example, if you were dealing with a burn, you would explain that cold water is used to cool the burnt area and surrounding tissue to reduce further damage. 'To take the heat of the burn away' would be an acceptable explanation for this.

*   As well as being able to explain the procedures for dealing with these three emergencies and why you would carry out these procedures, you must be able to demonstrate each procedure, relating the correct symptoms to each one. If you are unable to physically demonstrate the skills, you must be able to talk someone through exactly what you would do in the emergency situation.

(The emergencies and procedures used to deal with them are listed again at the end of this assessment brief).

Working towards a distinction grade

To gain a distinction you must complete the activities for the pass and merit grades. In addition you must carry out the steps to Activities 1 and 3 below.

Activity 1D

In the survey, you located and described hazards and a range of health and safety features in the workplace. In this activity at distinction level, you must now:

*   Show an understanding of the relationship between the location of the health and safety features to the hazards, and how this helps reduce risks. For example, you could identify childproof locks (health and safety feature) on cupboard doors in the nursery kitchen (location). The explanation would be that these features are necessary as bleach and cleaning agents are kept in the cupboards and if swallowed or spilt by a child could cause injury to the child.

    You could present this information in a table, with illustrations, if you wish.

*   In your survey audit of the workplace, you may have felt there was a need for certain improvements to be made. Make a list of these and suggest how they could be realistically made. For example, a corridor or entrance might be poorly lit. A realistic suggestion might be that higher wattage bulbs could be used, or additional lighting supplied.

Activity 3D

You must be able to demonstrate most of the first-aid procedures listed. If you are unable to physically do this, you must be able to talk through with another person your method of dealing with each procedure. You must not make any errors which could be life-threatening.

You will also be asked to demonstrate what you would do if the casualty had more than one symptom – for example, was bleeding and had a burn.

For students at all levels

When dealing with emergencies, you should always be able to show you know how and when to:

- use cardio-pulmonary resuscitation (CPR)
- place a person in the recovery position
- summon emergency services.

You need to be able to deal with these emergencies:

- asthma attack
- choking
- head injury
- burn and scald injuries
- fits
- electric shock
- broken bones.

You need to know the first-aid procedures for:

- no breathing
- no pulse or heart beat
- loss of consciousness
- choking
- bleeding
- burns or scalding.

Check your knowledge

1 Describe in a few words for each, two human factors and two environmental factors which could lead to accidents in a health or social care setting.

2 List four potential problems which could occur from carers using incorrect moving or handling techniques.

3 What are two responsibilities of employees under the Health and Safety at Work regulations?

4 What are two responsibilities of employers under the Health and Safety at Work regulations?

5 You become aware of a smell of burning in your college kitchen. You know that there is no class in there at the moment. List the first three actions you would take *in order of importance*.

6 The *best* method of reducing the risk from household chemicals is to store them:
   a   in the garden shed
   b   in a locked cupboard
   c   under the kitchen sink
   d   on a top shelf.

7 After you have made sure you are safe in an emergency situation, the next action to take is:
   a   keep the casualty warm
   b   take notes so you can describe the event afterwards
   c   assess the situation
   d   contact the emergency services.

8 The recovery position is:
   a   used for patients after an operation
   b   to ensure a casualty is kept breathing and will not choke
   c   used to support a casualty in resuscitation
   d   the position of the heart and lungs.

9 Arterial blood is visible because it:

   a dribbles gently from the cut

   b is blue in colour

   c is red and spurts from the wound

   d is never infected.

10 You have come across an accident and have dealt with it as far as you are able to, as a first-aider. Your role comes to an end when:

   a you have covered the casualty and talked reassuringly to him

   b the emergency services have been called

   c your friend arrives with a mobile phone

   d the emergency services arrive.

This unit is about something that all of us have experience of – food and drink. That is, it is about diet. The word diet is often used in a more familiar way as referring to 'going on a diet', or trying to lose weight. But in this unit, we use the word in its more correct sense. Here it means what you eat and drink.

This unit helps you add to your knowledge and understanding of what food and drinks make up a healthy diet. You will learn how to prepare healthy and appetising food, and will consider different client groups as you do this. You will also explore some of the health problems a person might have if the diet does not meet his or her personal and developmental needs.

This unit will be very useful in a job where you have to provide food and drink. It will also give you practical knowledge which you can use every day to help to plan menus for your friends and family.

You will need to learn about:

- what makes up a healthy, balanced diet
- the nutrients that are contained in each food
- where the nutrients come from
- planning meals which are healthy, interesting and which the client can afford
- preparing meals hygienically
- presenting meals to enjoy.

5.1 A healthy, balanced diet

We should eat 'a balanced diet' every day. This means eating a variety of food in the right amounts to provide you with your own particular needs. A balanced diet does not mean cutting out all the foods you enjoy because they are 'bad' for you, but it does mean including a range and variety of healthy foods in your diet to enable you to eat well and be healthy.

A balanced diet should therefore provide all the necessary nutrients we need. Nutrients include:

- protein, for growth and repair
- carbohydrates, the main source of energy

Think it over

Make a list now of your favourite food and drinks. They don't have to be food that you eat all the time, but food that you really like and enjoy.

Compare your list with a partner. Do you like the same kinds of food? Are there any foods which one of you likes and the other really dislikes? Why do you think this is?

Why is it important to enjoy your food?

Keep your list for later.

- fats, also for energy, and for other functions in the body
- vitamins and minerals, for good health and growth

- dietary fibre and water. These are not nutrients, but are essential for our bodies to work properly.

You will need to be familiar with nutrients for your assessment.

Food groups for a balanced diet

Food can be divided up into five main groups. In the pie chart you will see what the food groups are and what proportions of this food should be eaten each day. Later we will look at the nutrients in each food, so that you know why each is important in these particular proportions.

Malnutrition

If someone does not have a balanced diet with good nutrition they may suffer from malnutrition. Obesity, or being overweight, is one form of malnutrition. Being underweight can also be a sign of malnutrition, especially if it is caused by not having the right food to keep you healthy and full of energy.

Try it out

What I ate yesterday

Think about your own diet and how balanced it is by looking at what you ate yesterday or on a typical day in the last week.

List everything you ate from morning to night. Don't forget the snacks and drinks.

Then, organise the list under the five food group headings:

For example, if you had orange juice for breakfast you would list this under fruit and vegetables; if you had milk, cheese and butter, you would list this under dairy products, and so on.

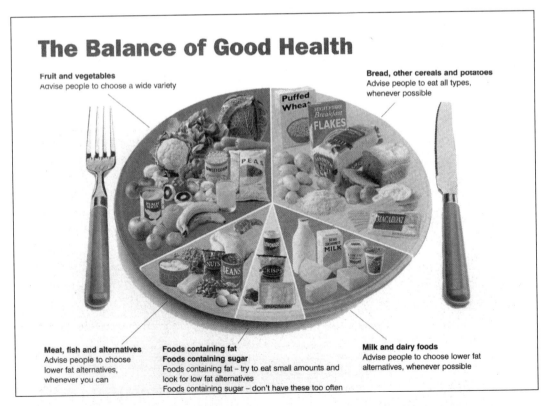

The Balance of Good Health

Fruit and vegetables
Advise people to choose a wide variety

Bread, other cereals and potatoes
Advise people to eat all types, whenever possible

Meat, fish and alternatives
Advise people to choose lower fat alternatives, whenever you can

Foods containing fat
Foods containing sugar
Foods containing fat – try to eat small amounts and look for low fat alternatives
Foods containing sugar – don't have these too often

Milk and dairy foods
Advise people to choose lower fat alternatives, whenever possible

The five food groups that you need for a balanced diet

The balance of good health

In 1994, the government published a national food guide, called *The Balance of Good Health*. It advises us on which food groups to choose from to have a balanced diet (remember the pie chart on page 144) and has some helpful information about how best to follow the advice.

These 'guidelines', as they are called, are also supported by the National Advisory Committee on Nutrition Education (NACNE) – you will come across their work later in the chapter.

The poster has eight guidelines to healthy eating. Let us look at these in more detail.

Guideline 1 Enjoy your food

How you can best enjoy the food you eat might include doing the following:

- eating food you like

- eating with family and friends

- choosing where and when you eat.

There may be others you could add.

Guideline 2 Eat a variety of food

The table below shows that each food group contains a variety of food to choose from. Some of it will be familiar to you, and some may be not, however all of it is available in this country.

Eating a variety of food is important because:

- you do not become bored with eating

- there is enough variety for you to take in the required nutrients.

Guideline 3 Eat the right amount to be a healthy weight

Weight can be a sensitive issue for some people. Most of us worry about our weight at some time. However many of us are comfortably within our recommended weight for height ratio.

Talk it over

Marilyn is 16 years old and always worried about her weight, because that's all her friends seem to talk about. She is 160cm tall and weighs 55 kilos. Her friend Olinda is taller than her. She is 170cm tall and weighs about the same. They both do lots of sport, in fact they are training for the school athletics championship at the moment.

In pairs, look at the height/weight chart, and see if you think either girl is overweight or underweight. Would you advise them to diet?

Food from food groups

Five food groups	Bread, other cereals and potatoes	Fruit and vegetables	Milk and dairy foods	Meat, fish and alternatives	Fatty and sugary foods
Types of foods	All types of bread rolls, chapati, crumpets, crackers rice cakes, naan. All types of grain, e.g. oats, barley, rye, bulgar wheat. 'Other cereals' means things like breakfast cereals, pasta, rice, noodles. (Beans and lentils can be eaten as part of this group.)	Fresh, frozen and canned fruit and vegetables and dried fruit. Fruit juice. (Beans and lentils can be eaten as part of this group.)	Milk, cheese, yoghurt and fromage frais. (This group does not contain butter, eggs and cream.)	Meat, poultry, fish, eggs, nuts, seeds, beans and lentils. Meat includes bacon and salami, meat products such as sausages, beefburgers. Beans such as canned baked beans are in this group. Fish includes frozen and canned fish, fish fingers and fish cakes.	Margarine, low-fat spread, butter, ghee, cooking oils, oily salad dressing, cream, chocolate, crisps, biscuits, cake, ice-cream, rich sauces, sweets and sugar. Fizzy soft drinks. Puddings.
Main nutrients	Carbohydrate (starch), fibre, some calcium and iron, B-group vitamins.	Vitamin C, carotenes, iron, calcium, folate, fibre and some carbohydrate.	Calcium, protein, B-group vitamins especially B12, vitamins A and D.	Iron, protein, B-group vitamins, especially B12, zinc and magnesium.	Some vitamins and essential fatty acids but also a lot of fat, sugar and salt.

The height/weight chart on page 69 should help you work out if you are within the limits for your height.

Guideline 4 Eat plenty of foods rich in starch and fibre

It is fairly easy to keep to this guideline. All the starchy food that most of us like, such as bread, rice, pasta, potatoes, are readily available (for energy), and if we eat the right kind, it can also give us enough fibre to keep our bowels regular.

However you can also:

- eat more bread, especially wholemeal bread

- eat more cereals

- try a combination of white and brown rice, to obtain the fibre from the brown rice

- experiment with different kinds and shapes of pasta and different sauces

- eat jacket potatoes with different fillings.

Why should we eat more starchy food and fibre?

They give you energy and are filling but not fattening.

Starches are digested slowly, so help fill you up. Fibre prevents constipation and there is evidence that a diet high in fibre may help prevent bowel cancer. Starches are also a good source of vitamins and minerals.

Guideline 5 Don't eat too much fat

Everyone needs some fat in their diet, however most of us eat too much of it. Remember food has fat you can see, such as fat on meat, and fat that is 'hidden', as in cakes, biscuits and ice cream.

Why all the fuss about fat?

Too much fat in the diet can lead to poor health and illness, such as obesity diabetes, liver diseases and some types of cancer. The fat causes the arteries to become 'furred up' and stops the blood circulating efficiently.

Guideline 6 Don't eat sugary foods too often

It can be quite easy to cut down on sugary food, rather than cutting them out altogether. Can you think of ways of doing this?

Tips for cutting down on sugar

- If you normally take lots of sugar in tea or coffee, start cutting down gradually.

- Eat less cakes and biscuits, have fresh or dried fruits instead.

- Use fruit that has been canned in natural juice.

- Read labels – there is a lot of added sugar in prepared foods.

- It is quite fun and enterprising to make your own desserts – look for recipes that are not high in sugar.

- Use sugar substitutes.

Why eat less sugar?

The sugar in food helps cause tooth decay. It may also add to your weight and cause health problems later on in life. However, we need some sugar in our diet, but much of what we need occurs naturally – fruit for example has its own sugar called fructose.

 Try it out | Collect some labels from cakes and biscuits and other snack foods that you eat and compare the amount of sugar and fat in them with what other members of your group eat. You might not have thought they were very sugary or fatty – but they probably are.

Guideline 7 Look after the vitamins and minerals in your food

If you have a balanced diet, you can get most of the vitamins and minerals you need from the food you eat. The main exception is vitamin D, which many of us get from sunlight.

How can you ensure adequate intake of vitamins and minerals?

Eating fruit and vegetables should be a major part of your daily diet. You should eat at least five servings of fruit and vegetables a day – including fruit juice. Go back to the 'Try it out' activity on page 144. Did you eat five helpings?

Why eat so much fruit and vegetables?

Vitamins and minerals provide you with natural protection against disease, help your body to function and help repair any damage to tissues and organs. They taste good and can be prepared in many different ways.

> ### ? Did you know?
> A golden rule is to think of colours to make sure that you are eating a variety of food with the nutrients you need – eat green and orange, yellow or red every day and you will be on the right track to health. And remember, 'fresh is best'.

Guideline 8 If you drink, keep within sensible limits

Here are the recommended guidelines for alcohol intake.

- 14 units per week for a woman
- 21 units a week for a man.

A unit is a glass of wine, a ½ pint of beer or a measure of spirits (see page 60).

Why is it advised to keep to these limits?

> ### ? Did you know?
> People tend to drink more alcohol at home because they are more generous with the measures! A glass of wine may be a very big glass, possibly well over 1 unit.

Too much alcohol:

- can damage your liver and kidneys
- can make your behaviour moody and unpredictable
- can slow down your reactions
- can contribute to heart disease
- can affect your social life and relationships
- can give you a hangover
- can become addictive.

So, although a little alcohol can be relaxing, and may even be good for health, an excess will almost certainly cause injury to the body and affect the way we function.

> ### ? Did you know?
> It is recommended that pregnant mothers do not drink. Alcohol will pass into the baby's bloodstream and can affect its growth and development.

Health problems resulting from an unbalanced diet

A person who does not eat a balanced diet can become ill over a period of time. Not eating the right nutrients or eating too much

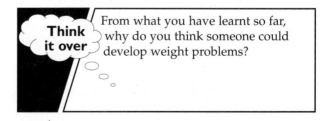

Think it over From what you have learnt so far, why do you think someone could develop weight problems?

Marilyn's father, Mr Bentham, is 42 and definitely overweight. He has a very sedentary lifestyle, that is, he works all day in an office. He also loves a good lunch and a couple of beers and at night a big dinner with some wine and perhaps a whisky. He rarely eats fruit and only a few vegetables. He loves chips and pasties and a big fry up on Sunday morning (which he cooks himself).

The other day he had to go to his doctor because he was beginning to have the odd pain in his chest and got out of breath easily whenever he decided (occasionally) to use the stairs instead of the lift at work.

The doctor gave him some diet advice about losing weight, and 'prescribed' exercise at the local gym instead of medication. He is going to see a trainer there next week.

In small groups discuss which of the guidelines you think Mr Bentham should take notice of? What advice would you give him to work within these guidelines?

of certain foods can lead to poor physical health, and even to mental health problems. Other problems might be:

- **Having an inappropriate weight for your height**

  This can mean being underweight as well as overweight.

Talk it over

In groups, discuss:

- Why is it not good for you to be underweight?

- Think of one major health problem which could develop if you were overweight.

- Think of a health problem which can develop if someone was trying to lose too much weight.

- Share your findings with the whole group.

- **Increased risk of heart disease**

  Heart disease may occur if you do not take enough exercise, if you eat too much fat, drink too much alcohol, or are overweight.

- **Increased risk of bowel cancer**

  One way of helping to prevent bowel cancer is to ensure that there is sufficient fibre in your diet. Dietary fibre is now referred to as NSP or non-starch polysaccharide. You should include about 18 grams of fibre a day in your diet. Look at the food table below.

Why does the body need fibre?

It helps keep the bowels functioning and therefore prevents constipation. By eating fibre you can also help prevent bowel diseases and cancer.

Fibre is the 'filler' in food. It helps give you a feeling of having eaten enough, and therefore can be useful as part of a controlled weight loss programme.

	Fibre (g/100g)		Fibre (g/100g)
Meat	0.0	Bread, white	1.5
Baked beans	3.7	Bread, brown	3.5
Beans, red kidney, boiled	6.7	Bread, wholemeal	5.8
Beans, runner, boiled	1.9	Flour, white	3.1
Cabbage, boiled	1.8	Flour, wholemeal	9.0
Carrots, boiled	2.5	All Bran	24.5
Potatoes, boiled	1.2	Porridge oats	7.1
Yams, boiled	1.4	Rice Krispies	0.7
Tomatoes, raw	1.0	Shredded Wheat	9.8
Apples with skin, raw	1.8	Weetabix	9.7
Bananas	1.1	Rice, white, boiled	0.1
Raisins	2.0	Rice, brown, boiled	0.8
Nuts, mixed	6.0	Spaghetti, white, boiled	1.2
Biscuits, digestive	2.2	Spaghetti, wholemeal, boiled	3.5
Biscuits, rich tea	1.7		

Fibre content of selected foods

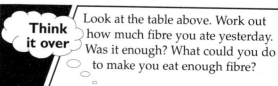

Think it over Look at the table above. Work out how much fibre you ate yesterday. Was it enough? What could you do to make you eat enough fibre?

Lack of vitamins or minerals in the diet

An unbalanced diet, lacking in minerals or vitamins can lead to health problems, such as those below.

A lack of:		can lead to:
vitamin C	→	**scurvy** – a disease where your gums are diseased and your teeth fall out
vitamin D	→	**rickets** – brittle, bendy bones which can break easily
iron	→	**anaemia** – not enough red blood cells so you feel tired and weak
calcium	→	**tooth decay** – where holes form in your teeth which can then break easily.

? Did you know?

The first commercial fruit juice was lime juice, given by Captain James Cook to his sailors on long voyages to prevent them getting scurvy.

Talk it over

Dan is 16 and has been having trouble with his teeth. He is a bit embarrassed because when he cleans them his gums bleed. He thinks that might mean bad breath, but he wouldn't know who to ask! He is also annoyed that he's had a cold for about a month and it won't go away. His nose is red and runny the whole time.

He lives with his parents, but he hardly ever eats at home, he's always out and only seems to grab a can of cola and some chocolate when he's hungry.

Sometimes he has chips and a bit of fish or a burger when he can be bothered. His skin is a bit spotty too. In fact, he's decided that he looks a bit grey: he'll have to do something about his appearance if he wants Olinda to go out with him this weekend.

In pairs, discuss why you think Dan is having the kind of health problems he describes? What would you suggest he does?

5.2 The nutrients in food

Nutrients are the 'building blocks' of food that are essential to keep us healthy and our body functioning.

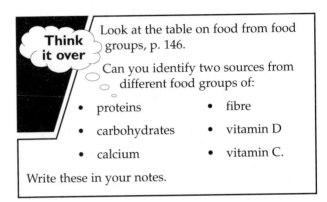

Think it over

Look at the table on food from food groups, p. 146.

Can you identify two sources from different food groups of:

- proteins
- carbohydrates
- calcium
- fibre
- vitamin D
- vitamin C.

Write these in your notes.

You can see that one nutrient can be found in more than one food group. This will be important when you are working out balanced meals for your assessment.

Proteins

Proteins are essential to all living things. We would not exist without them, because they provide the structure for the cells within our bodies.

Proteins are made up of chains of a chemical structure called amino-acids. These amino-acids are sometimes called the 'building blocks' of nature.

The body needs proteins

Every cell in the body needs proteins as part of the surrounding of the cell, called the cell membrane. Protein is also needed for body growth and to help in repairing damaged cells. It is needed for growth and repair of muscles, bones and to help the body fight infection. A protein called haemoglobin is needed to carry oxygen around the body.

The food sources of protein

There are two sources of protein: animal and plant.

Animal sources include red and white meat, fish, milk, eggs and dairy products such as cheese, milk and yoghurt.

Plant sources of protein include peas, beans, lentils, rice, wheat, nuts and seeds. Soya bean is particularly rich in protein.

Complementary protein

When a variety of vegetable proteins are eaten together to make up the amino-acids we need, it is called complementary protein. Many cultures which do not eat meat have been combining proteins for centuries. Traditional dishes such as dhal and rice (Indian) or rice and peas (West Indian) are examples of complementary proteins. So too are baked beans on toast and milk with cereal.

Carbohydrates

Carbohydrates are groups of substances made up of three elements: carbon, hydrogen and oxygen. Many different kinds of foods contain carbohydrates, as you will see below. Carbohydrates give us energy.

The body needs carbohydrates

The body needs carbohydrates because they provide energy to keep us going. They are essentially the fuel that keeps our cells and body processes running smoothly.

The food sources of carbohydrates

Carbohydrates are divided into starches and sugars. Some starch foods are very familiar and include:

*   bread
*   rice, maize and polenta
*   potatoes, including sweet potatoes and yams
*   breakfast cereals.

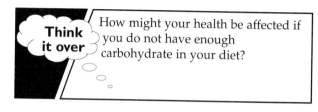

Think it over How might your health be affected if you do not have enough carbohydrate in your diet?

Sugars are easy to identify. They are sweet, as in the case of cakes and biscuits, sugary drinks, chocolate, sweets, jam and honey and ordinary table sugar.

Sugars that contain the table sugar we are familiar with are more harmful than others. These should be eaten sparingly.

Other sugars which occur within foods naturally, like lactose in milk or fructose in fruit, are not harmful to health.

Starches are better than sugars

It is better to take your energy from starches rather than sugars. Starchy foods are called complex carbohydrates and often provide other nutrients as well as energy-giving carbohydrates. These foods also release energy more slowly than sugars, and therefore 'last' longer. If you eat more starchy food, you feel less hungry and may not be tempted to eat quick energy-releasing foods (which also contain lots of fat) such as chocolates or crisps.

Carbohydrate and fibre

Starch sources of carbohydrate include those high in fibre, which are preferable to those lower in fibre.

Fats

The body needs fat

Fats are concentrated sources of energy and can be useful in the diet for that reason. Although we should not eat too much fat, it is still needed by our bodies to:

*   provide insulation against the cold, by preventing heat loss – so fats provide warmth

- protect body organs, e.g. kidneys, heart, liver

- help make the membranes of cells and nerve fibres

- store vitamins A, D, E and K in the body

- make some food more palatable and easier to eat, e.g. butter or margarine spread on bread.

Sources of fat

Animal sources

The main sources of fat in the Western diet come from animal and dairy products. These are called saturated fats and they are solid at room temperature. Examples are butter, lard, suet and the visible fat on meat. They are less healthy than those fats which come from plants because they can contain a substance called cholesterol which can contribute to heart disease.

Plant sources

These fats are usually liquid at room temperature and are familiar as oils, such as olive and sunflower oils. They are called unsaturated fats and are less likely to contribute to heart disease because they do not have the same furring effect on blood vessels as animal fats. Margarine is predominantly vegetable oil which has been treated to make it solid so that it can be spread on food and used for cooking.

Fish oil

Some fish contain a valuable oil which is unsaturated (and therefore liquid) and very good for your health. These fish include mackerel.

? Did you know?

Fish really is brain food. The oil which fish contains is thought to be good for your intelligence.

Types of fat

Vitamins

What vitamins are and why the body needs them

Vitamins are the keys to chemical reactions which help to keep the body functioning. They are identified by letters, although some also have scientific chemical names. The body only needs them in small quantities, but they are essential for health. In this unit you will be looking at vitamins C and D

The body needs vitamin C for the following:

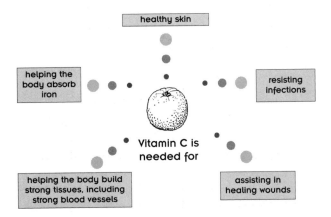

healthy skin

helping the body absorb iron

resisting infections

Vitamin C is needed for

helping the body build strong tissues, including strong blood vessels

assisting in healing wounds

Food sources of vitamin C

Vitamin C is found in many fruits and vegetables, such as:

- citrus fruits, e.g. oranges, lemons and limes
- green vegetables
- red peppers
- tomatoes
- blackcurrants and soft fruits
- potatoes.

The sources of vitamin D include:

- sunlight
- fish oils
- eggs
- margarine (added to)
- formula baby milk powder.

Minerals

Minerals are elements found naturally in the earth and in food.

They are needed by the body to enable it to work properly, and like vitamins you only need small amounts. In this unit we will be looking at the minerals calcium and iron.

Calcium

Calcium is one of the most important minerals needed by the body. It is needed to help form bones and teeth. It also helps muscles work. It is also used to help blood clot and to help in processes within cells. We therefore need calcium in our diet.

Food sources of calcium

Calcium comes from dairy products like milk, cheese, eggs, yoghurt. It also comes (not surprisingly) from fish where the bones are eaten, e.g. sardines and tinned salmon.

Vegetable sources of calcium include green leafy vegetables such as broccoli.

Iron

Iron is also essential for our bodies to function properly. Its main function is to help red blood cells to carry oxygen to all parts of the body. Oxygen is essential to life and gives the body's cells the energy they need to work.

Food sources of iron

Iron is found in a wide range of foods, some of which come from meat and fish, others from vegetables.

> **? Did you know?**
>
> Broccoli is a real wonder vegetable. It contains vitamin C, vitamin A, iron and calcium, has a good fibre content and is thought to protect against cancer. It is also available all the year round in greengrocers and supermarkets.

Water

About two-thirds of our bodies are made up of water, and we lose about 2 litres a day through sweat, breathing, speaking and passing urine.

We need to replace this daily. So we should have about eight glasses of liquid a day, some of which should be pure water. Water helps flush out the toxins in our system, and keeps skin fresh and clear.

5.3 Different diets for different needs

Not everyone eats the same type of food. You know from what we have discussed so far that different people have different needs at various times in their lives and according to custom, preference and tradition.

Vegetarian diets

A vegetarian diet is one in which no meat or fish is eaten. Most vegetarians drink milk and eat milk products and eggs.

Care with a vegetarian diet

Vegetarians should make sure they get the right amount of nutrients in their diet. This includes protein, calcium and iron.

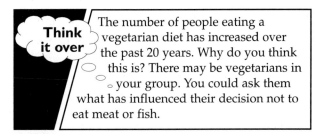

Think it over

The number of people eating a vegetarian diet has increased over the past 20 years. Why do you think this is? There may be vegetarians in your group. You could ask them what has influenced their decision not to eat meat or fish.

Protein

Sources may include beans, peas, nuts and seeds. Milk products are also a good source, as are cereals and potatoes. Eating a variety of protein sources should ensure that all essential amino-acids are taken in.

Calcium

Milk products are the best sources of calcium, but there is also calcium in green leafy vegetables such as watercress and cabbage.

Iron

For vegetarians, iron sources must come from vegetables such as spinach, peas and beans. Bread and fortified cereal, e.g. cornflakes, also contain iron.

Look it up

Marilyn and Olinda are 13 and have lots of friends who are Hindu and vegetarian. They love going to their friends' houses to eat curries and rice. They are thinking of becoming vegetarian together, but Marilyn's aunt told her that 'growing girls' should eat lots of meat for iron, otherwise they'll be too tired to do their work and play sport. This seems strange: Olinda is the brainiest girl in the class and really good at hockey.

To reassure Marilyn's aunt, look up the non-vegetable food sources of iron and plan a menu for a day which would ensure that Marilyn had plenty in her diet. Remember to refer also to the facts above about vitamin C, tea and coffee and iron absorption. Keep the menu plan in your portfolio notes.

Cultural differences

Britain is a multicultural society and as a nation we are fortunate to have such a wide range and diversity of foods available.

The table below shows the dietary requirements from different religious and ethnic groups.

You need to be aware of these restrictions if you are preparing food for people of different religious backgrounds.

Hindus	No beef	Mostly vegetarian; fish rarely eaten; no alcohol	Period of fasting common
Muslim	No pork	Meat must be 'Halal'; no shellfish eaten; no alcohol	Regular fasting, including Ramadan for one month
Sikhs	No beef	Meat must be killed by 'one blow to the head'; no alcohol	Generally less rigid eating restrictions than Hindus and Muslims
Jews	No pork	Meat must be kosher; only fish with scales and fins eaten	Meat and dairy foods must not be consumed together
Rastafarians	No animal products except milk may be consumed	Foods must be 'I-tal' or alive, so no canned or processed foods eaten; no salt added; no coffee or alcohol	Food should be organic

Differences in diet among certain religious and ethnic groups

Special diets for weight loss or weight gain

Most of us know someone who is going 'on a diet'. Dieting to lose weight should be done carefully, sometimes under medical supervision. It can be dangerous if it is too rapid, or if it deprives the body of essential nutrients.

Talk it over

In small groups or pairs discuss:

- Why do some people want to go on a diet?
- Why do some people need to go on a diet?
- Are these always the same thing?
- What might be the health benefits of losing weight?
- What might be some health concerns of losing too much weight?

Dietary needs of children

Children keep growing. Therefore a child's diet needs to have plenty of protein (for growth), carbohydrate (for energy), vitamins and minerals (for good health and growth).

The following tells you how much of each nutrient and food group a child should have every day. Go through it and then look at Josie Bentham's diet (page 169). Is her diet adequate for an active three-year-old?

Protein	Two servings, either meat or fish or complementary protein if vegetarian
Milk sources	Two servings, whole milk. Can be yoghurt, cheese sauce, milk pudding, cheese
Fruit and vegetables	At least four servings

Do's and Don'ts of losing weight

Do

- aim to cut down on fatty or sugary foods

- cut down gradually on the amount of food you eat

- drink a large glass of water half an hour or so before eating – you will probably eat less

- include lots of fruit and vegetables in your diet – use fruit or raw vegetables as snack food

- substitute low fat yoghurts and cheeses for full fat ones – these can also be good snack foods

- tell your family and friends you are hoping to lose weight, so they will help you and not insist that you eat lots of butter, cream, gravy and ice cream when you don't want it

- allow yourself an occasional treat – but keep an eye on how occasional it is

- seek advice from your doctor or practice nurse or from a well organised weight-loss programme – however some of these can be expensive, so check this before you start

- increase your physical daily exercise and you will not only feel better but your body will respond by losing weight more easily.

Don't

- skip breakfast – you need it for energy and overall body functioning. Having breakfast, even a slice of wholemeal toast or bowl of cereal with a piece of fruit, can put you in a good mood for the day. It's worth it!

- hope or expect large weight loss all at once – gradual weight loss will put you in better eating habits anyway and will be more permanent

- cut out carbohydrates – they are not fattening in themselves.

CASE STUDY — The desire to put on weight

Tejal is 16, weights 45 kilos (7 stone) and is 165cm (5ft 5in) tall. She feels she is too thin, and can't understand all her friends who are constantly going on diets. She wants to gain weight. She wrote a letter to a teenage magazine, to the Maxine column, and was really pleased when she saw her letter published. It made her problem seem less difficult to solve now that she was public about it (although she didn't use her real name, just initials).

This is what she wrote

Dear Maxine

I am 16 and I have a funny problem. I think I am too thin. I am 165 cm (5ft 5in) and weigh 45 kilos (7 stone).

I also fancy this boy, whose friend called me stick insect the other day – so there's probably no hope. But I would like to put on a bit of weight. I don't want to be fat or anything, just a bit rounder. All my family are slim, in fact none of us is any more than a size 10, and that's being optimistic. Do you think I can gain weight?

My friends can't understand me at all. They spend their life going on diets and seem to be irritated when they think I want to gain weight!! I can eat what I like, and still I stay the same weight. I do lots of sport, I'm training at the moment for the school's cross country race. I love sport, so I don't want to give that up. And anyway, the boy I fancy is into athletics too.

Please help me, and please don't tell me how lucky I am.

TS, Oxford
(Name and address supplied)

Dear TS

Firstly, I don't think you have a funny problem. Quite a few young people are like you. You simply have an 'ectomorph shape', that is, you are naturally slim.

You can do several things to give yourself more shape, if not lots more weight.

You could use weights in a gym (with the advice of a professional trainer) to give yourself more shape, particularly upper body strength, as you probably have good lower body shape with all your running.

You will need to increase the amount of calories you take in, but don't stop exercising. Exercise is important for your overall health.

Eat regular meals, and try to eat everything, not just bits of this and that. Perhaps slow down a bit when you are eating, which will help.

If you do snack between meals, make sure that they are good for you, like wholemeal bread and something nutritious like peanut butter or bananas. You can also eat full-fat yoghurts. But don't snack too soon before meals. It is important that you eat properly.

Don't be tempted to eat lots of fatty or sweet foods because they have lots of calories. They will probably make you feel unwell, will ruin your appetite for proper food and will not do you any good in terms of vitamins and minerals.

You are a **bit** lucky, but I do appreciate your problem.

I hope this has been helpful.

Regards

Maxine

Maxine

Questions

1 Why do you think Tejal hesitated to write her letter and didn't want her name to be published?

2 Plan a day's menu for Tejal which includes Maxine's advice.

Drinks   At least a litre a day –
600 mls should be
whole milk

Within these guidelines children should be
offered a variety of food. This helps maintain
their interest and enjoyment in eating and
encourages them to try new tastes.

Snack food

Snacks should be taken two or three times a
day to maintain energy levels. Healthy snacks
should be encouraged, but less nutritious
snacks, such as chocolate and crisps and
canned drinks, may be allowed occasionally.

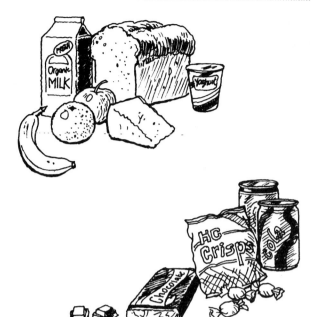

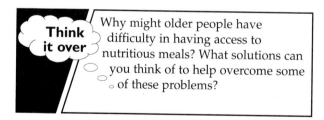
Make sure you eat the right snacks

important, as are fruit and vegetables and
fibre in the diet. Older people may naturally
eat less, which should not be a cause for
concern unless they are not taking in a
balanced diet. Vitamin D deficiency is
sometimes a cause for concern, and older
people should be encouraged to have exposure
to the sun for short periods, particularly in
the summer months. Oily fish is, however, a
good source of vitamin D.

<table>
<tr><td>
Try it out</td><td>Josie is three and very energetic! This
birthday, her family have decided to
give her a 'real' party. Her sister,
Marilyn, and her friend Olinda are
going to help. They think that 10
children altogether will be enough
for them to manage, but they are
looking forward to organising the
food and party games.

*In groups of three or four, think of some
varied and interesting ways of serving
healthy food for a children's party for
three-year-olds.*

*Keep a note of your ideas for this, as you
may want to use some of them for your
assessment.*

**WARNING: If you are going to
serve peanut butter in sandwiches,
make sure that none of the children
have a nut allergy. Also make sure
that you keep an eye on the
children if you are serving raw fruit
and vegetables, as they may
sometimes choke on these foods.**</td></tr>
</table>

Think it over Why might older people have
difficulty in having access to
nutritious meals? What solutions can
you think of to help overcome some
of these problems?

Pregnancy and lactation

While a woman is pregnant and
breastfeeding she needs to be able to supply
both herself and the baby with the required
nutrients. This does not mean 'eating for
two', but eating a normal balanced diet, with
protein, energy-giving carbohydrates, and

Dietary needs of elderly people

Older people have the same nutritional needs
as younger adults. However, they may be less
physically active and may need to cut down
on fatty or sugary foods which could lead to
weight gain. Calcium intake is particularly

vitamins and minerals from bread, cereals and plenty of fruit and vegetables. It is important that the diet includes food that contains vitamin C and D, calcium and iron. Extra folic acid is also needed to ensure the baby develops healthily, and this is usually given in tablet form. Vitamin supplements should only be taken under medical supervision, as too much vitamin A can cause birth defects. For this reason, foods rich in vitamin A, such as liver, should only be eaten very sparingly. Alcohol should be avoided, if possible.

No extra calories are needed for the first six months of pregnancy, and only 200 a day are needed for the last three months. That is the same as a jacket potato with 28 grams of cheese, or a slice of cheese on toast!

Food safety and pregnancy

There are some bacteria present in the following foods which might be harmful to a pregnant mother.

She should avoid:

- soft white cheese
- raw or soft boiled eggs
- raw or 'rare' meat

and make sure that all meat is very well cooked and that food is prepared hygienically (see further on pages 163–165).

5.4 Planning meals

You now have the basic information you need to be able to plan healthy meals for many different client groups, including yourself. Planning meals, however, has to take other factors into account as well as the content, although naturally that is a very important part of planning.

You might have thought about:

- **budget**, that is how much money you had to spend
- what was **available** for you to buy
- whether it was too much like the last meal you had (spaghetti bolognaise every night?)
- whether you were going to make the meal interesting or not
- who you were cooking for, how much time you had.

Budget

Most of us have to live within a budget, that is, we have a certain amount of money to spend on food, clothes, travelling to school, college or work, holidays, and so on. Dividing up the money we have to spend on certain items is called budgeting.

Budgeting to eat

How much you have to spend on food is an individual matter and one which each of us either decides for ourselves or decides within the family budget. The cost of food is something that is, on the whole, decided by those who grow and sell the food we eat. These are the factors we take into account when we are shopping.

> **Think it over**
> When did you last plan and cook a meal, or have some say in what you ate? What did you think about before you cooked or prepared it?

> **Try it out**
> In pairs do a costing on preparing a meal of spaghetti bolognese for you and a friend, using either meat or vegetables.
>
> How would you go about working out the cost?
>
> To help you two simple recipes are given below with a column for itemising the cost of each ingredient.

Some general budgeting hints

When you work out a menu, list the ingredients to ensure you will be able to afford them. You can then see when you have to substitute or leave something out. For example, the mushrooms and peppers are not absolutely necessary for this recipe.

Recipes and costs	
Spaghetti bolognese for 2	
Ingredient	**Cost**
200g dried spaghetti	
2 onions	
2 tablespoons oil	
200g minced beef	
I can tinned tomatoes	
pepper and salt, ½beef stock cube	
100g mushrooms	
½red pepper (optional)	
seasoning	
½beef stock cube	
Total Cost	
Vegetarian alternative	
Substitute for meat:	
I can of kidney or mixed beans	
100g grated cheese on the top of the sauce	
Wholemeal spaghetti	
Total Cost	

Shopping for food

Prices of some foods vary according to the time of the year. When foods are in season they are less expensive. However, many people now have access to a freezer, and so

A meal of spaghetti bolognese

much food is imported that most food we need is available throughout the year.

Shopping is an important part of meal planning. How and where you shop will influence the types of products that are available and the prices you pay for them. For example, some shops regard themselves as 'luxury' food shops and so have more fancy packaging and are more expensive. In others, the food is much cheaper, but they may not be so easy to get to.

Seasonal shopping

This means buying fresh fruit and vegetables when they are in season. Fruit and vegetables have more nutritional value if they do not have to be stored too long or have to be transported too great a distance. Buying fruit and vegetables in season may also be good

Try it out — Below is a list of fruit and vegetables which grow in the UK. See if you can write down which month they are 'in season'.

parsnips	spinach
strawberries	rhubarb
apples	carrots
Brussel sprouts	pears

economic sense for your local area as you may be supporting producers who live close to you. If they sell their produce locally they do not have to pay so much in transport costs so the food may be less expensive.

Seasonal foods may also mean foods that are eaten during a particular religious festival, for example at Christmas (e.g. turkey), or at the end of Ramadan.

5.5 Preparing meals

Here you will be introduced to essential kitchen hygiene rules and some commonsense skills for food preparation to make sure your practice in the kitchen is safe.

Before you start

Always make sure that you are familiar with the kitchen equipment you are going to use. This includes the cooker. For example, if you are using gas and you have not used this before, take instructions before you start and don't use it until you are happy that you can do so safely.

Similarly, make sure you are familiar with the unit of temperature: are you using the Fahrenheit or the Celsius temperature range?

Look it up

Find out how Celsius and Fahrenheit relate to each other and make notes of this to keep in your portfolio for later in the unit when you come to do some cooking.

Use of kitchen equipment

1 Safe use of knives

- Knives should be stored safely out of the way of children.

- They should always be washed carefully in hot soapy water and dried thoroughly to prevent rusting or contaminants remaining on the surface.

- They should also be kept sharp so that they can do the work they are designed for.

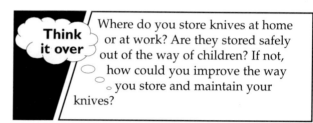

Think it over

Where do you store knives at home or at work? Are they stored safely out of the way of children? If not, how could you improve the way you store and maintain your knives?

2 Using blenders and mixers safely

There are many different kinds of mixing equipment available now, but the following guidelines will help to ensure you are using them safely.

- Ensure the plug is correctly fitted.

- Ensure the equipment has a British Standard kitemark.

- Read the manufacturer's instructions before using.

- Only use the equipment for the purpose for which it was intended – do not overload or overfill it.

- Make sure equipment with blades is stored away out of reach of children – the blades can be very sharp.

- Ensure all movable parts are carefully washed in hot soapy water, air dried if possible and replaced correctly. Careful washing and drying will mean less risk of cross-contamination taking place if the equipment is used for a range of different purposes with raw and cooked ingredients.

Choosing a cooking method

Boiling

Boiling is a way of cooking in water or stock, where just enough liquid covers the food and the liquid is kept at a temperature to maintain the boiling process.

Boiling is necessary for foods such as rice, pasta and potatoes, because it softens the starches in the food and makes them easier to digest. It has advantages and disadvantages as a method of cooking.

Advantages

- It is safe – if foods are boiled for more than one minute then any germs (bacteria) are killed.

- It does not destroy the flavour of the food because nothing is added (like fat).

- It can preserve nutrients, for example in lightly-boiled vegetables.

Disadvantages

- Boiled food can taste bland and boring.

- If food is overboiled (especially vegetables) it can become flabby and unappetising.

Simmering

This is also a cooking method using liquid, where bubbles rise up the side of the pan but the water is not actually at a rolling boil. Food can be cooked more slowly this way. Simmering is useful for stews and casseroles, hard boiling eggs and making soups. It also ensures that food does not break up while cooking.

? Did you know?

Kidney beans contain a toxin which can only be destroyed after boiling for at least 15 minutes. Uncooked kidney beans are poisonous.

Frying, grilling, barbecuing, baking

Frying is a method of cooking where fat or oil is used. It is quick and gives good flavour to the food. However, because so much fat or oil is used in frying it is advisable to cut down on fats and try to find other ways of cooking the same food.

Grilling, barbecuing or baking in foil do not require very much additional fat – often the fat in the food is sufficient, as in the case of bacon, sausages, chops or minced meat.

Frying can be hazardous

Household fires are commonly caused by chip pans overheating. This can occur when the fat is too hot, or if water or moist food is added to very hot fat or oil.

To avoid this type of accident, follow these sensible rules:

- Never leave a frying pan unattended while cooking is in progress.

- Lower the food to be cooked gently into the pan and do not cook too much at a time.

Frying, grilling, barbecuing and baking

- If a fire occurs, don't try to put it out with water, but throw a damp cloth over the top, and turn off the heat source. Don't try to move the pan until it has completely cooled down.

- Make sure frying pan handles do not extend over the edge of the cooker top where they can be accidently knocked or pulled down by a child (this applies to all cooking utensils).

- If the phone or doorbell rings, turn off the heat before answering.

Look it up

In a recipe book, find two recipes each for the methods used above (boiling, simmering and frying etc.). Why do you think these particular methods are used for these recipes?

Mixing ingredients and following recipes

Most recipes are written logically so that the ingredients are listed in the order in which they are to be used, and that the instructions for use mix the ingredients in the correct order for cooking. Below is a simple recipe, which will illustrate these points.

Read through the recipes and note:

Anzac Biscuits (an Australian favourite)

Preheat the oven to a slow cooking temperature: 150°C or 300°F

Ingredients

1 cup porridge oats	125 g (4 oz) butter or margarine
(rolled oats not instant oats)	1 tablespoon golden syrup or honey
¾ cup dessicated coconut	1 cup plain flour
1½ teaspoons of bicarbonate of soda	1 cup sugar
2 tablespoons boiling water	

Method

1   In one bowl, combine the dry ingredients: oats, sifted flour, sugar and coconut. Mix well.

2   In a saucepan, combine the golden syrup or honey and butter or margarine, and stir over a gentle heat until they are melted together.

3   Then mix the soda with the boiling water in a cup until dissolved and frothing and add to the syrup mixture.

4   Add the syrup mixture to the dry ingredients and mix together well.

5   Put dessertspoons of mixture onto a greased oven tray, leaving space for the biscuits to spread when they are cooking.

6   Put in the preheated oven and cook for 20 minutes. When cooked, put on a rack to cool while the next batch is cooking.

This recipe makes about 36 biscuits.

Discuss as a group:

- How does a packaged food instruction differ from the recipe given above?

- Are there any advantages of packaged foods over freshly prepared foods? When might packaged foods be useful?

- What might be the disadvantages of packaged food?

- How the ingredients are listed

- The method for cooking

- The weights and measures used

- The oven temperatures.

You could try this recipe if you like!

Following instructions on food packaging

Prepared foods must contain instructions which enable safe preparation of the food if the instructions are carefully followed.

These instructions will include how to prepare the food, the sort of container to use, the temperature to cook the food at and how long to cook it for.

Good hygiene in food preparation

It is very important that the food you prepare is safe to eat. There are some essential principles of good kitchen hygiene which you must follow when you are preparing meals. If you follow these principles you will protect those you are preparing food for from food poisoning, or other illnesses caused by contaminated food.

Bacterial food poisoning

Food poisoning occurs when you eat food that has been contaminated by harmful bacteria.

Not all bacteria are harmful. We have many useful bacteria living on our skin and in our bodies to help protect us and help our bodies function. However, some bacteria are extremely dangerous and can cause food poisoning. Examples are:

- Salmonella

- Staphylococcus aureas

- Clostridium perfrigens.

Sources of bacteria

Harmful bacteria come from five main sources. These are all common sources and ones which we all have contact with or are familiar with. They are:

- raw foods, especially raw meat (including poultry), shellfish, eggs and vegetables

- pets, and pests such as cockroaches, ants, rats and mice

- people

- air and dust

- rubbish, including food waste, and dirt.

By preventing the movement of bacteria from these sources we can prevent food poisoning.

Preventing cross-contamination

Cross-contamination means a harmful pathogen (e.g. bacteria, virus, fungi, yeast) being transferred from raw to cooked food. This could occur if you:

- use the same knife or equipment without washing it between preparing raw food and cooked food

- do not wash your hands between handling raw and cooked foods

- use the same preparation or storing surface for raw and cooked foods without cleaning thoroughly in between

- allow juices from raw meat to drip onto cooked meat.

Try it out

In pairs, rewrite the list of Don't's above into a list of Do's. Check your list with the rest of the group, and make a display chart. You can illustrate it if you want to make it more interesting.

! Remember!

5°C is the correct temperature for refrigerators.

? Did you know?

Bacteria can reproduce very quickly. The bacteria which cause food poisoning only need between 10 and 20 minutes to reproduce. They do this by simply dividing in two. Within a few hours one bacterium can become a few million!

The kitchen environment

A clean and uncluttered kitchen environment is a first step to ensuring that the food you prepare is safe to eat.

You should:

- make sure that all equipment, including knives, are washed and cleaned thoroughly before use

- check that the work surfaces and equipment you are using are not chipped or cracked and damaged in any way

- cover foods while awaiting preparation

- clean work surfaces with very hot soapy water

- clean floors with hot water using floor cleaner – if you use cleaning cloths, make sure they are only used for this purpose

- thoroughly dry mops and cloths outside if possible

- keep gloves for separate purposes – one pair for floors and another for dishes and surfaces.

! Remember!

Keep rubbish covered and emptied regularly.

Personal hygiene

Hands

- Handle food as little as possible.

- Always wash your hands in hot soapy water after going to the lavatory, or before starting to prepare food. Pay particular attention to fingernails, and wash your hands under running water.

- Dry with disposable paper towels, and dispose of these in a covered bin.

- Keep fingernails short, clean and unvarnished.

- Do not wear jewellery when preparing food.

- If you have a cut, cover completely with a blue or coloured plaster.

Hair

- Tie back so it does not dangle into food.

- Some establishments may want you to cover your hair with a hat.

Clothing

Wear clean clothing, with protection if possible.

Hazards and poor practice in the kitchen

Prevention of direct contamination if you are ill or unwell

- If you have diarrhoea or have been vomiting, you should keep well away from food preparation areas. You should not return to work until you are free from these symptoms.

- Cover mouth if sneezing or coughing, preferably with a disposable paper tissue. Then wash your hands before handling food again.

- Do not touch nose or mouth or any spots or sores while preparing food.

The illustration above shows ten different examples of poor kitchen practice. Can you spot them?

Try it out

In pairs arrange to visit an industrial or institutional kitchen and note what kitchen hygiene rules are displayed and what those working in the kitchen are wearing. You may be able to visit the kitchens in your own college or school. What other rules are followed in this kitchen?

---

10 tips for food safety – guidelines from the Ministry of Agriculture Food and Fisheries, MAFF

1 Take chilled and frozen food home quickly – then put it in your fridge or freezer at once.

2 Prepare and store raw and cooked food separately. Keep raw meat and fish at the bottom of the fridge.

3 Keep the coldest part of your fridge at 0–5°C. Get a fridge thermometer.

4 Check 'use by' dates. Use food within the recommended period.

5 Keep pets away from food – and dishes and worktops.

6 Wash hands thoroughly before preparing food, after going to the toilet or handling pets.

7 Keep your kitchen clean. Wash worktops and utensils between handling food which is to be cooked and food which is not.

8 Do not eat food containing uncooked eggs. Keep eggs in the fridge.

9 Cook food well. Follow instructions on the pack. If you re-heat make sure it is piping hot.

10 Keep hot foods hot and cold foods cold. Don't just leave them standing around.

If you follow these simple rules and use the knowledge you have gained from this unit you will not be a danger to yourself or others in the kitchen.

5.6 Presenting meals

One important part of planning any diet, or even one meal, is to think about what it is that makes the food appetising. That is, whether you want to eat the food or not!

What makes food appetising to you? What might 'put you off' eating a meal or some part of a meal?

Four important factors are:

- taste
- texture
- appearance
- portion size.

We use our senses when we eat, although this might not seem obvious! All five senses – *taste, touch, sight, smell* and *sound* – are used to decide whether we want to eat or not.

Taste

We do not usually eat food that we do not like the taste of. Taste is something that develops early, and is as much a matter of what we are used to than that some foods do not 'taste nice' and others do. Taste of food is often determined by food traditions. Some people dislike porridge with sugar and cream and you may detest vegetables cooked in rancid yak butter. Some people love spicy food, others do not.

Taste is often enhanced by use of condiments: pepper, salt, mustard, tomato ketchup, chili pickles, etc. The use of these is again determined by what we are used to.

Taste is connected to smell. If you have a bad cold, you probably won't taste anything, and you probably won't smell much of it either.

Texture

This is the sense that relates to touch. The touch is mainly in your mouth.

Babies, for example, cannot eat lumpy food because they cannot chew it. Likewise older people might avoid tough food, like crusty bread, because it is too difficult to chew.

Most of us probably do not like soggy chips or lumpy cheese sauce or very dry food, or perhaps very soft or 'sloppy' food. We also expect certain foods to have a certain texture: crisp apples or celery, crunchy crisps, meat that is easy to chew.

Appearance

We use sight to help us decide whether to eat the food or not. We are more likely to eat the

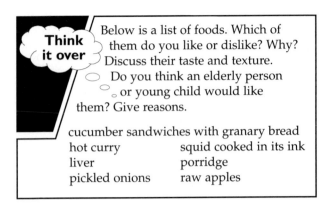

Think it over

Below is a list of foods. Which of them do you like or dislike? Why? Discuss their taste and texture. Do you think an elderly person or young child would like them? Give reasons.

cucumber sandwiches with granary bread
hot curry   squid cooked in its ink
liver   porridge
pickled onions   raw apples

food if it looks appetising or as we would expect it to look. A white plate of completely white food may look very unappetising. Presentation of meals, using different coloured vegetables or fruits or garnishes to enliven a pale plate, can make all the difference. You can even use different coloured dishes to help make the meal look attractive.

The way that food is placed on a plate is also important. Food can be arranged in an interesting way to make it look good to eat.

Appearance, like taste and texture, also depends on what we expect food to look like. We expect carrots to be long and orange in colour or bread to be brown, grainy or white. If food does not look 'right' we may not wish to eat it.

? Did you know?

When organic farmers started to sell their produce in supermarkets, people did not like the 'dirt' on the carrots. They did not look like proper carrots! Now customers accept the less than perfect looking vegetables because they want to buy the organic produce, no matter what they look like.

Portion size

The amount of food on the plate can also have an effect on whether you want to eat it or not. Too much can be as off-putting as too little, especially if you do not have a very big appetite.

Groups with special nutritional needs

The diagrams give an outline of how different factors might affect the appetite of three particular client groups.

Portion size
- Ask the client how much!
- Do not overload the plate
- Fill cups or glasses

Taste
- May lose some sense of taste and smell
- May prefer traditional foods rather than introduce 'new' foods
- Ensure condiments are available to enhance taste
- Teeth and gums may be a problem, so ensure food is of the right consistency for chewing and swallowing
- Crunchy food may not be appropriate

Appearance
- Ensure food looks attractive on the plate
- Provide the best utensils for eating with, with favourite or special cutlery or plates if required

Older people

Older people may be less active, which means that they need less energy from food, and may have smaller appetites. This does not mean that their nutritional requirements are any less. It may mean that particular care should be taken to make the food tasty and appealing.

Children

Children develop eating habits from very early on. It is important to introduce them at an early age – as young as a few months – to different tastes and smells and textures. They may not be fussy eaters later.

Children's appetites do vary from day to day. One day a child might be very hungry all day, the next he or she might not feel like eating at all. It can depend on lots of different things in a child's life – the amount of exercise, a cold coming on, teething, feeling excited about an event like a birthday party or a new friend coming to play, or something happening at school. Some eight-year-olds can sometimes eat as much as an adult!

You need to have patience. Scolding a child who does not eat can make mealtimes an unhappy time, when they should be fun.

Portion size
- Try smaller portions of new foods first, allowing room for 'seconds'
- Do not overload the plate, or overfill the glass or cup
- A portion may be an apple, a carrot, a slice of bread, a rasher of bacon
- Let the child help themselves so that they get an idea of how much is 'enough'

Taste and texture
- Provide a variety of different tastes and texture for children, which will help them have a wider range of eating habits in later life
- Don't give extra salt or sugar
- Let children experiment with food by helping in the kitchen, or with shopping
- Let smaller children have finger food as well as using spoons and forks. They may make a mess, but they will also be enjoying new tastes, textures and temperatures

Appearance
- Colour and shape can make all the difference, so try a variety of shapes in toast, pizza jigsaws, celery 'boats' and 'gardens' made out of green and coloured salad.
- Try healthy snack food and allow the child to help prepare portions of raisins, fruit, toast and smooth peanut butter which look fun and are healthier than crisps and chocolate

The client who is ill or recovering from illness

A client who is ill or recovering from illness will need access to nutritious food that allows him or her to make a good recovery. Protein, possibly fish or white meat rather than red meat, vitamins and minerals from fruit and vegetables, and some carbohydrates should be included. The old phrase 'a light diet' is a good way of describing this.

Choice should be provided if possible. If the client is in hospital, he or she might have a special diet provided by a dietician. It is important to follow the guidelines set out as the diet has been chosen to help the patient's own particular needs.

Think it over

Think about how hungry you felt when you last had an illness of any sort. If it was just a cold, it was probably difficult for anyone to persuade you to eat or drink.

It is important for you to be aware of the factors which might encourage someone who is ill or recovering from illness to start eating healthy food.

Portion size

- Allow the client to select how much he or she eats. Eating a little is better than eating nothing at all. If the client is not very hungry, being presented with an overloaded plate could probably take the appetite away altogether

Taste and texture

- Some illnesses and medications change normal taste, so the client may want additional seasoning to compensate for these changes, or may not like the taste of food he or she normally likes

- The client may prefer bland and easily digestible food rather than spicy food

- Give lots of choice, if you are able to, especially within the main food groups. Choice will encourage intake

- Constipation may be a problem if the client is not very mobile. Ensure there is fibre in the diet, but make it appetising!

- If food is to be served hot, make sure it is hot. Tepid food is not only unappetising, it can also become easily contaminated

Appearance

- Carefully and attractively presented food is an encouragement to eat

- Carefully presented food also indicates that you have thought about the client and his or her needs

- Provide garnishes, colour and cheerful china and serviettes to enhance the appearance of the food

- Take away uneaten food as soon as possible

Unit 5 Assessment

You will be externally assessed (tested) for this unit.

You will have the opportunity to work towards a pass, merit or distinction grade.

The activities based on the scenario below are ordered in such a way as to guide you through this assessment. The levels of assessment are clearly indicated as:

- P for Pass

- M for Merit

- D for Distinction

You may wish to discuss with your tutor the level of the activities you do. All students must complete the first three P activities to achieve the minimum for Unit 5.

SCENARIO

The Bentham family

Josie

Josie Bentham is three, healthy and active. She loves running and jumping games and especially playing with her brother Sam's football. Josie's favourite food at the moment is fish fingers and mashed banana and yoghurt.

Sam

Sam is eight, and he is very active too. Sam says he is hungry all the time, and doesn't care what he eats. He does like chips and peas though – he'd have them with everything. They have a sister called Marilyn who is 13.

Marilyn

Marilyn is quite careful about what she eats. Sometimes she thinks she needs to go on a diet, but they are always being told at school it's not good for you to diet! She gets a bit confused about what she hears about what is good for you and what is not. She and Sam sometimes cook at home, and they both enjoy that. Her favourite foods are spaghetti bolognese, cauliflower cheese and chocolate ice cream (not together).

Mrs Bentham

Mrs Bentham works in a nursery, and has to plan the menus for the children every day. She tries to prepare food that everyone will like. The nursery has children from lots of different countries. She finds that interesting and uses suggestions from the parents about what to put on the menu.

Mr Bentham

Mr Bentham has a problem. He works in an office, and is finding that he is not getting as much exercise as he would like. The other day he had to go to his doctor who suggested that he was overweight and not only needed to lose weight but should take more exercise. Sam and Marilyn think that he should take up football!

Olinda

Marilyn's best friend is Olinda, whose family come from Jamaica. Olinda's grandmother lives with them, and does most of their cooking. She is a wonderful cook but says she is not getting any younger. She certainly doesn't eat very large meals, although they are delicious.

Gran and Pop

Mr Bentham's parents, Gran and Pop, live quite close. They have just started to have meals on wheels, which comes to their house four times a week. Gran says it saves her having to cook so much, and the food always seems nice and healthy, and just the kind of things they like.

Working towards a pass grade

Activity 1P

Make a list of the components of a healthy balanced diet. You may illustrate this if you like to make it interesting to look at and learn from.

Activity 2P

For this activity, you are going to create a plan for a day's diet, within a given budget, for a chosen individual.

- Think of a person from within the client groups you have been studying. It may be someone you know, even yourself, or you may wish to use a member of the Bentham family.

  Describe in about 50 words the client you are going to plan a day's diet for and what his or her particular dietary needs are.

- Now decide the budget. By this time you should have some knowledge of how much various food items cost. Discuss this with your tutor. You will have to be realistic in your budget, and show that you can work within it.

You are going to create the plan. You can do this in a grid.

Time of day	Meal	Ingredients	Cost

You will need to ensure that the overall food to be included makes up a balanced day's food for the individual, including nutritional content and energy requirements. This activity will need quite a lot of thought and preparation.

Activity 3P

Identify a range of factors which might affect an individual having access to a balanced diet. You can do this in a spidergram if you like, or as a chart. You can make this apply to any individual, not someone in particular.

Activity 4P

Having a varied and interesting diet is important, otherwise you become bored with what you eat. Answer the following questions which relate to variations in a normal diet.

Can you give:

1 three autumn and winter fruits and three summer fruits that you can buy in season

2 two ways of cooking meat without frying

3 a healthy substitute for cake as a snack for children

4 a substitute for chocolate or crisps as a healthy snack for you

5 dairy produce which is not full fat for an adolescent

6 details of a high protein lunch for an elderly inactive woman

7 one way of serving fresh vegetables without destroying the vitamins

8 a way of providing a non-meat iron-rich supper for a pregnant mother

9 one vegetarian and one animal alternative to red meat?

Imagine you are entering a slogan competition for a large supermarket chain. Complete the following slogan in 10 words.

Eating a varied healthy diet is good for me

because ....

....

....

....

Activity 5P

You are now going to describe how to prepare one of the meals for your chosen individual. Ideally it should be a cooked meal.

If possible, you should try to prepare the meal at your school or college. You could use the meal you planned in activity 2P.

Describe:

- any safety features in planning the menu
- any food hygiene and food safety features you will need to consider when preparing the menu
- any food hygiene or food safety features you will have to consider when serving the menu
- how you would ensure everything is cleared away safely
- what arrangements you might make for storing leftovers safely and hygienically.

Working towards a merit grade

To achieve a merit grade you must complete all the activities in the pass section. In addition you must complete the steps for Activities 3, 5 and 6 below.

Activity 3M

Having identified some factors which might affect an individual's achieving a balanced diet, now describe why these factors are important to the individual. For example, if you said economic factors were important, you now need to describe how this might affect an individual's ability to buy the food he or she requires.

Activity 5M

In Activity 5P you planned, prepared and served a meal for an individual client. Can you now describe how you would make sure the food you prepared was attractive and palatable to him or her? If you have prepared the food, you

could include photographs as part of the evidence for this activity, or illustrate it in some other way.

Activity 6M

Write a short case study of someone who does not have a balanced diet, explaining what he or she eats in a day and why this diet is unbalanced. You can refer to Dan on p. 150 if you do not wish to write your own study, and put this into your own words. Explain what possible effects this unbalanced diet could have on the health of this individual.

Working towards a distinction grade

To achieve a distinction you will have to complete the activities for the pass and merit grades and carry out the steps for Activities 2, 6 and 7 below.

Activity 2D

You have created a budgeted, balanced diet for an individual in the pass section (Activity 2P).

Looking at the day's diet you have planned, can you now say why this is a balanced diet by justifying the food choices you have made.

Activity 6D

In Activity M6 you wrote about the effects of an unbalanced diet on the health of an individual.

Make suggestions about how this individual could improve his or her diet.

Activity 7D

Britain is a multicultural nation. Within any given care setting (e.g. a nursery, hospital, residential home) there may be a need to cater for many different dietary requirements. Choose one care setting and describe how, within a day's dietary provision, you would ensure that the needs of the following cultural and ethnic groups were met. Give a brief description of the care setting as an introduction to this activity.

- Jewish groups
- Muslim
- White Christian
- Hindu
- One other of your choice.

Check your knowledge

Questions 1–10 require short answers.

Questions 11–20 are multiple choice questions. There is only one correct answer.

Short answer questions

1 When thinking abut preparing a meal, which of the food groups should be the largest on your plate?

2 Which food group should you eat more sparingly and why?

3 List four ways to reduce fat in your diet.

4 List four sources of carbohydrate which could give you additional nutrients. Use the table below to set out the answer.

Carbohydrate source	Additional nutrient

5 Summary questions on nutrients.
Tick the boxes below to say whether the following are **true** or **false**.

		True	False
a	Sugar contains many vitamins and minerals.		
b	Vitamin D is found in sunlight.		
c	Foods rich in protein include plant as well as animal food.		
d	Carbohydrates are needed for growth and repair.		
e	Fat is needed to store some vitamins.		
f	Spinach is a good source of iron.		
g	Calcium contains vitamin C.		
h	Baked beans on toast is an example of complementary protein.		
i	Carbohydrates are fattening.		
j	Children need milk products for healthy teeth and bones.		

6 Suggest three essential rules for good personal hygiene practice in safe food handling.

7 What might the advantages be of grilling over frying when preparing meat or vegetables?

8 What are the four conditions that pathogens need to thrive?

9 List three ways to encourage a client who is recovering from illness to eat and enjoy her food.

10 What foods are not allowed by the following religious groups.
   a People of Muslim faith
   b People of Jewish faith
   c People of Hindu faith.

Multiple choice questions

11 Scurvey is a disease caused by:
- **a** lack of protein
- **b** lack of vitamin D
- **c** lack of iron
- **d** lack of vitamin C.

12 Fibre is essential in your diet because:
- **a** it helps you enjoy your food
- **b** it prevents anaemia
- **c** it helps prevent constipation
- **d** it is a good source of energy.

13 Fish oils and sunlight are a good source of:
- **a** vitamin D
- **b** energy
- **c** vitamin C
- **d** healthy teeth and bones.

14 A glass of wine provides:
- **a** two units of alcohol
- **b** ½ a unit of alcohol
- **c** one unit of alcohol
- **d** three units of alcohol.

15 The coldest part of the fridge should be kept at:
- **a** −18°C or below
- **b** 3°C or below
- **c** 5°C or below
- **d** between 5 and 7°C.

16 Salmonella is:
- **a** a fish found in fresh water
- **b** a potentially lethal virus
- **c** a sexually transmitted disease
- **d** a bacteria which can cause illness.

17 When cooking frozen chicken you should:
- **a** put it straight into the hottest part of the oven to cook
- **b** defrost thoroughly before cooking
- **c** ensure that all pets are kept away from the kitchen
- **d** stuff with breadcrumbs and herbs.

18 When costing a meal for a client you should:
- **a** ensure you only buy what is in season at the time
- **b** buy the most nutritious food at the price your client can afford
- **c** always use a good recipe book
- **d** take into account bargains at the supermarket.

19 A healthy snack for a child could be:
- **a** chocolate
- **b** crisps
- **c** a plate of chips and ketchup
- **d** raisins and apples cut into shapes.

20 A pregnant woman needs in her daily diet:
- **a** a glass of red wine to help a healthy heart
- **b** some sugar for energy
- **c** plenty of protein and calcium
- **d** a full complement of vitamin tablets.

Exploring Recreational Activities for Clients

This unit explores the importance of recreational activities for good health and well-being. In it you will find out about the different things that people do in their recreation time and the benefits that they can expect. You will also have the opportunity to find out about the recreational facilities that are available in your own area. Another section of the unit will offer you the opportunity to discover and learn about the barriers that stop people from taking part in recreational activities, as well as finding out about the health and safety requirements for people who are joining in with recreational activities.

The whole of this unit of work aims to help you carry out the exploration into recreational activities in your local area. To help you collect your information so that you can put your evidence together you need to learn about:

- the benefits of recreational activity
- the recreational facilities available in your community
- how these facilities can be used by clients to enhance their well-being
- the barriers that might make it difficult for people to use health and recreation facilities
- the health and safety factors associated with health and recreation facilities.

6.1 Benefits of recreational activity

Before we can examine the benefits of recreational activity it is important to have a good understanding of the word 'recreation'. What exactly does it mean? If we look in a dictionary we will find that recreation is a word that has several meanings, such as:

- play
- diversion
- entertainment.

So we can say that recreational activities are those things that we do for pleasure. Our recreation time is that special time in a day, or week, when we have no work to do and we can carry out those activities that give us pleasure.

People carry out recreational activities for a wide range of reasons. Most often they spend their leisure time doing the things that:

Look it up

Look the word 'recreation' up in a dictionary of your own. Make a note of the explanation given and then compare your definitions with another person's.

- gives them pleasure
- helps them learn a new skill
- helps them to learn new information
- keeps them physically fit
- helps them to meet other people.

If we put these reasons together we can clearly see that there are three main reasons for people participating in recreational activity. They are:

- to improve their mobility (physical activities)

- to improve their relationships (social activities)

- to keep their minds active (intellectual activities).

Talk it over

Lisa and Dougie have taken up dancing lessons. They are fed up of going to parties and being the only ones who cannot dance. They have learned how to do modern dance as well as other dances, such as 'rock and roll'.

They have also learned how to 'line dance' which they really enjoy. They always have a good laugh whenever they go wrong! They have met loads of new people and have become very friendly with another couple. They often go out with them on a regular basis, usually to the cinema or for a meal or bar snack.

Working with another person put Lisa and Dougie's different recreational activities under the headings of 'mobility', 'social', 'intellectual'. Which activity do you think they enjoy the most?

Lisa and Dougie are clearly getting many benefits from their recreational activity. They started off by wanting to learn how to dance, so that they could join in more at parties. However, we can see that there are many more benefits than just learning to dance. This is important for us to remember that most recreational activities improve all three parts of our lives at the same time!

Lisa and Dougie have improved their physical ability and mobility because dancing is quite energetic. They have also improved their relationships because they have made many new friends, as well as the two special ones, and of course they have learned a new skill and can follow the 'rules' of the dancing.

Improving mobility through physical activity

Some people say that physical activity is exercise or sport, but these are usually different from physical activity. For example, sports are usually planned, formal activities that have a leader or a coach to help you. In many cases exercise is the same. There is often a leader to help you do the exercise – for example in step aerobics there is usually someone who guides the class.

Physical activity is best described as 'doing something active'. If you want to improve your fitness and your health, through doing something active, you may want to achieve:

- having strong muscles

- being able to bend and turn easily (flexibility)

- looking 'toned up and good'

- having a strong heart.

The 'something active' needs to make you hot and sweaty and a bit puffed for breath. You would need to do an activity like this regularly to get the physical benefits.

Think it over

Nancy has decided that she wants to take up running in her spare time. Six weeks ago she could not run 100 metres without getting out of breath and feeling sick! She thought it was because she was a little overweight as well as being out of condition.

She now runs (and walks a little bit) four times a week. When she went out running last night, she completed her first 5 kilometres in one go. She is feeling very pleased with herself and is now determined to get herself fit enough to run 8 kilometres in one go. She knows the weight she has lost will make it easier for her to keep going now.

How often is Nancy going out running in a week? How long has it taken for her body to adapt to regular physical activity? Make a list of the benefits Nancy is getting from her recreational time.

Nancy's physical recreational activity can bring her many benefits. For example:

- increasing strength, especially in her legs (making the muscles stronger)
- increasing stamina (improving the body's staying power)
- increasing mobility (suppleness and flexibility)
- helping to maintain (or lose) weight
- helping to sleep well at night.

Nancy's physical recreational activities have not just improved her physical body. They will also have contributed to:

- increasing the sense of well-being (feel good factors)
- increasing self-esteem (feeling good about ourselves)
- effective stress management (coping with life better).

Some people like to become involved in physical activity that includes other people. This could be through playing team games, such as:

- badminton
- tennis
- football
- netball.

Compare your findings with those we have identified in the spidergram.

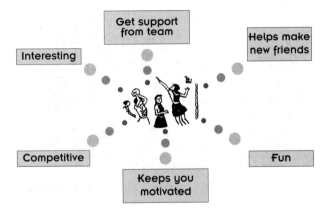

Talk it over

Terry is an 18-year-old wheelchair user. He is a member of the local basketball team. They are in the first division, so playing matches involves a lot of travelling around the country.

He has had a busy day at work and does not feel like going out to practice tonight, but he knows he cannot let the team down.

After the game he and a few friends had a snack in the club bar. He felt really fresh and full of life after the game and now he was having a few laughs with his mates. He was so glad he had decided to come!

Working with another person discuss the benefits to Terry of physical recreational activities. It might be helpful to think of the PIES whilst you are carrying out this activity.

Talk it over

Discuss with another person some of the benefits of joining in with physical activities that involve other people.

Not everyone is happy participating in physical recreational activities with others. For many people having others around all day is part of their job, for example teachers. If this is the case the person might want to participate in an activity that can be carried out alone.

Activities carried out alone

Remember, sometimes these are done as part of a team as well!

The benefits of doing activities alone can be:

- stress management
- time to think
- improved stamina
- peace and quiet

- improved mobility

- improved strength.

If you are trying to help a client carry out more recreational activities you should check whether they want to be with others or alone. People usually want to do different things. Sometimes we even want to do different recreational activities at different times.

Improving relationships

For some clients developing and having a good relationship can be difficult. Many people are shy and do not know how to go about making new friends. This is especially difficult for those people who have moved house and gone to live in another town.

Taking part in recreational activities can be a good way to meet with friends or to develop new relationships. So it will be important to choose recreational activities that allow you to meet other people.

Think it over

Colin moved house with his parents six weeks ago. He used to live in Lancashire but now he has moved to London. He feels like he has lost all his friends and does not know where to begin making new ones.

He has left school and is going to be registering with a college in September, but he still has to wait for another two months before that starts. He is really 'bored!'

His father has suggested that he visit the local community centre, but he does not want to go in there on his own. He has been to the cinema twice but says 'that is no fun on your own'.

Colin has clearly chosen the wrong recreational activity for meeting other people. Make notes on why you think he will not make new friends easily by going to the cinema.

It is likely that you have identified many factors about the cinema that will stop Colin making new friends. Compare your list with ours to see if you have identified the same things.

- The cinema is dark

- Talking is not allowed

- People sit separately

- Everybody rushes in before the start of the film and then rush out when it has finished.

Talk it over

Colin's father had a good idea when he suggested going to the local community centre, but it can be hard going for the first time on your own.

Colin's father offered to go with him to see what kind of recreational activities were on offer. Once they arrived they found a list of the activities pinned on a notice board.

'Hey, look', said Colin, 'they have got a new acting group just starting. I really fancy that. I think I will go along and offer my services to the leader, somebody called Sam. I really enjoy being in plays and things!'

Discuss with another person why you think Colin agreed to visit the community centre with his father. Why do you think he feels comfortable going to the acting group when he does not know anyone? Make notes of your discussion for your portfolio.

Joining an amateur drama group is one way of making friends

Think it over

When Colin arrived at the acting group he found six other people all standing around. He could tell that they did not know anyone either.

Soon they were joined by the group leader, who said his name was Sam. He helped them to introduce themselves to each other.

The first play they had a look at was really funny and they were all laughing for most of the night. By the time Colin came out he had the telephone number of three members of the group. 'That's been brilliant', he thought to himself!

Colin has clearly made three new friends already. Why do you think this has happened on the first night? You might have to think about Sam's role in this.

Talk it over

Discuss with another person the benefits to Colin of taking part in the acting group on a regular basis. Make notes for your portfolio.

It is not always easy for people to improve their relationships through social activities. Sometimes they need some help to 'get going', like Colin did. Having Sam to contact on arrival was helpful, but as a group leader part of Sam's job was to help people meet each other and relax.

Think it over

What happened when you started studying on your present course? Was anyone available to help you meet with others and relax?

We need to recognise that it is important for clients to take part in recreational activities that will help them to develop good

relationships with others because they can learn:

- how to mix with others

- acceptable social behaviour (how to behave in public)

- a 'picture' of how other people see them

- to feel good about themselves if they have a lot of friends

- how to share

- how to support others and accept support themselves.

Recreational activities don't just help people to make new relationships, they can also help people to improve existing relationships.

Talk it over

Shazia is seven years old. She has just joined the girl's brigade and is feeling silly because she does not know what to do. All the other children are wearing a uniform, but her mum says she cannot have one until she is sure that she is going to stay.

Right now, she just wants to go home. Then the group leader came up, took her hand and introduced her to one of the others, a girl called Michelle. 'Michelle will look after you', she said.

Michelle explained what to do at games time and again at break time. She even shared her biscuits with Shazia.

By the end of the evening Shazia was skipping out to meet her mother. She could not wait for the next session.

Six months later Shazia was helping another new girl to settle into the group.

Discuss with another person why Shazia managed to settle into the group so easily. Make a note of the social skills both Michelle and Shazia are learning in this situation.

Lilly and Burt share community sheltered accommodation for people with learning disabilities. They have lived in the group home with three other people for nearly two years. They do not get on at all well.

Their carer has tried all kinds of things to help them but nothing has worked.

Two weeks ago they both joined an interior decorating course at their local college. The tutor explained about colours and paints and the best way to improve a room in your house. Soon they were chatting away with another group member called Ray.

Lilly and Burt asked Ray to visit them in their home to discuss how they are going to change their house.

Two weeks later the carer noticed how well Lilly and Burt were getting on, now that they are decorating the house together with their new friend Ray. Thank goodness for shared interests she thought!

Working with another person discuss the factors that have helped Lilly and Burt to become friends after all that time sharing the same house. Make notes for your portfolio.

Zafar is still in bed! The care worker is really worried about him. He has been in the residential care home for six weeks now and still has not settled in properly. She has tried everything!

Ahmed, a 74-year-old resident of the home had noticed Zafar arrive but hadn't really seen him since. So he decided to make an effort to be sociable and invite him to a social evening at the local community centre.

It took him ages to persuade Zafar to go with him. But Zafar gave in and went along. When he got there he found two people he had not seen for ages, as well as finding out about other social events planned for the next religious festival.

He was so pleased that he had decided to accompany Ahmed.

Working with another person discuss why you think Ahmed felt he had to make an effort to be sociable.

What immediate benefits will Zafar gain from attending this social activity?

What might be the long-term benefits to Zafar from continuing to attend the community centre?

Make notes for your portfolio.

It is clear that going to the same recreational event and having a shared friend has helped Lilly and Burt get to know each other better. They have even found that they share the same kinds of interests – decorating their house.

The recreational benefits to an individual come in two forms: short term and long term. There are immediate or short-term benefits, for example read about how Zafar got out of bed and began to get to know Ahmed right away and met two people on the first visit to the community centre. The long-term benefits could include:

- motivation (looking forward to the next visit)

- interest in life

- making more friends

- settling into the residential home better.

There is a whole range of benefits to be gained from joining in social activities. Use the chart to identify some benefits linked to dancing, social clubs, walking groups and going on day trips.

Think it over

Can you think of any other short- or long-term benefits for Zafar from participating in the recreational activity? Make a note of them for your portfolio.

Talk it over

Working with another person make your own chart with three different social activities listed. Then identify the benefits to yourself and other people from joining in them. You will need to think about the benefits to mobility as well as relationships.

Social activities are an essential part of good health and well-being. Life can involve having many problems and having someone to share them with can help a great deal! Social activities don't just improve our relationships, they can also improve our mobility, as in the case of dancing and walking.

Keeping the mind active

Intellectual activities help us to keep the brain working. If we do not use our mind and brain regularly, we can easily become bored, and be boring ! It is important for our mental and intellectual health to keep ourselves interested in the things that are around us.

We can keep ourselves interested by carrying out intellectual activities, such as:

* studying (that is what you are doing by reading this!)

* going to evening classes (learning to paint or draw or other creative activities)

* learning to play a musical instrument

* joining in pub quizzes

* doing the crossword in the local newspaper

* reading books, magazines and newspapers

* watching information programmes on the television

* taking an interest in news programmes.

Social activities	Benefits to self	Benefits to others
Dancing	Improved fitness Fun Making new friends Better self-esteem Less stressed Learning new skills	Less grumpy Good to be with Maintaining good relationships Partners for dancing
Going to clubs	Making new friends Gaining new hobbies Better self-esteem Fun Less stressed Getting out of the house	More interesting person to be with Maintaining good relationships
Walking groups	Improved fitness Making new friends Discovering the countryside Better self-esteem Fun Less stressed	More interesting to be with Maintaining good relationships
Day trips	Making new friends Discovering different places Better self-esteem Keeping yourself interested in life Fun Less stressed	More interesting to be with Maintaining good relationships

Pub quizzes are a way of using your mind

Think it over

Make a list of all the things that you like to do in your recreational time that help keep your mind active. Compare your list with another person. Do you share the same interests or do you both prefer different intellectual activities?

Compare your list of benefits with ours. Have you identified the same ones, or something different? Our list includes:

- learning new information

- saving money

- making new friends

- learning a new skill

- taking up a hobby

- avoiding boredom.

Talk it over

Billy is 18 years old and has Down's syndrome. He has been working for three years at a local waste paper recycling plant. He heard some of his work colleagues planning to go to a cyber café to learn how to use the Internet. He is really interested in going along as well.

He asked Jim, who was three years older than him, if he could go with him. 'Of course you can', said Jim.

Billy found the cyber café really interesting. He had to learn how to use the computer from step one, but Jim said he would be delighted to show him.

Billy can now find all kinds of interesting information on the Internet and Jim has found that he really enjoys teaching information technology skills. Jim has decided to ask the local college about teaching qualifications for himself!

Discuss with another person the benefits of the cyber café to both Billy and Jim. Make a note of your discussions for your portfolio.

Talk it over

Molly is 64 and has had a hip replacement. She cannot get out and about as much as she used to do, so she is living with her son and his family. She has developed a new recreational interest that she can do at home. She has decided to do a healthy living course to find out more about diet, exercise and stress management. She tells her daughter-in-law all about the information she collects.

She has also joined a distance learning course at her local college. She has a computer and she emails her essays and assignments to her tutor.

Her family cannot believe what she is doing. Twelve months ago, when her grandson got the computer, she couldn't even switch the 'thing' on, now she is teaching him to email on the computer instead of always playing games!

Discuss with another person the benefits to Molly and her family of her intellectual interests. Make a note for your portfolio before comparing your benefits with ours.

Learning how to use the Internet is one way someone with Down's syndrome can use their intellectual abilities

The benefits of intellectual activities can be far-reaching. In other words, we don't always know where an intellectual activity might take us. For example, Jim started off by being kind to Billy and showing him how to use a computer. But he also found out that he was good at teaching others. Who knows, maybe Jim will become a teacher because his intellectual activity involved showing Billy how to become involved!

Molly is not the only one to benefit from her intellectual activity! The information she gains from doing a healthy living course can all be shared with her family so that they can learn about healthy living as well. She is also keeping herself interested in life, which is likely to make her caring needs easier to be met. And of course her grandson is benefiting from her knowledge of the computer!

6.2 Local recreational facilities and activities

There are many different recreational activities available to our clients and us. If we are going to use them effectively we need to know where we can find the kind of recreational activities that interest us. This may not be as easy as it sounds. Let us start by thinking about where we can find recreational activities that will allow us to improve our mobility.

The kinds of places where physical activities can be found are very varied. They include:

- Sports centres
- Youth clubs
- Community centres
- Colleges
- Private gymnasiums and health clubs
- Swimming pools
- Parks and playgrounds.

Look it up

Norma is a nursery nurse. She and other care workers care for 10 children, who are all aged between five years and nine years of age. She works in an after-school club which is held in a secondary school in Anytown.

As the weather is good today she decides to take the children to the sports field running track so that they can run around and let off some 'steam'.

The children enjoy racing each other on a real track, as well as playing at doing the long jump in the sand pit area.

Find out if any of your local schools have these kinds of facilities which members of the public can use. Or do they have these kinds of facilities only for those who attend the schools.

Think it over

Rita and Shaheen have a young child each. They met in Mitton Park one summer when the children were using the climbing equipment there.

When they got talking with other mothers they found out that there was a 'fitness trail' available for everyone in the park.

Now they meet on a Monday (even when its raining) to follow the trail.

They walk around a 3-kilometre circuit. At different points there are notices that tell them what to do. The first one says 10 knee lifts gently, the second one tells them to jump in and out of the tyres on the floor, and the third one tells them to swing over a metal archway using arms only.

Rita and Shaheen really enjoy this activity and feel they are actually getting fitter because of it.

Think about the kinds of recreational activity that will help you to improve your mobility. Write them down. Remember it is likely to include some kind of exercise or sport as well as other things. Now make a list of the places that you could visit in order to do the activities you have thought about.

Look it up

Working with another person find a map of your local area and mark in red the places where physical activity can be carried out. You might need to use a Yellow Pages or some other kind of directory to find out exactly where they are.

You could also visit a local information centre or tourist centre (if you have one close by) or a borough or town council and ask for a list of places to visit. You should find places for physical activity listed in the information.

Try it out Ask about ten people where they go for their recreation time. Make a note of the answers they give you. Try and add these places to your map.

Places for social activities

Sometimes we find that the places that offer physical activities also offer social activities. We have already discussed that one activity might cover all three benefits (improving mobility, relationships and intellectual ability). In general, social activities can be found in any place where lots of people meet regularly. However, there is also a range of places dedicated to social activities. The newspaper advertisement gives you some idea of these.

Sources of intellectual activity

Any recreational activity that involves learning a new skill or new information is classed as keeping the mind active. Climbing the wall in a sports centre requires the person to work out each move in order to get to the top. And of course picking up the newspaper to find out about places to go and things to see is an intellectual activity in its

---

YOUR GUIDE TO SOCIAL ACTIVITIES ACROSS THE COUNTY
Places to Go, People to See!

Entertainment Halls

King Edwards Hall	Line Dancing, Jazz Night, Meet and Eat evening
Queen Vics Place	Drama Group meetings, Magic for All, Beetle Drive (all ages welcome)
The Charter Theatre	Music by Lloyd and Dibner

Libraries

Anytown Library	Family Tree Searchers meeting, Poetry for Fun, Books for the Family
Alltowns Library	Book Writers Club meeting, for budding writers

Museums

Anytown Museum	Art Appreciation Society meeting, Egyptology for the Beginner
Alltowns Museum	Metal Detector Club meeting, Roman Coins Talk, for all ages

Nature Reserves

Anytown Nature Reserve	Butterflies in Close Up, talks for the collector
Alltown Nature Reserve	Brave the Birds, a guided woodland walk

Leisure Centres

Anytown Sports Centre	Football, Basketball, Swimming, Badminton
Alltowns Tennis Centre	Lawn Tennis and Indoor Tennis
Images Leisure Centre	Gymnasium, Climbing Wall, Swimming and Sauna
Daisyfold Swimming Pool	Lengths Only, Canoeing for Beginners, Diving for Beginners

own right – it's called reading the newspaper!

- Entertainment halls
- Newspaper
- Museum

Talk it over

Working with another person discuss which places you would approach if you wanted to make

a   new friends

b   improve mobility and make new friends

c   improve intellectual ability and make new friends.

Make notes of your discussions for your portfolio.

Think it over

Look back at the newspaper advert and make a list of the places where you or a client could go if you want to improve your intellectual ability. Then compare your list with ours.

- Library
- Nature reserve
- Leisure centre.

Talk it over

Stuart is really interested in finding out about his family tree. He wants to know about his family members who lived hundreds of years ago.

He has been to his local church and collected records of family members who had lived in the area 150 years ago, now he is trying to trace a member called Jackson who emigrated to America in 1800.

The members of his family tree club have suggested that he tries to use the Internet to see if he can find any trace of them that way. If that fails he will have to think again!

Discuss with another person the skills and knowledge that Stuart is developing as a result of his intellectual interests. Name the places he uses to help him with these interests. Make a list of them for your records.

Look it up

Collect newspapers from your own area and examine them for advertisements of places to go and things to see. Cut the adverts out and then discuss them with another person. You could make a wall collage of all the activities available in your area.

Stuart is using a wide range of places to help him with his activity, such as:

- the church
- the Internet
- the family tree group.

He is probably using books and other records as well. Each time he visits or uses one of these places he is developing his skills further. He is talking to people, learning to use the Internet and learning how to research church records.

Other people develop their intellectual skills by carrying out simpler activities. For example:

- reading books and magazines
- watching TV documentaries.

6.3 Recreational activities for different client groups

It is important to recognise that all people are different. This is likely to mean that your friends, clients and other people will be interested in different recreational activities. They will not want to do the same things as each other unless they happen to share some of the same interests. We have already said that for many people friendships actually start because of a shared interest or hobby.

It is likely that the different social classes choose activities that fit in with their lifestyle. For example, men in the professional and intermediate classes are more likely to garden or do DIY because they are more likely to have a garden and have the money to spend on it!

As well as social class differences, we should also remember that our clients and friends have different cultures and different abilities. In other words, some people will not be able to join in the recreational activities available because they:

- are not physically developed enough (old enough)

- do not have the skills required to join in

- are not culturally acceptable

- do not have the mental ability to join in

- are too old and frail to join in safely

- have special learning needs

- have physical disabilities.

Research by the Office for National Statistics (1995) has shown that there is a difference in the way different social classes spend their recreational time. (Do you remember reading about social class in Unit 2?). Have a look at the chart below and then answer some questions about it.

We should be aware of the different needs clients have in relation to recreational activities. For example, we know that our clients are likely to want to improve their mobility, relationships and intellectual ability, however the way they choose to do this can vary from one person to another. It is the need to recognise client diversity, ability and motivation that is important for

Time use[1]: by social class[2] and gender, May 1995

	Hours and minutes per day							
	Professional and intermediate		Skilled manual and non-manual		Partly skilled and unskilled		All social classes[3]	
	Males	Females	Males	Females	Males	Females	Males	Females
Sleep	8:26	8:25	8:29	8:46	9:02	8:59	8:40	8:48
TV and radio	2:16	2:07	2:53	2:18	2:50	2:57	2:37	2:28
Eating at home	0:59	1:00	1:01	1:06	0:56	1:03	0:58	1:05
Gardening and DIY	0:59	0:19	0:56	0:29	0:50	0:26	0:54	0:25
Cooking, routine housework	0:39	2:05	0:48	2:23	0:40	2:38	0:42	2:24
Personal care	0:38	0:43	0:44	0:49	0:36	0:46	0:39	0:47
Care of children and adults	0:23	0:36	0:12	0:43	0:10	0:36	0:16	0:39
Other home leisure[4]	1:23	1:12	1:08	1:00	1:02	0:51	1:11	1:01
Paid work	3:58	3:24	4:14	2:14	3:00	1:42	3:46	2:16
Travel	0:57	0:47	0:44	0:49	0:45	0:32	0:50	0:43
Socialising[5]	0:50	1:17	0:53	1:10	1:05	1:13	0:55	1:12
Shopping	0:30	0:36	0:22	0:48	0:33	0:54	0:26	0:46
Eating or drinking out	0:36	0:29	0:32	0:28	0:54	0:14	0:38	0:24
Other out-of-home leisure[6]	1:14	0:51	0:58	0:47	1:24	0:50	1:16	0:51

1 Components do not add to 24 hours due to rounding and activities not stated.

2 Social class of own occupation.

3 Includes people in the armed forces, those who never worked and those who did not state an occupation.

4 Includes study at home.

5 Includes telephone conversations.

6 Includes education, voluntary work and various other leisure activities.

Source: *Omnibus Survey*, Office for National Statistics

Talk it over

Working with another person make a note of your answers to the following:

- Which social class females watch the most television?

- Which social class is most likely to have care of children or adults?

- Which social class men do the most gardening and DIY?

matching the right recreational activities to the right client groups.

When we are matching the different client groups to different recreational activities we need to be careful not to stereotype people (thinking that everyone is the same). For example, Shaheen is not happy to attend a mixed sex swimming session, but another Muslim person may not object. People are different and have different needs. As carers

Talk it over

Shaheen is a Muslim girl aged 17. She enjoys going out with her friends to dances and evening classes at the local college. Her brother often gives her a lift to the college and then arranges to collect her and her friends if he can. The family likes to make sure all the girls are safe.

Last week Miriam suggested that they should all go to the local swimming pool for a mixed sex event being organised by the local council.

Shaheen is not going to go because she does not find swimming with people of the opposite sex culturally acceptable.

Discuss with another person ways in which Shaheen could go swimming if she wanted to without compromising her cultural needs. Make notes of your discussion.

we will usually be working with one or more of the following client groups:

- children

- adolescents

- adults

- elderly people

- people with special needs.

So we should have a good understanding of the recreational activities that are likely to meet their individual needs.

Recreational activities for children

Talk it over

Lucy is in her first stage of training as a nursery nurse. She is doing her first week's placement at the Little Tykes nursery school.

She has been asked to organise a recreational activity for the children, aged three and four years.

She decides to give them a book each and tells them to read the stories quietly so that they do not disturb the babies who are sleeping next door.

Within five minutes the children are all running around creating a great deal of noise.

Discuss with another person what has happened to Lucy in this case. Do you think she chose an appropriate activity for three and four year olds? What would you have chosen for the children as a recreational activity?

In general, children like to carry out recreational activities that keep them busy and physically active. Small children often need to have a change in the activity every 10 minutes or they become bored and fed up.

Often it is a range of factors that influences what recreational activities a child chooses to do.

Talk it over

> Hinna is six years old. Her mother has decided that it is time she learned to swim. She saw an advert the other day at the local swimming pool offering free lessons to all children under the age of 10.
>
> This offer is part of an accident prevention programme to cut down on the number of children who drown each year in their area.

Discuss with another person what you think are the major factors influencing Hinna's recreational activity. Make a list of these factors for your portfolio.

We can see that her mother decides what Hinna should do, so it is not really Hinna's choice at all. This is often the case for small and young children. Other influences in making the decision are:

- safety campaign
- fear of the child drowning.

However, there are other factors that will influence a child's decision as to which recreational activities to take up. These are often called needs. However needs are not always needed, sometimes they are more like wants, such as:

- wanting to start a new hobby
- wanting to meet other children
- needing to learning new skills or information
- needing to keep safe
- needing to learn how to share with other people.

Many recreational activities help a child to grow and develop. They learn about their place in the world through recreational activities.

It is interesting to note that children watch the least television of all age groups. This is because when watching the television they need to sit still and take the information in, something they often do not like doing! In most cases television can only hold their attention for a short time before they get bored.

Recreational activities for adolescents

A MORI survey carried out in June 1996 showed that 8 out of 10 teenagers aged between 15 and 19 have a TV in their bedroom. However teenagers still do not watch as much television as adults!

Children need to have a variety of activities to do

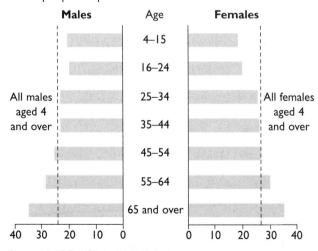

Source: BARB; AGB Ltd; RSMB Ltd
Television viewing by gender and age in the UK, 1996

Teenagers use some of their recreation time at discos

Teenagers seem to have a range of things that they like to do with their recreational time, such as:

- meeting up with each other
- discos and other dance clubs

Talk it over

Dan and Edward have decided to visit the cinema to see the latest release. On the way there they noticed a museum in the street close by. 'Hey I've never noticed that before', said Dan, 'I wouldn't mind going in there some day to have a look.'

'Well, don't think I am going to go with you, it sounds really boring to me', said Edward.

'Give it a chance, I've been in some really interesting museums with my dad.'

Discuss with another person why you think Dan and Edward had never noticed the museum before? What might be the benefits of Dan visiting there?

Did you know?

160 million CDs were sold in the United Kingdom in 1996.

- listening to music
- visiting the cinema.

It is likely that Dan and Edward have been far too busy doing the usual things that teenagers do to have noticed other forms of recreational activity. However, it is possible that once a person has been introduced to a new activity they may go on pursuing it if it interests them.

Talk it over

Discuss with another person how Dan could persuade Edward to go to the museum with him. What might be the benefits to Edward of attending with Dan?

Teenagers also enjoy visiting places such as theme parks. A great deal of their recreational time is spent on day trips once they are old enough to go alone.

Talk it over

Nigel and Fiona have decided to visit Blackpool Pleasure Beach. It is free to get in so they do not have to worry about the cost.

They can't wait to meet up with their partners, Rosie and Tracy. They have never been before and are looking forward to the day out.

Discuss with another person the benefits all four teenagers will get from this recreational activity. Make a list for your portfolio. Don't forget to include mobility, social and intellectual benefits.

The fun of the fair

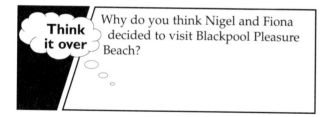

Think it over

Why do you think Nigel and Fiona decided to visit Blackpool Pleasure Beach?

We can tell from these cases that adolescents spend their recreational time doing a great many different activities. The needs they have differ from children because the teenage years can be a time of growth and personal development as well as uncertainty. Sometimes teenagers join in recreational activities to:

- feel that they belong to a certain group
- impress their friends
- learn new skills
- gain qualifications
- prepare for work or further study
- gain reassurance from their friends.

Recreational activities for adults

Adults have many different needs that will influence their choice of recreational activity, such as:

- how much time is available
- how much money is available
- what skills and knowledge they have
- physical ability
- mental ability

Think it over

Howard and Andrea have two small children. They both have full-time jobs and find that caring for the home and children as well is exhausting.

These days money is a bit tight, so they do not get out as often as they would like, as they have to pay for baby-sitting.

They look forward to renting a video and spending the evenings together once the children have gone to bed.

Why do you think Howard and Andrea spend time watching the television? Make a list of all the factors that have influenced this choice of recreational activity.

The chance to relax

189

- motivation
- planning for the future
- time out for themselves.

Just like adolescents, adults are interested in a wide variety of recreational activities. However, there may be some constraints on adults that do not usually apply to adolescents.

Have you guessed by now who watches the most television? Yes it is adults! We can see that there are clear reasons for adults choosing the kind of recreational activities that they do. In Howard and Andrea's case lack of money, caring for children and lack of energy are the main reasons why they chose to watch the television.

However, time, cost and child care are not the only reasons for adults choosing a particular activity.

Talk it over

Monica is a wheelchair user. She took up horse-riding in her recreational time 10 years ago. She started because it helped to strengthen her back muscles, but over the years she has come to love horses, especially Pandora.

This is her own horse, which she has had for three years now. She enjoys meeting other horse-riders at the stable and finds riding a welcome break from the office and home.

Working with another person discuss the benefits Monica is getting from her choice of recreational activity. Include in your discussions her original need for taking up horse-riding and how that need has changed. Make notes for your portfolio.

Monica developed her recreational activity because she needed to improve her mobility, but over the years her recreation time has become very precious because she has developed an emotional attachment to her horse.

Talk it over

Lynda enjoys running by herself on the hills. She usually takes along her large dog for company and safety.

She works as a teacher and in some of her spare time helps to organise local running events for her club. She spends a lot of time talking to people during the normal working day.

Discuss with another person why you think Lynda chooses to spend time running on the hills with her dog instead of going to group events. Make notes of your discussion for your portfolio.

Lynda, on the other hand, wants to have time to herself, or what we call 'space'. This is the time to 'recharge the batteries'. It is not always beneficial to spend all your time with other people. Having some personal space can be good for us.

Recreational activities for elderly people

All the age groups we have explored so far enjoy doing the same kinds of things with their recreational time. There should be no question of age in the kinds of things we choose to do with our recreational time. Older people are just as likely to choose the same activities as children, adolescents or adults. However, their reasons for making their choices might be different.

Very often older people find themselves in a position where they need to find new company and develop new social relationships because they have lost their partner through old age.

Many older people carry on doing the same recreational activity that they have always done.

Some older people look forward to retirement, seeing it as a whole new world of opportunities. For them recreation becomes

Talk it over

Ronnie has got divorced. It has all come as a bit of a shock to him. After all you don't expect to get divorced when you are 69 years old.

He cannot cook, except for beans on toast, so he has decided that he will go to the local college and join a cooking for beginners class.

He loves it. Last week he learned how to prepare and cook vegetables. This week it is going to be egg dishes.

Discuss with another person the needs that influenced Ronnie into spending his recreational time learning to cook. What other benefits do you think Ronnie is also getting? Make a list of them for your portfolio.

Talk it over

Paul and Ann have both retired. They started planning for retirement three years before because they did not want to find themselves bored with nothing to do. They saved up and bought a caravan so that they could spend more time away from home without it costing too much.

They have both been to classes to learn how to map read and about safety on the mountains. This has given them the confidence to walk up mountains in the Lake District and Scotland.

They are planning to go to France next year and do some walking in the Alps.

What was the need that encouraged Paul and Ann to take up walking and to learn about caravanning and map reading? How do you think these activities have affected their lives? Make notes for your portfolio.

more important, they plan how they are going to fill their time and begin to develop new skills and collect new knowledge.

If older people have the opportunity to plan for retirement they can use their recreational time to good effect. For example, Ann and Paul have both learned new skills, they are keeping themselves fit and healthy and they are learning about the world around them. It is likely that they are also meeting new people and attending new kinds of activities – for example they could have become members of the caravan club.

We have to take care not to see older people as 'past it' and having no life. This is definitely not the case.

We have seen from the above cases that older people have the same kind of needs as adults,

adolescents and children. We can see that they need to:

- feel pleasure
- be sociable (have friends)
- keep themselves fit
- feel good about themselves
- keep themselves intellectually stimulated (learning new things).

Age does not really change the things people like to do with their recreational time. The most important factors affecting recreation are likely to be ability and cost. However, even these can be handled so that they do not prevent people from doing what they want with their recreation time.

Recreational activities for people with special needs

Everyone has special needs of some kind. In some cases these are hidden, but for others

Think it over

Do you know any older people? Make a list of the things they like to do with their recreational time. Now think about why they are carrying out these activities. In other words what 'needs' are driving them.

they are more obvious. For example, a person with physical disability or a person with learning difficulties may need more support with their recreational activities than a person with needs centering around self-esteem or confidence.

Talk it over

Mishka is a wheelchair user. She is really keen on amateur dramatics and wants to join the local amateur drama club in her area. She would like to be an actor when she leaves school.

Her brother has told her that she probably won't be able to join because they won't want someone in a wheelchair.

She discussed this with her teacher at college and he said she should apply just like anyone else.

She is now playing a part in the Christmas pantomime and cannot wait for the performances to begin.

Discuss with another person why you think Mishka wanted to join the drama club. What need is she demonstrating? Make a note for your portfolio.

Mishka wants to learn about acting. She wants to gain the experience she needs for applying for a place in a drama school that will train her. Being a wheelchair user should not stop her from developing her intellectual knowledge and skills about acting. However, there may be occasions when Mishka could not join in certain activities, however much she wanted to. For example, Mishka could not enjoy physical activities that include running and walking. But she could enjoy team or individual activities that use the wheelchair, for example basketball and marathon racing.

We have said before that every person is different. The way they spend their recreational time will depend upon what interests them and what they need to get out of life at that

Think it over

William lost a leg in an industrial accident three years ago. Since then he has learned to walk with an artificial leg. At first he was very conscious and depressed about his disability. He found his friends were too embarrassed to talk to him, so he felt he had to prove that nothing had changed. He has realised that it does not stop him from doing the things he likes.

His favourite activity has always been motor-bike racing. He came third in the Isle of Man TT races this year. He has every intention of coming first next year, so he is looking for sponsorship from a wealthy company.

He spends much of his recreation time writing letters and making phone calls to suitable companies. One day someone will help!

What is the need that is making William carry out his recreational activities? You will need to think about his personal development and his future plans.

point in time. For example, William wanted to show that losing his leg had changed nothing as far as he was concerned. He also wanted to show his friends that there was nothing to be embarrassed about. He probably needed their friendship more than ever.

Wheelchair users can be active

Clients with learning disabilities can also join in many social and physical recreational activities. In some cases it may be necessary to make sure they are supervised to maintain their health and safety. It is possible that some clients with learning disabilities may not recognise the dangers in certain situations, such as jumping into the deep end of a swimming pool when they cannot swim.

Some clients with learning disabilities will not be able to fully join in all the intellectual recreational activities that are available. For example, if a client cannot read then they will not be able to use the written word. This could mean that they will need books that are picture-based. It is likely that the carer would have to 'read' the book for them and explain the pictures and stories involved.

It is also possible that clients with learning difficulties may not understand some games with complicated rules.

People with special needs have exactly the same requirements for their recreational activities as children, adolescents, adults and older people. The only difference is likely to be the support they require in order to carry out their choice of activity.

People with special needs still need to:

* have an interest in life
* improve their mobility
* make new friendships
* feel good about themselves.

Therapists who use recreational activities

Recreational activities are so important to physical and personal development that there are health and social care professionals employed to use recreational activities to assist clients to improve their lives.

The health and social care professionals who can help both you and your client with recreational activities are:

* physiotherapists
* occupational therapists
* play therapists.

Physiotherapists

A physiotherapist is usually employed by the health and social care sector. Some have their

---

Talk it over

Roy is an adult with learning difficulties. He is also profoundly deaf. He lives and works in a residential care home.

In the evenings he likes to play cards with the staff and other residents. They play a range of different card games which means Roy gets confused with the rules. His carer, Sharon, explains them to him at the start of each game. Sometimes she has to help him part way through the game as well.

Discuss with another person the needs that Roy has to enable him to play games in an evening. What other kind of games could Roy play? Is he likely to need support from his carer? Make a list of his support needs to match the games you have suggested for him.

SNAPSHOT

Mark is recovering from a stroke. He is only 33 years old, which is very young to have a stroke.

When he was first admitted to hospital both a doctor and a physiotherapist examined him to try and find out what had happened.

The physiotherapist could tell from his muscle movement and reflexes that he probably had a stroke. The doctor was able to confirm this through her diagnosis.

own businesses and are self-employed. Physiotherapists are especially trained to help clients overcome physical disability or to recover the use of certain parts of their body after an accident or illness.

We can see in the case of Mark that part of a physiotherapist's work is to assess a patient's needs. They always work with or under the guidance of a doctor.

A physiotherapist also uses recreational activities as a way of helping clients to overcome their physical difficulties.

A physiotherapist often suggests different recreational activities and exercises that will increase the strength, stamina, mobility and balance in different parts of a client's body.

Recreational activities that could be used by a physiotherapist are:

- ball games (to improve the use of hands and arms)

- football games (to improve the use of legs and feet)

- swimming (to improve full body stamina and mobility)

- using weight training (to improve muscle strength).

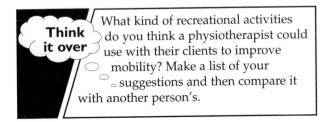

Think it over What kind of recreational activities do you think a physiotherapist could use with their clients to improve mobility? Make a list of your suggestions and then compare it with another person's.

Occupational therapists

These health professionals are also employed by the health and social care services to help clients improve the quality of their lives. Sometimes this means making a client's environment more suitable for them. For example, making changes to the height of worktops in a kitchen for a client in a wheelchair, as well as widening doorways and fitting stair lifts. The occupational therapist does not actually make the changes, they recommend the kind of work that should be done to improve the client's life.

Another part of their job is to recommend suitable creative recreational activities that will help a client to improve their physical or mental ability, such as:

- making toys

- wood-carving

- sewing, knitting

- clothes designing

- painting and drawing.

Some occupational therapists work with clients from the community, as in the case of Christine.

Weight training is used to build up muscles after an illness

Talk it over

Beverley is 18 years old. She is in hospital on the long stay ward because she broke her legs, one arm and the fingers on one hand in a motorbike accident.

The occupational therapist assigned to her ward has been helping her to recover from these injuries. The physiotherapist has organised walking aids and the occupational therapist has organised aids to her everyday living, for example adapted cutlery and drinking cups. Music is available through a portable CD player that is easy to reach and books rest on a book stand that is placed over the bed.

The thing that Beverley has appreciated the most is the typewriter that she has been given to keep her up to date with her assignments for college.

When the occupational therapist organised the typewriter she was not thinking so much about the assignments but more about keeping Beverley motivated and interested in life.

The typewriter has also proved useful in getting Beverley's arm and hand working again.

Working with another person discuss the role of the occupational therapist in the treatment of Beverley's recovery. Make notes on the recreational activities that Beverley is carrying out. How will they help her recovery?

Talk it over

Ranjit is losing his eyesight, which worries him a great deal. He enjoys reading so much.

His occupational therapist has arranged a large magnifying glass for him to use for the moment. This is very useful as it enlarges the letters and he can see them very well.

The therapist has already identified that he will need to become a member of a talking books scheme when he is no longer able to read, but he does not know this yet.

Working with another person discuss how the occupational therapist is supporting Ranjit with his failing eyesight. What will be the benefits to Ranjit of being a member of a talking books club? You might need to think about social and intellectual needs.

Think it over

What skills and knowledge do you think you would need to be a good occupational therapist?

It is important for an occupational therapist to be aware of a wide range of recreational activities and the way they can be used to support clients with their everyday living.

Problems created by serious injury can be overcome by special aids

Play therapists

A play therapist is also employed by the health and social care sector. They usually work with younger clients, especially children. They organise recreational activities that will help the child to learn about their environment or develop new skills through the use of play. The child can also be helped to overcome some learning or social development problems through these kinds of activities. The kinds of recreational activities that could be recommended are:

- books and pictures
- water play

- painting
- role play
- physical play
- theatre.

Play can be a good way to help younger people learn about the world around them and their roles and responsibilities in it.

All the therapists we have just looked at can make your job as a carer much easier. They are there to advise and help you. If you have a client that needs help but you do not know what to do, ask the therapist!

Look it up

Find out how children are supported through crisis by play.

6.4 Barriers to recreational activities

Many people have no problems accessing the recreational activity of their choice. As long as they know where to go and have enough money to pay for it they can gain access to a wide range of activities. However, there are clients who will need support to access the recreational activity of their choice.

We have already touched on some of the difficulties experienced by clients who want to take part in recreational activities but for some reason cannot. We have identified the need for certain physical and mental abilities and of course the age to match the chosen recreational activity. However, there are other barriers to participation, such as:

- cost
- physical access
- availability of recreational activities

- specialist equipment
- specialist clothing
- transport
- social pressure
- cultural pressure
- stereotyping.

Remember!

The activity must match the client's ability!

Cost

Some recreational activities can be costly. For example, if your recreational activity at the

Think it over

Make a list of the recreational activities that you or your friends and family do. Now try and think about the cost of each one. If you do not know the cost you can find out and make a note for your portfolio.

Talk it over

Gillian is a single parent with a low income. She finds it very difficult to make ends meet. Her daughter, who has just started secondary school, wants to learn how to play the guitar.

She has come home from school with a note from the teacher explaining the cost of the equipment. There is just no way Gillian can find the amount of money required.

She has explained to her daughter why she cannot take up guitar classes. Shelley understands, but is still very upset because all her friends are staying behind after school to learn and she wants to join in.

Working with another person discuss the problems that lack of money has caused in this case. You might like to include issues around personal development, peer pressure and guilt.

weekend is attending a football match the cost could be very high. You have to consider the cost of the ticket and maybe the cost of getting to the ground. Not everyone has money to spare for this kind of activity.

It is possible for people to choose recreational activities that are free of charge, especially if cost is the major barrier to participation in other activities.

> **Think it over**
> Make a list of all the free recreational activities that you can think of. Keep it in your portfolio for information.

As health and social care workers we should be able to recommend a range of free or very low cost recreational activities that people can take part in. It is very likely that it is the clients without money who need the recreational activities the most!

Physical access

Clients who have a physical disability may not be able to gain access to some buildings

> **Think it over**
> Nasim is planning a visit to the textile museum in Anytown. He has not been before but has been told that it is really interesting.
>
> He uses walking aids but thinks this should not affect his visit. When he arrives at the museum there is a ramp into the front entrance, which is very useful. However, once inside he finds that the museum has four floors and there are two flights of stairs to each floor.
>
> 'I cannot make it past the first flight', Nasim thought. He went and asked if there was a lift anywhere. 'I am afraid not', he was told.
>
> *How do you think Nasim's recreation trip would have affected him?*

and places. For example, a client who uses a wheelchair for mobility may find that the recreational activity they have chosen takes place in a building with stairs and no lifts. Also some buildings and shops have very narrow doorways that a wheelchair will not fit through.

It is likely that Nasim would be put off trying other places just in case the same thing happened. Even if he decides to check each place first (before turning up) he is still restricted in his development because he cannot make the most of such trips.

In some cinemas, it is still possible to find there is no access for clients with a physical disability because of lack of space. Wheelchairs in aisles can cause a blockage if there is a need to quickly empty the building because of fire. Nowadays most cinemas have removed some seats to make space for people with physical disabilities. However not all recreational places have access for all the people who want to use them.

> **Talk it over**
> Stella is 42 years old and has three young children. She has taken them to a theme park for the day. When they try to go on some of the exciting rides they find that there is a height restriction. Stella is 135cm tall and therefore was not allowed on any of the rides requiring a certain height.
>
> Although her children are taller they were not allowed on because they had to be accompanied by an adult.
>
> Working with another person discuss why you think access was denied to Stella and her children.

Another barrier to physical access is the one Stella experienced.

There are occasions when health and safety have to come first. It is not always about being correct and making sure everyone can do the same things. If there is a real safety risk, then that must be dealt with appropriately.

Availability of recreational activities

Even if a client has access to the recreational activity of choice and they have enough money to pay for it, there is still something that might stop them! It could be that their recreational activity is just not available in their area. So now availability and travel become barriers for the client.

Clients who live in rural (country) areas may not have a great deal of choice about the activities available to them. Country areas do not usually have the same amount of facilities as do town and city areas. For example, if clients live in a city they may have a sports centre close by, but in the country they might only have a church hall in which to play a particular sport, such as badminton.

People who live in town and city areas might have more choice of creative activities, but they have other problems to face.

- Some clients may not be too happy about leaving their homes after dark.

- Other clients might not like to travel alone, especially if they have to go down dark lanes and travel through unsafe areas of the town.

Specialist equipment

Many recreational activities need specialist equipment, materials or other resources. Clients need the money to buy these in order to participate.

It is essential that as health and social care workers we recognise the importance of

Talk it over

Bill lives in a rural area. He has spent all his life there and finds plenty of things to occupy him. His wife has always lived in the town and she is feeling really fed up. She cannot find anything to interest her. Bill is also fed up because his wife is always moaning about having nothing to do.

Whenever she wants to go out she has to drive 16 kilometres to the nearest town. It is costing her a fortune in petrol, which she really cannot afford. Sometimes she does not pay her bills because she wants to keep the money for fuel. Bill has suggested that she tries to find some recreational activities close by.

Because nothing is available, Bill's wife decides to start her own group for people who are interested in creative writing. At the first meeting there were eight people present.

Discuss with another person how the lack of available recreational activities has affected Bill, his wife and other people. Make notes of your discussion for your portfolio.

Think it over

Mrs Mason really enjoys pottery painting. She has just joined an advanced painters class and now needs to buy the following things:

- White china dishes and plates
- China paints including gold leaf paint
- Six different sized paint brushes
- Glazing materials
- A book of painting designs to copy from.

The teacher has said that she will be able to use the kiln (oven) on the premises but will have to pay £2.50 for each item fired.

What other recreational activities can you think of that require specialist equipment? Make a list of them for your portfolio.

clients using the right equipment and clothing. Never take short-cuts with specialised equipment as lives could be lost by using the wrong equipment. It is better to suggest that clients change their recreational activity if they cannot afford to buy the correct equipment and clothing.

Specialist clothing

The cost of specialist clothing and the kind of clothing itself can be a real barrier to recreation for some people.

Talk it over

> Beryl is 18 years old and desperately wants to lose some weight. She has been told by her doctor that she is clinically obese and that swimming would be the best activity for her until she has lost some weight.
>
> When Beryl tried on her swimsuit she just knew she could never go swimming unless she had the pool all to herself.

Discuss with another person the problems Beryl is facing over the need to wear a special outfit. Make notes of your discussions for your portfolio.

In some ways a swimsuit is not specialist clothing because so many people have one. However, Beryl would argue that it is the need to wear a swimsuit that is putting her off swimming because it makes her conscious of her body shape.

For other people specialist clothing is not necessarily about how they look but how they feel.

We have already mentioned cost as a problem in the need for specialised clothing. However, there are some recreational activities in which small changes could be made to allow more people to participate.

Talk it over

> Phillip wants to play lawn tennis with his friends at the local tennis club. He has saved enough money to buy himself a good tennis raquet.
>
> When he goes along to join he is told membership is £150 a year, but he can pay for it monthly through his bank.
>
> 'I can manage that', he thought. But his next shock came when he was told he could only wear white clothing on the tennis court. This included his shorts, tracksters, shirts and sweaters. 'I can't possibly afford that as well', he thought. 'I give up!'

Discuss with another person ways in which the tennis club could have helped Phillip overcome the need for specialist clothing. Make notes of your discussions.

Look it up

Working with others choose two of the following activities and find out what clothing is required for each of them. You could make a poster to present your findings to others.

- Diving
- Horse-riding
- Ice hockey
- Painting for small children.

Transport

We have already touched upon the need for easily available transport for people to be able to reach the recreational activity of their choice. Do you remember the case of Bill's wife (page 198). She had to travel long distances to her choice and it was costing her a fortune!

It is possible that the friends could ask a parent to collect them after a concert but that is not really fair to the parent concerned.

Another option might be to ask a parent to meet them at the railway station when they arrive at midnight, but that still has problems. What about a taxi as a solution?

> **Think it over**
> What other problems would organising a taxi raise?

We have now come full circle back to the cost of the night out. It might be that in this case there is no suitable solution until one of the friends learns to drive. What do you think?

Social pressure

We all like to do similar things to our friends. If our friends like to play football, so do we. If our friends take up photography, so do we (if we can afford it!).

This type of pressure is called 'peer pressure'. Your friends may suggest that you do the same things as them or that they join you in the things that you are doing! Peer pressure is very strong when we are adolescents, but it can also be important to adults.

This kind of pressure can work against us when we want to take up a recreational activity that will make us different from the crowd.

Social pressure is very strong. It is hard to go against the expectations other people have of us. But we need to remember that our recreational activities are for us and not for other people.

When we are encouraging our clients to do activities it would be helpful if we could suggest activities that fit in with society's expectations, however we need to be careful not to stereotype individuals. As carers we should be aware of the social pressures on our clients and support them in overcoming these if necessary.

> **Talk it over**
>
> Selina is a care worker in a sheltered housing complex for older people. One of her client's, Veronica, has decided to take up line dancing as a recreational activity.
>
> Her friends think that this is really funny. Sometimes Veronica gets a bit depressed because she cannot get anyone to go with her.
>
> Selina suggested asking the organisers of the line dancing to put on a session in the sheltered housing community room. When they arrived and started playing the music several residents went to see what it was all about.
>
> Before you knew it three of them were having a go at the dancing.
>
> Discuss with another person the way Selina has helped to overcome some of the social pressure barriers to Veronica's recreational activity. Make notes for your portfolio.

Line dancing is a beneficial activity

What other actions could the care worker have taken to help support Veronica with her chosen recreational activity?

The way we are brought up by our families or guardians can affect the kinds of recreational activities that we want to do. For example:

- if a person has been brought up to go walking every weekend it is possible that when they become adults they will do the same with their family

- if a client has been brought up to sit in front of the television each night of the week they will probably do that all of their lives, and so will their family (unless they can be encouraged to change!).

Cultural pressure

In some cultures it is not acceptable for people to mix with others during recreational activity – for example, keeping males and females separate during recreation time. It is important that these cultural barriers are recognised and appropriate action taken that will allow people to fully participate.

Talk it over

Last week, Shaheen's best friend, Miriam, told her that the council had agreed to a 'women only' swimming session twice a week.

Shaheen cannot wait to go, especially as her family are happy for her to attend with Miriam.

Working with another person discuss the reasons why you think the council had agreed to a women-only session in the first place. Include in your discussions the effects this could have on Shaheen and her family.

Do you remember Shaheen on page 186? She felt that mixed sex swimming wasn't suitable for her. The good news is that her town council has agreed to women-only sessions.

? Did you know?

You can show respect for a client by accepting the way they live and trying to help them obey the rules of their culture.

Stereotyping

Stereotyping people is something we should try to avoid. We already know that people are individuals, that we all like doing different things for our recreational activities, no matter what our age or our ability.

It is possible that you have heard some people (especially older people) talking about stereotypical differences between males and females. Boys for example like to:

- play with cars
- mend things
- play rough games
- climb trees and do other dangerous activities.

Talk it over

Ann is a wheelchair user. But she wants to participate in the paraolympics and has begun her training as an athlete.

Last week she overheard two people talking about her. They were laughing and saying that no-one could be an athlete if they were in a wheelchair.

'Just wait until I come back with an Olympic gold medal,' thought Ann, 'I will show them!'

Discuss with another person how Ann is likely to have felt when she heard these stereotypical remarks. How could they have acted as a barrier to her determination?

But girls are not like this! They like to:

- clean the house
- cook meals
- play with dolls
- carry out safe, gentle activities.

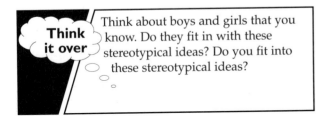

Think it over
Think about boys and girls that you know. Do they fit in with these stereotypical ideas? Do you fit into these stereotypical ideas?

The chances are that the people you have thought of do not fit easily into these stereotypical beliefs about what they should or should not do or like. It could be they enjoy a mix of different things. Most of us do!

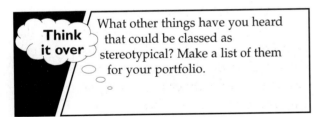

Think it over
What other things have you heard that could be classed as stereotypical? Make a list of them for your portfolio.

It is possible that Ann could have been so upset that she withdrew from her chosen activity. She might have felt the need to act as these two people expected her to!

Think about Veronica who wanted to do line dancing. It should not have mattered that she was an older person, but her friends were behaving in a stereotypical way by laughing at her because they felt she was too old.

Try it out Working with another person ask 10 people from different age groups about the recreational activities that the following people are likely to choose.

- People over 65
- Wheelchair users
- Teenagers.

When you get your results find out if the answers are stereotypical. For example, have all 10 people said older people like to carry out a gentle activity or teenagers have loads of energy?

We need to be careful to always see our clients as individual people. Just because they are male or female, have or have not a particular ability, or belong to a certain group of the population, does not mean they will be the same as the others from their group. Everyone is different!

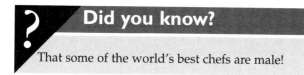

Did you know?

That some of the world's best chefs are male!

6.5 Health and safety factors in recreational activities

If you are involved in suggesting recreational activities for your clients you should know about health and safety recommendations.

Look it up

Read Unit 4 to find out more about health and safety rules and regulations.

It is possible that some physical (exercise-based) recreational activities could be a danger to the client or other people involved in the activity. For example:

- Rugby players often suffer from head and neck injuries. They usually have teeth missing!

- Skiers may break a leg.

- Bungee jumpers can damage their backs and eyes.

Any recreational activity that involves people running, jumping and twisting can be a danger, if only from pulled muscles. However, if there is more than one person involved the

Bungee jumping can cause injury

dangers become more serious. People often crash into each other. Teeth are knocked out and skulls have even been fractured.

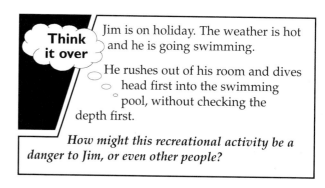

Think it over

Jim is on holiday. The weather is hot and he is going swimming.

He rushes out of his room and dives head first into the swimming pool, without checking the depth first.

How might this recreational activity be a danger to Jim, or even other people?

Jim has not taken care to check that the water is deep enough for him to dive into the pool safely. It is possible for a person to break their neck from this kind of action. There is also the added danger of landing on someone who is already in the water.

Many physical games are played and carried out according to certain rules and regulations. These must be followed to keep safe. Look at the spidergram to identify the kinds of activities that have safety rules and regulations.

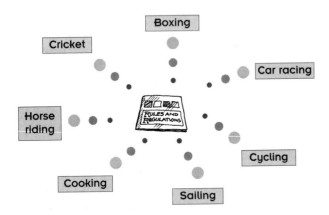

The kinds of things you are likely to have found out are:

- Cooking — health and hygiene rules, fire safety
- Boxing — gloves, mouthguard, no hitting below the belt
- Cycling — helmet, joint pads, gloves, following laws of the road
- Rugby — protective helmet, mouthguard, tackling according to the rules
- Canoeing — helmet, life jacket, wet suit, safety personnel on duty
- Cricket — protective pads, helmet, gloves
- Horse-riding — helmet, protective clothing

It is not just 'dangerous' activities that have safety requirements and special equipment. Any recreational activity that requires physical movement needs to meet health and safety requirements. If physical recreational activity is being planned you will need to think about:

- the space available – is there enough room to move safely?
- suitability of the floor surface – is it polished and slippery, could it cause an accident?
- the state of the equipment – is it in a good state of repair or is it broken and unsafe to use?
- if the activity is inside – are there any fire exits?
- where the fire extinguishers are kept – and can you use one?
- is there a 'first-aider' available – do you know where to find one?
- how you can get help if you need to.

Another thing we should think about is the health and fitness of the client who wants to participate in the recreational activity. The last thing we want is a client's health being harmed because of the recreational activity they are engaged in.

It is always useful to check that a client is:

- using the right equipment

- wearing the right clothes

- physically fit

- capable of the activity

Think it over

Brian has had a heart attack within the last five years. This has left him with angina. He gets chest pains whenever he tries to do too much.

He has decided that he wants to play cricket for the local team! His care worker suggests that he visits his GP to make sure that he is OK to go ahead. His GP suggests that the short sharp running involved in cricket might be a problem and suggests swimming instead.

What do you think the benefits are of Brian checking out with his doctor the suitability of his chosen recreational activity? How do you think Brian will feel about his care worker suggesting he visit the doctor?

- the right age

- requiring supervision.

If you are ever in any doubt about a client's health, fitness or capability for joining in physical or other activities, you should check with a senior member of staff. They will be able to find out from the client's doctor if it is acceptable for them to join in. It is especially important to check safety for clients who have:

- had a heart attack

- asthma

- muscle diseases

- joint problems (such as arthritis)

- breathing problems

- just got over an illness

- just had an operation

- may be pregnant.

There are many more conditions that you would need to check for. If ever you are in doubt, ASK. It is always better to be safe than sorry!

Unit 6 Assessment

For this assessment, you need to produce a report about **locally** available recreational activities and facilities. It must include:

- details of how the activities and facilities could benefit clients

- description of available activities for a client group

- identification of barriers to participation

- consideration of health and safety features for the clients.

For this unit you will have the opportunity to work towards a pass, merit or distinction grade.

The activities are ordered in such a way as to guide you through this assessment. The levels of assessment are clearly indicated as:

- P for Pass

- M for Merit

- D for Distinction.

You may wish to discuss with your tutor the level of activities you do.

All students must complete the first four pass activities to achieve the minimum for Unit 6.

Activity 1P

- Describe your local area. This area will have been identified by your group and your tutor. The description could usefully be in a map or some other kind of visual form. The area will have to be realistic in terms of area and distance, because you will have to investigate the recreational facilities available within this area.

- Within this local area, you need to correctly identify what local facilities are available. You do not have to consider particular client groups at this stage. Useful sources of information are outlined at the end of this unit. You will need to go out to research

this, and this can be done in groups with the information pooled at the end of your researches. However, you will need to produce your own report of available facilities. You can make this part of the report as visual as you like, with photographs, images, different text, colours.

Activity 2P

- Consider one particular client group: this could be children, elders, people with special needs, your own age group. You are now going to describe how this client group benefits from at least two different facilities you have identified.

Physical, social and intellectual benefits should be described.

You could carry out this activity by drawing up a list or table, and entering the various parts of the activity within the table.

Activity 3P

- Correctly identify any health and safety issues related to the activities available within the facilities you have described. These issues could be for specific client groups or for the activity. For example, swimming for children or people with special needs would require constant supervision by high levels of qualified staff. Swimming might also involve use of special equipment which may need checking each time before use.

Activity 4P

This activity relates to your client group and activity/facilities you identified in Activity 2P.

- Identify any common barriers to participation in the activities at this facility. It could be that the activity is very expensive, or is not on a bus route, or is only open at certain hours of the day which would not make it commonly accessible.

The barriers may also be health and safety features: for example, certain equipment might be needed for health and safety purposes which might be expensive or not easily available.

You can provide this information in a list or table.

Working towards a merit grade

To achieve a merit grade you must complete all the activities in the pass section. In addition you must complete the steps to Activities 2, 3 and 4 below.

Activity 2M

- Consider either recreational activities for one client group or recreational activities in general, and describe why you think they are beneficial to health and well-being. Use the headings: physical, intellectual or social to demonstrate that you understand the benefits of recreation. If you are going to undertake a general description, use three or four activities (e.g. walking in the country, going to the cinema, swimming) to guide your work.

You must be able to demonstrate a sound understanding of benefits of recreation in this section.

You could carry out a small survey of people undergoing an activity to make this interesting for you. Discuss this with your tutor. You could also make use of your own involvement in recreational activities to guide your work.

Activity 3M

- In Activity 2P you described some health and safety issues relating to the facility/activity you were working on. Describe how these health and safety issues could be addressed. For example, if you identified the need to supply a number of qualified staff at a swimming class for children, you might suggest that parents with swimming skills or lifesaving or first-aid qualifications could accompany the children/class to ensure everyone has an opportunity to participate.

Activity 4M

In Activity 4P you identified some barriers which might prevent individuals taking part in certain activities or accessing facilities.

- How can these barriers be overcome? Relate this to specific recreational facilities. For example, a cinema might not have wheelchair or disabled access. You could suggest that a ramp be made available and that space be provided for wheelchairs.

You may obtain some information from local council offices, for example a guide, to access in your local area. You could use this as a basis for this activity, but you will still need to visit at least two facilities yourself. This can be done in groups or pairs, but you will need to provide an individual report.

Working towards a distinction

To gain a distinction you must complete the activities for the pass and merit grades. In addition you must complete the steps to Activities 2 and 4 below.

Activity 2D

In Activity 2M you looked at the benefits of recreational activities, either in general or specifically. To extend this, you are now going to analyse the use of recreational benefits by describing how the needs of a client group are met by taking part in a particular recreational activity. For example, one client group may be elderly people living alone or in relatively isolated circumstances. Their need might be for more social interaction.

The recreational activity might be going to a day centre once or twice a week to meet friends for lunch and have a quiz or games afternoon.

The benefits could well be intellectual as well as social. If they took part in any physical activity, like swimming at a leisure centre close by as part of the weekly range of activities offered by the day centre, the benefits would be physical as well as social and emotional.

You cold present this in small case studies or 'snapshots' as given in the textbook.

Activity 4D

Looking back at barriers to using facilities which you did in Activity 4M, can you suggest alternatives to this facility, and explain why (justify) you think they could be alternatives? For example, if you looked at the cinema and found that it was not able to provide disabled access, perhaps you could suggest that a film or video club could be set up. Or if you found that the local leisure centre had limited hours of opening and was very expensive, you could suggest that the local school, which opened its pool at alternative times and was very inexpensive, would still provide a venue for swimming.

You need to relate this to one particular client group: in the examples above, the groups might be disabled teenagers, or elderly people hoping to start a swimming club.

Some useful sources of information

Church/religious group newsletters
Cinemas/theatres
Community volunteer groups
Craft centres
Day centres
Directories of local organisations
Health education services
Leisure centres
Libraries
Local shops
Newsletters
Newspapers
Nurseries

Physically handicapped and able-bodied (PHAB) youth facilities
Post offices
Schools and colleges
Sports centres
Youth clubs.

Check your knowledge

1 What does the word recreation mean?

2 Describe one recreational activity which would help with mobility (physical) for a toddler.

3 Describe one activity which would help improve relationships (social) for adolescents.

4 Describe one activity which would help keep an active mind (intellectual) for an older person.

5 In one or two sentences, describe the work of:
   a   a play therapist
   b   an occupational therapist.

6 Kitty is being discharged from hospital following a car accident where she badly injured her hand. How could a physiotherapist help in her rehabilitation?

7 Tom cannot afford to go ten-pin bowling with his friends because the bus fare is so expensive.
   This is an example of:
   a   lack of interest
   b   social behaviour
   c   financial barrier
   d   health and safety regulation.

8 Specialist equipment for recreational activities means:
   a   having to provide transport for the event
   b   certain items may have to be provided before the client can participate

c social services will be required to provide the equipment

d health and safety regulations must be maintained.

9 All Jane's friends try to make her go clubbing with them, but she does not like the places they visit.

This is an example of:

a intellectual pressure

b social pressure

c financial pressure

d family pressure.

10 Motivation to do something means:

a going fast

b a nervous disorder

c something only business executives are involved in

d being stimulated to act.

Exploring Physical Care

Unit 7

This unit explores why some people need help and assistance with their everyday physical care. You will find out about the kinds of everyday activities that clients with physical care needs may require help with. At the same time, we will explore the kinds of equipment and aids to everyday living that can be used to improve the quality of life for the client.

You will also find out about the best ways to make sure that health and safety requirements are met. These include ways of keeping both yourself and your client safe whilst using aids for everyday activities.

You can also practice your skills and apply your knowledge for providing physical care. You can demonstrate your ability to help clients with their eating and drinking, or to support them whilst they are dressing and maintaining their personal hygiene routines.

The unit helps you carry out an investigation into the care needs of an individual and the kinds of physical care aids that are available to you.

You need to learn about:

- the reasons why people need physical care
- the settings, agencies and personnel involved in physical care
- the relevant health and safety issues.

7.1 Reasons why people need physical care

The reasons why people need physical care are likely to be broad and varied, however we can say that in general most people need physical assistance for one (or more) of the following reasons:

Age-related reasons for needing physical care

Infants and young children

We already know that babies, infants and young children cannot take care of themselves.

Talk it over

Jason is three months old. He has been crying for over an hour now. His nappy is wet and badly needs changing. The blankets and sheets on his bed are wet underneath him.

He is also due a feed and so is feeling very hungry and sorry for himself.

Discuss with another person the reasons why Jason needs help to have his care needs met to allow him to be comfortable. Make a list of them under the heading of 'Babies: reasons for physical care'.

This is the most vulnerable time of our lives. We are completely dependent on someone else meeting all our physical care needs.

Have your discussions highlighted the fact that Jason:

- cannot feed himself
- cannot change his bedding
- cannot get out of his wet nappy
- cannot change into dry clothes himself.

Advancing age

Loss of mobility

Many people who reach the other end of their lives (old age) need help and support to meet their physical care needs. The problem is it can be very difficult to accept or even ask for help when we become older. Many older people are proud that they have never had any assistance in their life.

Read the diary of Lizzie, who is aged 82, to see what she feels are her physical care needs.

Lizzie is in real need of help with her physical care needs and her everyday activities. It is easy to see that she is not eating properly and her hygiene routines are not good. She is old and tired – she says her age 'has caught up with her'. It looks as if her arthritis has affected her mobility as she cannot manage the stairs anymore and everything has become a real effort for her.

Loss of mobility for older people usually means that the person requires help and support with some part of their physical care needs.

We can see that Lizzie needs a lot of support with her physical care needs. She needs help with:

- washing and personal hygiene
- dressing

Monday 15 May 2000

I wish I did not have to spend so much time on my own. I miss Jim, now that he has gone! I know I should pull myself together and get on with life but it is so hard. I cannot get to the shops without help any more and I don't like bothering my neighbour too much. Anyway, there is no point going out without Jim.

I feel tired all the time. I do not have the energy to get washed every day so now I just wash myself when I can. I suppose it's enough. It will have to be, I don't have anyone to help me. Oh dear! I think it is about 3 weeks since I last had a good wash, but I can't get upstairs to the bathroom any more. I don't think I've ever seen the house so dirty. What would Jim say I wonder?

It would be easier if I didn't have this blooming arthritis in my hands and back. But it is just getting worse. I cannot open tins and jars any more, I am really fed up of jam sandwiches, soon I won't be able to make food to eat! And then what will I do?

I can't remember the last time I fastened all the buttons on my dress.

The doctor is due to visit next week, maybe I will ask him for some iron tablets. They should help. I do hope so. I am really frightened of what the future holds for me!

- shopping
- cleaning and cooking
- moving about the house (getting up to the bathroom).

Talk it over

Working in pairs discuss with another person the reasons why Lizzie needs help with her care needs. Make a list of them under the heading of 'Older age', and keep the list.

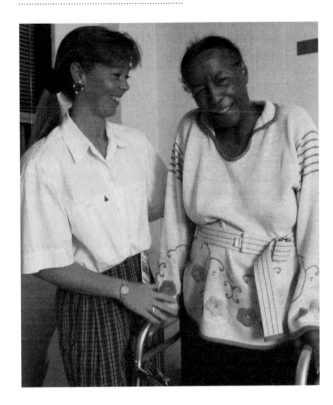

We can say that lack of mobility is a major reason for Lizzie needing care from others.

Deteriorating sight and hearing

When something deteriorates it means that it is not working as well as it should, often because it is 'wearing out'. This 'wearing out' can happen to the human body as well as to mechanical things, such as car engines. Common parts of the body that often 'wear out' are eyesight and hearing.

Think it over

What do you think happens as eyesight and hearing begin to deteriorate? It might help to think about older people you know who wear glasses or have cataracts, and maybe you know someone with a hearing aid. Make notes of your thoughts for your portfolio.

Deteriorating eyesight

If deterioration in the eyes is very severe, people can lose their eyesight altogether. This means that they are likely to need support with their physical care and their everyday living activities.

People who have deteriorating eyesight can easily injure themselves, especially if they are not used to the changes in their vision. They forget to look for obstacles in their path, or they move too quickly not realising there are dangers around them, like Debrah, who has burned herself twice.

Talk it over

Debrah is 72 years old. She has been wearing glasses for 30 years. Each time she has gone for an eye test the prescription has become stronger and stronger.

Now she can only see a few inches in front of her. Everything is blurred and very faint. When she is walking or moving around the house, she needs to feel her way very carefully. She has burned herself twice when she has been cooking her meals.

Working with others discuss the reasons why Debrah needs help with her physical care needs. Make a list of these and put them under the heading 'Deteriorating eyesight'.

Deteriorating hearing

People who have lost or are losing their hearing will also need assistance with their physical care needs for everyday living. They are likely to need help to communicate with others in a variety of different settings – for example, when out shopping, in the home or in day care settings.

The amount of care and support they need will depend on how severe the deterioration is. For many older people hearing loss starts off gradually and they find themselves asking people to repeat what has been said. However, as the hearing loss becomes greater they will no longer hear sounds made by things such as the telephone, door bell and television.

People having difficulty hearing are likely to need some kind of help and support from carers. They may need someone to tell them when the phone is ringing or when there is someone at the door. These are simple things and yet without them the quality of life for the affected person is poor.

We need to think about the safety of deaf people. They cannot hear fire or smoke alarms and when preparing and cooking food they will not hear the sound of 'boiling'.

Talk it over

Rose is completely deaf. But she has begun to get used to it. Tomorrow she is going on a day trip with the other residents of Holly House Sheltered Accommodation to do their Christmas shopping.

She has to be up and ready to travel by 8.00am. When the warden goes to check that everyone is ready she finds that Rose is missing. All the residents have been knocking on her door to tell her to get a move on but she has not responded to anyone. The warden dashes off to get the key to the door.

Discuss with another person the reasons why Rose needs to have her physical care needs met by others. Make a list of them and put them under the heading of 'Deteriorating hearing'.

Not only does Rose need help with being awakened in the morning (for special events), but she is also likely to need help when she is out shopping. For example, having a conversation with shop assistants will be difficult, as will asking for directions or ordering food in cafe.

Memory loss

People suffering from 'memory loss' will need help with their everyday living activities and physical care needs. Loss of memory can happen at any age, particularly if a person has suffered head injuries in an accident. However, the most common kind of memory loss is the sort brought on by diseases such as Alzheimer's. This disease destroys the cells of the brain so that eventually the person will lose all their faculties.

Talk it over

Megan is 69 years old. She developed Alzheimer's disease two years ago. Her husband is caring for her.

When Megan is feeling well she loves to do the preparation and cooking of all the meals. The problem is she often forgets half way through what she was doing and goes on to do something else.

The last time that Megan went out on her own, she forgot how to get home again. Fortunately one of her neighbours saw her wandering the streets and brought her home safely.

This morning Megan has dressed herself but has forgotten to put any underwear or shoes on.

Working with another person identify the reasons why Megan has to be helped with her physical care needs. Make a list of them for your portfolio. Use the heading 'Memory loss'.

Long-term illness

Some people need to be given assistance with their everyday living because of long-term illness. Such an illness is unlikely to respond to treatment over a short period of time. Long-term illnesses that need physical care include arthritis and Parkinson's disease.

Arthritis

Many people suffer from some form of arthritis. This is a disease which affects the joints of the body and they become painful. The most common joints to be affected are:

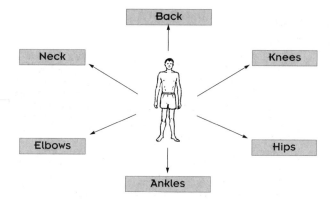

These joints are under the most wear and tear. The knees especially have to cope with all the physical activities that we do. The knee joints carry our weight every day and are the joints in the body most likely to suffer injury.

Talk it over

Stephen has had rheumatoid arthritis since he was 32. His doctor told him that this form of arthritis was the most severe kind. It was likely to cause major mobility problems for him in time.

At first his joints would swell and he would feel hot and sick, and as time has gone on his joints have become very swollen and stiff.

He has good days and bad days. Sometimes he can go for weeks looking after himself. On other occasions he needs more support from his carers because movement is difficult and he feels so sick and unwell.

Discuss with another person the reasons why Stephen needs to ask his carers for help. Make a list of them in your portfolio under the heading 'Arthritis'.

Stephen needs physical care when he has a bad attack of arthritis. This is when he feels sick and in pain. It is also the time when his joints are stiff and cannot move. So we can see that the reasons for Stephen needing physical care are lack of mobility and illness.

Parkinson's disease

This is a condition of the brain that slowly causes the muscles of the body to become rigid (stiff and solid). This means that the person's face becomes stiff and expressionless and they find it impossible to make the muscles move into a smile or frown. Arms and legs also stop working properly and the person may look as if they are going to fall over.

Many people also develop 'the shakes', which are known as tremors. Drugs can help many people who have Parkinson's. However, someone with the disease is going to need more care as the disease gets worse.

The after-effects of a stroke or heart attack

A person usually has a heart attack when the blood vessels in the heart have become too narrow to let the blood pass through. So the heart is starved of oxygen and the person has a heart attack. A stroke is exactly the same thing, except the narrow blood vessels are in the brain.

Many people need help with their physical care needs as a result of strokes and heart attacks.

Strokes

People who have had a stroke may be affected in some or all of the following ways:

- loss of movement down one side of the body

- loss of some speech

- possible loss of some memory

- paralysis down one side of the face

- not be able to see properly

- experience some mental disability.

When a client is recovering after a stroke, they will need a great deal of support with their everyday living activities, especially if

Talk it over

John Bishop is 56 years old. He had a stroke three weeks ago and has been in hospital ever since.

He is due to go home today and his wife is coming to collect him at 10.00am. She has been talking to the doctors who have told her that John will need a lot of support and help over the next few weeks, to help him recover from the effects of the stroke.

Mary Bishop knows it is going to be hard work helping John, because he will need most things doing for him for the next few weeks. He is feeding himself now but still needs help to get dressed and wash himself. He cannot walk without help so he will need assistance going to the toilet.

His speech is still 'slurred', so Mary finds it hard to understand him. But the speech therapist has explained that his speech will get better with practice.

Hopefully, John will make a good recovery and be able to care for himself before too long.

Discuss with another person the reasons why John has to be helped with his care needs now that he has had a stroke. Make a list of the reasons and put them into a list in your portfolio.

Talk it over

Brian is 50 years old. He has just had a heart attack. He was in hospital for two weeks but now he is home again. The heart attack has left him frightened of it happening again.

He has to take things easy for a while. He has been told not to lift or push anything heavy and definitely not to drive for the next six weeks.

He is going to take more regular exercise now, with advice from his doctor, and watch his diet – less fat and a bit less alcohol.

Working with another person make a list of all the reasons why Brian has to have help with his physical care needs over the next few weeks and months.

the stroke was a severe one. On the other hand, if the stroke is very mild it is possible for people not to realise that they have had one.

Heart attacks

Many people who have a heart attack make a good recovery. But they may need help and care for the first few weeks of their recovery. Most people however can still care for their own everyday living needs.

? Did you know?

Heart attacks are the biggest killer in this country.

It is usually men aged between 35 and 64 who are most 'at risk' from a heart attack. Why do you think this is?

Brian is going to need help with the housework because he must not lift or push heavy things, such as a hoover. He is not allowed to drive for at least six weeks, so he is going to need help with transport.

In some cases, people can be very ill, especially in the early days following a heart attack. In such cases they will need to have all their physical care needs met by another person.

Accidents

Accidents happen suddenly, which is why they are called 'sudden events'. The results can be devastating for the victim and their family. Serious accidents, such as car crashes, can leave the victim requiring constant care for the rest of their lives. Imagine the care needs required for accident victims confined to bed with little or no body movement.

Of course not all accidents are that serious, even so in many cases the victim will need some kind of support until their injuries are healed and they can care for themselves again.

Christopher Reeve

Acute illness

An acute illness means 'sudden' illness. This is often a short-lasting illness that happens without warning. For example, a young person (or older one) may suddenly develop acute appendicitis (inflammation of the appendix) and have to have it removed.

Try it out

Prevention of accidents is seen as a priority area for government health targeting.

1 As a group, make a list like the one below, to identify as many physical care needs as you can that arise from accidents. You may think of accidents you or your friends and family have had that resulted in needing physical care.

2 Why do you think the government is keen to promote accident prevention in its 'Healthier Nation' document?

Accident	Resulting physical problem	Resulting physical need
Slipped on ice	Broken leg	Personal hygiene, dressing

SNAPSHOT

Shamina has been rushed into hospital with a high temperature and pain in her eyes when she looks at lights. She looks very ill and has no energy.

The doctor believes she may have developed meningitis. She has been given antibiotics and will need to be in hospital for some time.

• *Is this acute or chronic illness?*

• *What physical care needs might she have?*

! Reminder!

Acute   = Short, sudden, less than 3 months
Chronic = Slow, long-lasting, more than 3 months

Long-term disabilities

Long-lasting disabilities mean the person has to have their care needs met for a long time, if not permanently. These disabilities include:

- osteoporosis
- arthritis
- chronic bronchitis
- emphysema
- heart disease
- cerebral palsy.

Talk it over

Miriam is 12 years old and is a wheelchair user. She has been diagnosed as having a serious heart condition that requires a heart transplant so that she can live a full and active life.

At the moment she cannot walk without getting out of breath, she cannot climb stairs at all and has to be carried if there is no lift.

All her school work is carried out at home as she cannot stay in school because she needs to have a carer with her all the time.

Discuss with another person the reasons why Miriam has to have her physical care needs met by others. Make a list of them for your portfolio.

Types of activity requiring help

The types of activity that people need help with varies from one person to another, however there are some activities that need more help than others, such as:

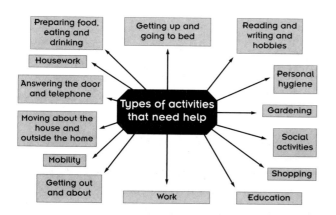

Talk it over

Irene has been involved in an accident that has left her with severe memory loss.

Her husband is frightened of leaving her in the house alone. The last time he left her, while he went shopping, she left the house in her night-clothes and the police found her wandering in the street. Fortunately, they knew who she was and brought her straight back home.

Irene still likes to do the cooking but she can never remember how to do it. She becomes angry and aggressive because she cannot remember and she thinks that she should. The last meal Irene cooked consisted of rice pudding and baked potatoes because she became confused with the first and second courses.

If Irene's husband does not remind her, she forgets to wash and get dressed in a morning. She would be quite happy just sitting in a chair all day.

Working with another person make a duty roster for Irene's husband that will remind him of the activities that she needs help with. You could start with the first thing in the morning. So the first one on the list might look like this:

7.30am: Help Irene to get out of bed, take her to the toilet.

When you have finished the duty roster compare yours with another pair's work. Are there any differences?

Now that we have some idea of the activities that clients might need help with let us take each one individually and explore them further.

Getting up and going to bed

Some people are not able to get up or go to bed because of physical disability.

If you are helping people to get up in the morning it could be as simple as passing them a stick or moving a wheelchair close to the bed so that they can climb out of bed themselves. In some cases you might need to use lifting equipment, such as a hoist, so that the client can be moved from the bed to a chair. If this is the case you will need to have had training to carry out this kind of support for clients.

Dressing and undressing is often part of getting up or going to bed, and so is washing and toileting. There are also many other activities that can help to support our clients at this time. It could be simply passing a client their book and reading glasses once they are in bed or getting them a drink if one is requested.

Personal hygiene

Many clients need help with maintaining their personal hygiene. For some people this could mean complete support with a bath or shower (the carer washing and drying them) or just help getting into a bath or shower.

Whatever the help needed, clients should be treated with sensitivity and care so that they feel supported and valued.

Talk it over

Working with another person make a list of the feelings a client might have if they have to be assisted with:

- washing themselves
- combing and washing their hair
- being taken to the toilet.

Think it over

How would you feel if you had to rely on another person to take you to the toilet?

Getting out and about

Many clients need help getting out of the home. For example, a client might need to visit the hospital or require support with their shopping or gardening. In many cases clients will also need help to carry out their social activities, such as visiting friends or social clubs.

Think it over

Agnes is 74 years old. She lives in a rural area with hardly any public transport service. She is a member of Bury Ladies Association and enjoys going to the music concerts and other events they organise.

She has to rely on Tony the Transport man. He is the husband of one of the members. He says he does not mind collecting her and taking her home once a month. However, Agnes is beginning to feel embarrassed about having to keep asking him.

Why do you think Agnes needs transport help in this case? Why do you think she is beginning to feel embarrassed at having to keep asking Tony for a lift?

Shopping

Shopping for food, clothes and other items is an essential part of everyday living, but for some clients going shopping can be a difficult task.

Talk it over

Billy is 56. He had a stroke several months ago and he is recovering quite nicely now. However, he still gets confused if he goes out of doors on his own.

He has just noticed that he has used the last of his tinned soups and vegetables. He finished the food in the fridge and freezer three days ago.

He has a pile of bills still waiting to be paid. He just does not know how he is going to manage.

Discuss with another person the type of activities that Billy needs support with. Make a list of them for your portfolio.

Billy needs support with a range of activities. He could definitely benefit from someone doing the shopping for him, and it would also be helpful if someone could take him to do his own shopping. The bills need to be paid so that he can stop worrying. It might be necessary to ask a carer to pay the bills for him whilst they are out shopping.

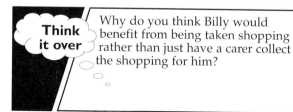

Think it over

Why do you think Billy would benefit from being taken shopping rather than just have a carer collect the shopping for him?

Helping with the garden

Gardening

For many people gardening is a pleasurable activity, but for some clients having a garden can bring problems as well as pleasure.

Talk it over

Megan cannot stand looking at her garden anymore. If Gareth was still alive it would not look like that at all. The trouble is she cannot get down on her hands and knees to weed the garden herself, and it grows so fast.

The last time she went down the garden path she tripped over the branches of a small bush that had grown across the path. She finds it difficult to lift her feet high enough to step over the branches.

Her grandson, Tom, slipped last week on the green stuff that has formed on the path.

Working with another person discuss the kind of help that Megan would benefit from. How would the help you have suggested improve her life? Make notes for your portfolio.

Social activities

Taking part in social activities is central to the health and well-being of everyone. People who need care from others could definitely benefit from taking part in social activities.

A social activity usually involves other people. For example, Agnes going to the Bury Ladies meetings is a social activity. Going out to visit friends or having them come to visit you is also a social activity.

Remember that people from different cultural groups are likely to choose social activities that suit them and their beliefs or their society's expectations. For example, it is not always appropriate to suggest activities that involve both sexes or alcohol. This means that as carers we should be aware of the needs of our clients and try to accommodate their cultural diversity.

Think it over

Make a list of all the activities that you like to do that could be classed as social. Compare your list to another person's to see if there are any differences.

Talk it over

Javed has been housebound for seven years now due to a serious accident when he was 17. He cannot walk at all and only has limited movement in his left arm. Fortunately he is right-handed, so he can still write and draw. He loves anything at all to do with painting and artists.

He is feeling very lonely as no-one except his family visits him. Most of his friends have stopped coming round because he found video games boring.

The last time Ash came round he brought bottled beer with him which upset Javed's mother and made her ban him from the house.

Working with another person make a list of social activities that would be suitable for Javed. Remember to take into account his preferences and likes and dislikes.

In your discussions did you think about social activities that could take place outside the house as well as indoors? It might be that Javed just needs help with transport to enable him to take part in many more activities.

Moving about the house and outside

For many clients with physical care needs help to move around their home or outdoors is essential if they are to lead fulfilling lives. For example, someone might need help to get out of bed and get dressed in the morning. Other people might need help to get from one room to another, and some people might have a problem getting up or down the stairs.

Preparing meals, eating and drinking

Some clients need support to prepare their food and drink. This could be in the form of a carer providing physical assistance, such as lifting heavy pans on and off the cooker, or providing special equipment, such as a potato-peeling machine.

However, some clients need very specific assistance with eating and drinking. For those who have no movement in their arms or hands this may mean holding cups and cutlery for them.

Talk it over

Jade is 13 months old and learning to hold her own cup. Fortunately it has a lid attached to it as Jade is in the habit of swinging it around and 'putting it to bed with teddy'.

Working with another person discuss the type of help Jade needs with her drinking activities. Can you think of the support she is likely to need with her food preparation and eating as well? Make a note of your discussions for your portfolio.

Housework

Many clients require help with housework. The type of help required will depend on the client's ability to carry out certain tasks themselves. It might also depend on how much money they have to spend on house-cleaning support.

Talk it over

Virginia has been ill for three months. She lives on her own and cannot cope with the housework.

She is managing to prepare and cook all her own meals now, but cleaning the windows and stairs is out of the question.

She dusts and hoovers about once a week, which is fine by her, but she hates the thought of the bathroom not being cleaned properly, especially as her illness involves using the toilet a lot.

Working with another person discuss the type of assistance Virginia needs. How often do you think Virginia will need help – every day, once a year? What do you think? Make notes of your discussions for your portfolio.

Talk it over

Working with another person discuss the importance of being able to see to read and write.

Make a list of all the daily activities you can think of that would require being able to see to read or write. Compare your list with our spidergram.

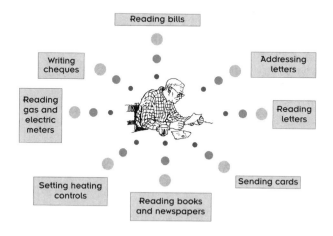

Reading bills

Writing cheques

Addressing letters

Reading gas and electric meters

Reading letters

Setting heating controls

Reading books and newspapers

Sending cards

Hearing and answering the telephone and doorbell

For people who are deaf, hearing and answering the telephone or doorbell can be a problem. It can also be a problem for people with physical care needs, such as those who cannot move around the house easily. For example, they cannot answer the telephone unless it is within reach!

Seeing to read and write and take part in hobbies

Many clients need help to see to read and write and to take part in their hobbies. As people become older they often find that their eyes have changed and they need glasses to be able to see clearly. Sometimes clients need more than glasses to help them to see clearly.

Did you think of these daily activities? They are the kind of things a client would need help with if they were unable to read or write through loss of eyesight.

Going to work

Many of the clients who have special care needs are able to work if they are well supported. It is important that clients are encouraged to participate in as many everyday living activities as possible. Going to work is clearly an activity that is worth participating in.

Try it out Working in a small group make a poster that shows the kind of hobbies that would need to be supported for a client who is losing (or has lost) their eyesight. Compare your work with another group's activity.

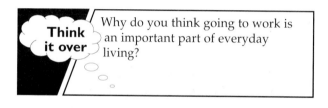

Think it over Why do you think going to work is an important part of everyday living?

Being able to work allows a client to earn money and be as independent as possible.

They are often with other people and can socialise as well as earn a living.

Rob has Down's syndrome. He is 18 years old and has just started work in a sheltered workshop. He is taken to and from work by minibus.

He is assembling plastic corners for fitted kitchens. A very important job. He has to be good at using a screwdriver to make sure that both parts of each corner are fastened together.

He has a supervisor who helps him when things go wrong. His supervisor also tells him when to take a break and where to go for lunch.

He will get his first wage this week. He has already decided what he will spend it on.

Working with another person discuss the types of activities that Rob needs help with. How does the support he receives allow him to participate in work? Make notes of your discussions for your portfolio.

Taking part in education

An essential part of participating fully in life is finding out about the world we live in and the way we can contribute to society. The way we find out about the world and our roles in society is through education. For most people this means going to school and then perhaps to college. Some people also take part in education through their workplace.

Education does not stop when we have completed school or college. For many clients education is something that continues all their lives. Clients with physical care needs are still going to need to learn new skills or to acquire knowledge. This might be so that they can participate in life again or so they can start a new way of living.

Lillian is in and out of hospital being treated for a tumour in her brain.

She is studying for her GCSEs. Most of her education is taking place at home or whilst she is in hospital.

A home tutor visits her four times a week and her teachers send work to her so she can keep up with her studies.

Working with another person make a list of the activities that Lillian is being given help with. Why do you think it is important for Lillian to receive help at this time in her life?

Sue is almost ready to go home following her rehabilitation from a stroke.

She is spending some time with the occupational therapist learning how to carry out tasks in the kitchen.

This is to make sure that she will be safe from harm, and so that she can prepare food and drink for herself in between visits from her carer.

Why do you think this is classed as an educational activity? Make notes for your portfolio.

Providing physical care

Settings

Providing physical care for people who need it can be very hard on the carer as well as the client. For this reason care is provided in a variety of settings, such as:

- client's own home
- residential care homes
- day care centres
- nursing homes
- hospitals.

The type of care setting used will depend on the needs of the client.

Since the NHS and Community Care Act 1990, many clients have been cared for in their own home. The government tries very hard to make sure that people who want to be cared for at home are given as much support as possible.

In general, we can say that people who use residential care homes are:

- older people

- people with learning difficulties

- people with physical disabilities.

Day care centres are used by any person, of any age or ability, who needs social care (and sometimes treatment, such as physiotherapy) once or twice a week but usually lives at home with their carer.

Nursing homes are for anyone, of any age, who needs residential medical care (nursing).

Hospitals are for anyone, of any age, who require medical assistance or treatment (treatment by doctors and nurses).

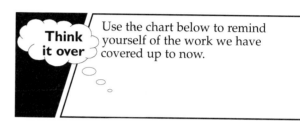

Think it over Use the chart below to remind yourself of the work we have covered up to now.

Reasons for needing physical care	Type of care needed	Length of time care needed
Age-related (babies, young children, older people)	Warmth, shelter, cooking, cleaning, feeding, washing, dressing, shopping, getting out and about, moving about the house	Babies and young children until the care is no longer needed. Older people until the care is no longer needed
People who have lost their mobility, memory	Warmth, shelter, cooking, cleaning, shopping, getting out and about, washing and dressing, social activities, hobbies	All the time
People with a long-term illness	Warmth, shelter, washing, dressing, cooking, cleaning, shopping, getting out and about, social activities, hobbies	For as long as the illness lasts
People who are suffering from the after-effects of a stroke or heart attack	Warmth, shelter, cooking, cleaning, shopping, getting out and about, exercise, hobbies, washing, dressing, reading and writing	Until the person is fully recovered (or as recovered as they can be)
Sudden events (accidents and acute illness)	Warmth, shelter, washing, dressing, cooking, cleaning, moving about the house, shopping, getting out and about (if necessary), hobbies	Until the person is recovered
People with long-term disabilities	Warmth, shelter, cooking, cleaning, washing, dressing, getting out and about, moving about the house, answering the door, hobbies	For as long as the person needs the care

Specialist equipment

Physical care can involve supporting the client's weight, helping them move from one place to another, or any other kind of physical assistance that may be needed.

A hoist is one example of an aid to mobility that lifts a client in and out of difficult places, for example a bath.

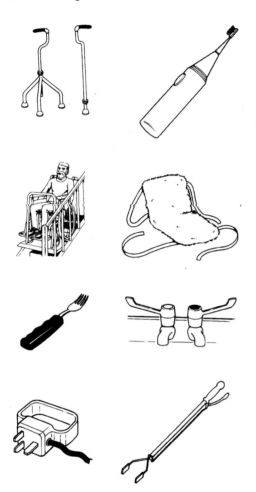

Some aids to physical care

Talk it over

Working with another person discuss the kind of aids to mobility you have seen. These could be in the workplace, in the home, on the streets or in books. Make a chart of the aids to mobility you have discussed.

Talk it over

Gail is a new care worker at Happy Days Residential Home for people with physical disabilities.

Her supervisor has asked her to complete an inventory of all the specialist equipment that the care home holds for helping clients with their everyday living. Gail has been told to list the equipment under the following headings.

- Mobility
- Sitting
- Comfort in bed
- Dressing and undressing
- Bathing
- Using the lavatory
- Seeing and hearing
- Transport.

Gail has decided to start with mobility because she thinks she can easily recognise this kind of equipment.

Working with another person discuss why you think Gail might have chosen to start with special equipment that assists mobility. Write your reasons down and then compare your reasons with Gail's.

 Try it out

Find out how three pieces of the equipment you have put on your chart help a client to be more independent. Write your findings down for your portfolio.

 Try it out

Using the headings in Gail's list find out about aids that are available to the client after each heading she has written.

Examine the chart to make sure that you have not missed any off your list and that we have not missed any off our list!

Physical need	Types of equipment available
Sitting comfortably	Special cushions Rubber rings Chairs with adapted backrests and seats Chairs with neck supports and arm supports Chairs that recline
Comfort in bed	Air mattresses Water beds Specially shaped pillows Leg rests Beds that tilt Bed tables for eating Book rests Lightweight blankets
Dressing and undressing	Long-handled shoe horns Zip extensions Velcro fasteners Large buttons
Bathing	Bath lifts and hoists Bath stools for sitting on Non-slip bath mats Steps to get in the bath Handles in the bath Adapted taps Adapted shower taps Wider doorways Baths that fill after you have stepped into them
Using the lavatory	Raised seats Higher/lower toilet bowls Handles by the side of the toilet Low-flush tanks Wider doorways Foot pumps for flushing the toilet
Seeing and hearing	Glasses, magnifying glasses Hearing aids Flashing fire alarms Vibrating alarm clocks Fax machines Mini-com systems Audio loops Braille books Talking books Guide dogs Hearing dogs
Transport	Adapted cars, gear change on the column Automatic gear change Handles on the steering wheel Adapted foot pedals Motorised wheelchairs

Specialist equipment used as aids

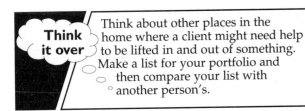

Think it over: Think about other places in the home where a client might need help to be lifted in and out of something. Make a list for your portfolio and then compare your list with another person's.

Have you noticed how many of the physical aids we use for convenience are essential for maintaining the independence of a client who needs help with their physical actions?

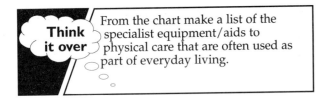

Think it over: From the chart make a list of the specialist equipment/aids to physical care that are often used as part of everyday living.

7.2 Settings, agencies and personnel involved in physical care

Just about every worker in the health and social care profession provides physical care in some way or another to their clients. The main providers of physical care are:

- Informal carers
  - Family
  - Friends.
- Formal carers
  - Doctors
  - Occupational therapists
  - Physiotherapists
  - Nurses
  - Care assistants
  - Support workers.
- Voluntary organisations
  - Age Concern, for example.

For more details about carers see pages 19–27.

Think it over: What do you think might be the difference between an 'informal carer' and a 'formal carer'? Make notes of the differences for your portfolio of evidence.

Informal carers

Informal carers do not usually get paid for the care they give. It is usually family ties and responsibilities, as well as love and caring, that encourages them to provide physical care for a relative or friend.

The government tries to protect and care for informal carers through the Carers (Recognition and Services) Act 1995. That they should be given as much support as possible is seen as important. Professional carers can provide help and advice and in some cases training to help informal carers care for their relatives and friends in the best possible way.

Talk it over

Hilda and Harold have been married for 50 years. Hilda has developed arthritis in her hands and now finds it very difficult to dress herself in the morning.

Harry helps her to get up and puts her clothes on for her. He says that it is quicker that way. During the day they cook and clean together with Harry carrying out all the jobs that Hilda cannot do.

The only thing that Hilda really hates is being helped to go to the toilet. She finds that kind of assistance really degrading and embarrassing.

Working with another person discuss the physical care that Harry is providing for his wife. Make a list of the care given. You could use the headings Gail used, e.g. mobility etc.

Think it over: What kind of a carer is Harry?

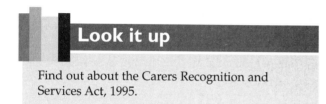

Look it up

Find out about the Carers Recognition and Services Act, 1995.

Formal carers

Formal carers have chosen to care for the physical needs of their clients. For them it is a job of work and they are paid for doing it. However, in most cases professional carers do the work because they also enjoy helping and supporting others who need their assistance. All formal carers should be trained and qualified to do their job properly and to a high standard.

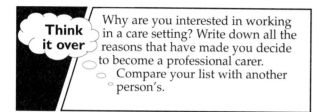

Think it over Why are you interested in working in a care setting? Write down all the reasons that have made you decide to become a professional carer. Compare your list with another person's.

As you can see from the spidergram there is a wide range of health professionals who all provide some kind of care with physical activities. The kind of training they have will be different depending on the work they carry out.

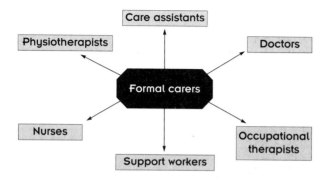

For the role of **doctors** see Unit 1.

Occupational therapists are mostly concerned with improving the quality of everyday living for their clients. Their work might include:

- recommending changes to the client's accommodation
- suggesting suitable specialist equipment for the client
- recommending suitable creative activities
- helping clients become independent
- assessing client's physical and mental abilities.

Physiotherapists are mostly concerned with helping a client regain or increase their mobility and movement. They work with clients to:

- improve muscular strength
- increase stamina
- improve flexibility.

Nurses work under the supervision of a doctor and provide physical care assistance in health centres, hospitals, nursing homes and the client's own home. They help with:

- assisting a client to eat
- mobility
- promoting independence
- personal hygiene routines
- medication
- treatment.

Care assistants usually help in a wide variety of ways. They work under the supervision of another health professional to assist a client with their everyday living activities, such as:

- feeding
- mobility
- personal hygiene
- recreation
- dressing and undressing.

Support workers are available to help and assist both the health professional and the client. They can provide care under the supervision of another health professional.

> **Talk it over**
>
> Working with another person discuss the work that a support worker carries out. How do they support a client's physical needs? Make notes for your portfolio.

For more on formal carers see pages 20–25.

Voluntary organisations

Many voluntary organisations also provide help with physical care assistance. Age Concern is a good example of an organisation that provides volunteers (unpaid workers) who will visit a person's home to provide help with:

* shopping
* getting out and about
* gardening
* social activities
* hobbies.

Sometimes they may even provide assistance with cooking and cleaning. Personal hygiene routines would normally be left to an informal or professional care worker.

Other organisations that provide similar support are:

* Alzheimer's Disease Society
* The Red Cross.

7.3 Relevant health and safety issues

Whenever you are working with clients to provide physical care and assistance you need to think about the health and safety requirements involved. It is important that you understand how to:

* keep yourself safe from harm or injury
* keep your client safe from harm or injury
* keep the work (or home) environment safe and free from harm.

Legislation

There are laws to help us maintain a safe environment, for ourselves and our clients, when we are working. The main law is the Health and Safety at Work Act of 1974. The major result of this Act is that employers and employees both have a duty and a responsibility to protect and care for the health of themselves and their clients. For more on laws covering health and safety see pages 122–125.

> **Look it up**
>
> Working with another person find out about the Health and Safety at Work Act 1974. Make notes about the responsibility of employees in the care of themselves and other people.

Safe practice in moving and handling techniques and use of equipment

The Health and Safety at Work Act makes it clear that employees have certain responsibilities when it comes to health and safety in the workplace. These are:

- if you know an action will be dangerous don't do it!

- always take reasonable care of the safety of others

- always follow the correct procedures and safety rules

- report anything that you think might be a risk to health and safety

- always wear the correct protective clothing

- report any accidents to your employer immediately

- never tamper with equipment and machinery that you are not qualified to deal with.

In January 1993, the European Union **Handling and Lifting Regulations** became law in the United Kingdom. This means that all **employers** have a duty to maintain the health and safety of their staff. The law also says that you as an **employee** have a duty to keep yourself, your work colleagues and your clients safe.

An employer must follow these rules

- Manual moving and handling tasks that could cause injury should be avoided if at all possible.

- Manual handling or lifting should always be assessed before it is carried out.

- Students are not allowed to lift clients unless they are assisting a qualified member of staff.

Assessing manual handling

Is lifting really required?

If so, what needs moving (a client or an object)?

How heavy is the weight?

Can lifting equipment be used for this task?

Is lifting equipment available?

Who will do the lifting?

Are they trained to lift correctly?

How much time and space is required?

Look it up

Find out about the 1993 European Union's Handling and Lifting Regulations. Make notes for your portfolio of your findings.

Moving or handling a client or an object is not an easy task. Those who think it is usually end up with back injuries!

Handling and lifting should never be carried out until you have had the proper training. It is important that you learn to use all equipment safely and in the correct manner.

Hints and tips for safe practice when using specialist equipment

- Always follow the manufacturer's guidelines.

- Never leave equipment lying around.

- Always store the equipment in the correct way.

- Never 'play games' with it!

- Only use the equipment with the client who should be using it.

! Remember!

Reading about safe handling and lifting is not as good as being SHOWN how to do it!

Personal, general and food hygiene

Another part of health and safety is personal, general and food cleanliness and safety. If you are going to keep yourself and your client safe from harm, then you will need to know about the importance of maintaining a clean and hygienic environment. This includes the need to keep yourself and your client clean as well.

Personal hygiene

Let us start by exploring the importance of your own personal hygiene. Keeping yourself clean and appropriately dressed for the job is an essential part of being a carer. You need to:

- wash every day

- tie hair back

- keep your finger nails short and clean

- always wash hands after going to the toilet and before preparing food

- wear gloves when dealing with body fluids

- always wash hands after helping one client before you move on to helping another client

- make sure all your clothes are clean and well repaired

- wear comfortable shoes.

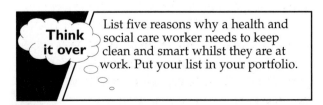

Think it over List five reasons why a health and social care worker needs to keep clean and smart whilst they are at work. Put your list in your portfolio.

General hygiene

This is about keeping your environment clean, tidy and safe. It is fairly simple to keep a workplace hygienic and free from hazards if we follow a few golden rules.

Golden rules of general hygiene

- Keep working areas clean and tidy.

- Help clients keep their personal spaces clean and tidy.

- Clean up immediately if there is a spillage.

- Make sure work surfaces are clean and hygienic, by using, for example, a suitable disinfectant.

- Make sure equipment is clean and ready for safe use.

- Put equipment and materials away after they have been used.

- Store equipment, materials, chemicals, drugs etc. in a safe place and according to the manufacturer's guidelines.

- Floors should be cleaned carefully and any potential hazards reported to management (for example, loose carpet, trailing wires etc.).

- Make sure hands are washed after workplace cleaning duties.

Food hygiene

This is a very important part of good hygiene. Safe food handling is an essential skill for carers who help to feed clients in either the workplace or their own home.

For more on safe handling of raw food see page 163.

When working with food in any situation we need to:

- store the food safely before and after it is cooked

- make sure fridges and freezers are kept at the right temperature

- take care not to store cooked and uncooked meat together on the same shelf

- avoid using 'out of date' food

Look it up

Mumtaz is preparing a meal for the children today. It is her turn to cook the evening meal for when they get back from school.

Mandy's favourite food is chicken with potatoes and vegetables. Mumtaz makes sure the work surface is clean and tidy. She has her cooking equipment ready for use. The oven is switched on and ready to use.

Mumtaz prepares the chicken next to the sink, she makes certain that she uses a special knife and chopping board. She does not want the raw chicken to touch anything else, neither does she want the equipment that the chicken has touched to be used again until it has been washed thoroughly.

Find out why Mumtaz is so particular about preparing and cooking the raw chicken. Make some guidelines for your colleagues on handling raw food. You could put them in a prominent place for everyone to see.

- cook food thoroughly

- always defrost frozen food

- make sure cooking equipment is clean and suitable for the task

- make sure working surfaces are clean and tidy

- make sure our hands are clean.

Dealing with body waste

Dealing with body waste from a client needs to be carried out quickly, efficiently and sensitively. A carer must dispose of the waste in the appropriate place. In hospitals there are special rooms set aside for disposing of bodily waste. They are known as 'sluice rooms'.

Bed pans or commodes should be removed as soon as possible after the client has finished with them.

Talk it over

Lillian is in hospital. She is feeling dreadfully embarrassed. She has been given medication that is making her go to the toilet every 30 minutes or so.

She has to share a ward with four other ladies but to save her from keep running to the toilet she has been given a commode. It has been put next to her bed.

The care assistant has just helped her to get on the commode and although she has closed the curtains there is a big gap down one side and the visitors at the next bed can see her.

Working with another person discuss how Lillian is likely to feel. How could the care assistant have handled the situation more carefully? What should the care assistant do with the body waste once Lillian has finished on the commode?

Demonstrating the skills of physical care

Helping people within the limits of their wishes for assistance

One of the central skills a carer needs to develop is the ability to be able to talk to their clients. Communication is the 'key' to good relationships and caring skills. Many clients with special care needs are able to carry out many tasks for themselves. Often a carer is providing assistance rather than doing the complete activity for a client.

Ensuring people make choices about their care wherever possible

It is important to give your clients choices. This is important in demonstrating value and respect to clients. We should always try and encourage our clients to make their own choices to ensure that they are taking an active part in their own lives. Many people who have become older or have a disability feel that they are no longer of any use. It is important to avoid this situation wherever possible.

Having special care needs has been known to make people dependent on others when there is no need for this to happen. An important part of the caring process is trying to help people to live as independently as possible.

There are many ways we can encourage a client to make their own choices. We can:

- make sure the client achieves tasks where possible

- always ask about the kind of help required

- offer appropriate help when it is required

- use positive body language

- give plenty of encouragement.

It is important to remember that encouragement and support for making choices includes:

- never 'taking over' something the client can do

- always respecting the client's decision

- always offering the client a choice if there is one.

SNAPSHOT

Tracy has learning difficulties and lives in supported housing. Nick is encouraging Tracy to choose her own holiday destination this year. Last year she ended up in a holiday camp by the seaside and she did not enjoy it at all. Someone else had made the decision!

Nick knows that Tracy loves trying out adventurous things when she is offered the opportunity. She enjoys horse riding and swimming.

Nick has brought in a brochure for an outward bound centre that specialises in holidays for people who are wheelchair users.

By the time Tracy had finished looking at the brochure the decision was made. She would be going to the outward bound centre with two carers whilst the others in the care home went somewhere else.

- *Why is it important for Tracy to make a choice of holiday?*

- *How is Nick supporting her is this choice?*

Unit 7 Assessment

You need to produce evidence in the external assessment that shows your understanding of:

- why people need physical care

- the range of settings and persons providing physical care

- empowerment and health and safety issues that apply to the provision of physical care.

This assessment will give you the opportunity to consolidate your knowledge and understanding of the many issues surrounding giving physical care to clients.

For this unit you will have the opportunity to work towards a pass, merit or distinction grade.

The activities are ordered in such a way as to guide you through this assessment. The levels of assessment are clearly indicated as:

- P for Pass

- M for Merit

- D for Distinction.

You may wish to discuss with your tutor the level of activities you do.

All students must complete the first four pass activities to achieve the minimum for Unit 7.

The following three case studies provide a setting for the assessment.

CASE STUDY 1

Eve is 83 and lives independently in her bungalow in a small village. She has had problems with her sight and is registered blind. This does not mean she has no vision, but many activities of living are becoming difficult for her. She feels secure in her bungalow because she knows where everything is. However there are a few emerging problems. Cooking a main meal has become rather difficult. Eve likes a hot lunch, and is unable now to cook the way she would like to. She also feels the house is getting a bit grubby, she can't see the dust the way she used to.

Her other health problem is arthritis. This isn't too bad, but she occasionally has difficulties in turning on taps and doing up buttons. Her GP has said that he will refer her to the occupational therapist at the community hospital. Apparently there are all sorts of aids to help people with arthritis.

She is going next week for her first appointment, and then the occupational therapist will probably visit her at home for a home assessment.

Eve has many friends in the village, and also loves listening to the radio. She watches the news on television, but can't make out all the images on the screen. There is a lively over-60's club in the village hall twice a week, and she can get there by herself because there are no busy roads to cross. The shops are more of a problem, but they are thinking of installing lights at the corner which would make it much safer for her.

Joelene lives around the corner. She pops in to see Eve every morning and evening, just to make sure she is safe and for a bit of company. Eve looks forward to this: Joelene often makes her a cup of tea, and prepares a flask of hot chocolate.

CASE STUDY 2

Will is 14, a very lively and energetic young lad. Last week he had an accident and broke his right leg and badly injured his right arm. And, of course, he is right-handed! He is going to be in hospital for a few weeks while his leg mends. He will be in a special adolescent unit.

He is already finding it frustrating. He is unable to attend to his personal needs: even eating is a problem, let alone washing and personal hygiene. He has been told that it is possible he will be able to go out later, but in a wheelchair . . . with his leg sticking out. How embarrassing. And he has no idea when he'll be able to play cricket again.

CASE STUDY 3

Sunny is a care assistant working for a care agency whose clients are based in the community and in residential settings. She has a case load of regular clients, who range from Rosie, a young girl with cerebral palsy, who lives at home and who requires almost total care (her mother helps Sunny), to an elderly couple, Mr and Mrs Bhatti, who need help with bathing three times a week. One of Sunny's clients, Mrs Browther, has a big garden that she is very proud of, but which is getting too much for her. Sunny's son, Eddie, now goes there once a week to help in the garden and do any heavy shopping.

Sunny also works one afternoon a week in a residential home which also provides respite care for clients and their families. She helps run a social afternoon, providing music and other activities for the residents. Milly Brown, one of the residents who comes for respite care, has Alzheimer's disease. She particularly enjoys the music and joins in all the songs. The residents choose the activities. Sunny has built up quite a range of contacts who can do everything from running quiz afternoons to driving the minibus on outings.

Working towards a pass grade

Activity 1P

From the case studies above, identify the activities of daily living that **four** people need support with. You could do this as a table. Try to include as wide a range as possible.

Activity 2P

The subjects of the case studies may require equipment to support their different needs.

Identify what equipment might be available to support the following:

- Jenny
- Will
- Eve
- Mr and Mrs Bhatti
- Mrs Crowther.

Activity 3P

In the case studies above, the work of both formal and informal carers is outlined.

- Who are the formal carers? Give reasons for your answer relating this to the care they give.

- Who are the informal carers? Give reasons for your answer relating this to the care they give.

- What is the value of providing informal care? You may like to think both of the carer and the person being supported.

Activity 4P

The following list includes some of the physical care given to a range of clients. For each one, describe what health and safety issues must be considered. You must show an awareness of current requirements for: moving and handling, food hygiene, dealing with waste.

- A client needs help moving to a comfortable position in bed.

- A client uses a commode in her room. The waste must be removed.

- At 09.30 a carer prepares a cold chicken salad for a client's lunch.

or

- Choose one example from each of the case studies to show how a carer should demonstrate awareness of moving and handling, food hygiene and dealing with waste.

Working towards a merit grade

To achieve a merit grade you must carry out the pass activities and the additional steps to Activities 1 and 2 below.

Activity 1M

Using the examples of the four clients described above in Activity 1P describe:

- why they require physical care

- how their dignity and independence can be maintained while receiving this care and why this is important

- how carers can ensure that the client is fully empowered while receiving this care and

why empowerment is an important aspect of care delivery.

Activity 2M

The clients above have been cared for in a range of care settings. Using these settings to focus on, or using care settings that you are familiar with or have discussed in class:

- describe the reasons for providing care in a
  - domestic setting
  - sheltered accommodation
  - hospital
  - residential home
  - nursing home

  You must clearly describe the reasons for providing care in the community as against care at home in a residential setting.

- describe the advantages and disadvantages of providing care in each of these settings.

  You can do this in a list if you like.

Working towards a distinction

To achieve a distinction grade you must carry out the pass and merit activities and the additional steps for Activities 1 and 2 below.

Activity 1D

What do you think are the issues that affect whether a client is empowered or not within his or her care setting or by his or her carer?

You may like to think of this under a range of headings, for example:

- Staff attitudes
- Staff training
- The attitudes and values of the institution
- Resources (time, facilities, staff numbers)
- Client's expectations from care.

There are other factors which contribute to a client being empowered or not in care.

For each heading that you use, give actual or fictional (but realistic) examples of how these could affect the care the client receives.

Activity 2D

• Using the case study of Eve explain why you think supported care at home would be the best option for her, and how this care could be provided.

• Using the case study of Milly Brown, explain why she might need respite care, and why it would be preferable to carry this out in a residential care setting.

You need to show that you have grasped the advantages and disadvantages of different care settings and that supported independence in a client's home is the preferred method of care.

Check your knowledge

1 List four types of physical care that might be required by a client who has lost mobility.

2 What is arthritis and how does it affect physical health?

3 Jill has had a stroke and needs some help with her daily care. A stroke is:

   a a condition of the lungs which affects breathing

   b an inflammation of the liver

   c a condition resulting in not enough oxygen getting to the brain because of a blood clot

   d another name for a heart attack.

4 An example of an acute illness is:

   a osteoarthritis

   b tonsillitis

   c Alzheimer's disease

   d multiple sclerosis.

5 Name three kinds of physical care that could be carried out in a day centre.

6 Which professionals would carry out that care?

7 Before she goes to work each morning, Jenny pops into her mother's house to help get her up and prepare her breakfast.

   Jenny is an example of:

   a a carer employed under the NHS and Community Care Act

   b a formal carer

   c an informal carer

   d an occupational therapist.

8 What are three responsibilities of *employees* under the Health and Safety at Work Act 1974?

9 Maintaining good personal hygiene as a care worker is essential because:

   a it is part of the community care legislation

   b carers look better in a uniform

   c you are protecting yourself and others

   d clients won't trust you if you don't look smart.

10 Giving a client choices about the care he or she receives is an example of:

   a good personal hygiene

   b assisting when a client's health has deteriorated

   c the care value base

   d the role of the informal care assistant.

Answers to questions

Unit 1

12	d
13	c
14	b
15	c
16	b
17	b
18	c
19	b
20	d
21	c
22	c

Unit 2

11	a
12	b
13	b
14	b
15	b
16	b
17	c
18	c
19	b
20	c

Unit 3

12	d
13	b
14	a
15	b
16	d
17	c
18	b

19	c
20	a
21	d

Unit 4

6	b
7	c
8	b
9	c
10	d

Unit 5

11	d
12	c
13	a
14	c
15	c
16	d
17	b
18	b
19	d
20	c

Unit 6

7	c
8	b
9	b
10	d

Unit 7

4	b
7	c
9	c
10	c

Glossary

Abuse: This word is used in a variety of different situations. It always has a negative meaning that is usually applied to the way people treat other people. For example, physical abuse usually means hitting another person or neglecting their physical needs, mental abuse could mean insulting and humiliating them.

Active listening: Listening so that you have taken in what is being said.

Agenda: A list of items to be discussed in a meeting.

Aims and objectives: A set of goals or targets we are trying to achieve.

Attitude: A basic view about life which can affect the way you deal with people and situations.

Balanced diet: A diet that contains the essential nutrients from different food groups, enabling the body to function effectively.

Benefit/beneficial: Something that is helpful to you.

Body language: The way we send messages to another person by using our body.

Bonding: Forming an emotional attachment to another person. Babies usually form an emotional attachment to their carers in the first year of their life.

Brainstorming: Putting together everyone's ideas. These days a 'brainstorm' is usually called a 'quick think'.

Carbohydrates: Nutrients which supply the body with energy. These are divided into starches and sugars.

Care value base: A set of principles of good practice which help guide carers to give the kind of care each individual client needs. It includes the promotion of antidiscriminatory practice, respecting individual beliefs and cultural backgrounds, confidentiality, giving individuals choices about the care they receive and respecting individual rights.

Clarification: To make something clear.

Client rights: All people have the right to be different and free from discrimination. They have the right to be treated fairly and respectfully. They should be given choice, safety and security and their development needs should be met. At all times they have the right to confidentiality of their information.

Community Care Act, 1990: A law that changed the way the health and social care services were provided and purchased. The major principle behind the changes was that people are best cared for in their own homes or other familiar surroundings.

Component: The parts that make up a whole.

Confidential/confidentiality: Keeping information which you have about others to yourself. Confidential information may be shared with others who genuinely have a 'need to know' or if other people were at risk if the information is kept to yourself. Confidentiality is a key part of the care value base.

Confront: To face up to something.

Consensus: Reaching a general agreement.

Constructive criticism: Helpful and meaningful criticism which is directed towards issues which can improve the situation rather than towards any particular individual.

Contaminant: Anything in food that makes the food harmful to human health.

Contaminate: To introduce something into food that will make it harmful to human health.

Conversion tables of weights and measures:

Imperial	Metric
1oz	28.35g
1lb	453.59g
2.2lbs	1 kilogram (1,000grams)
1pint	568.26 mls
	1litre = 1,000mls

(These figures are often rounded up for practical use.)

Culture: The customs and beliefs which shape how we view the world around us. It may also include our lifestyle.

Defensive: Being concerned with protecting your ideas and responsibilities.

Designate: To give someone a particular task or role.

Detrimental: Not beneficial or good for you.

Diet: The food and drink that is normally consumed each day.

Dietary intake: The food and drink that your diet consists of over a given period of time.

Dietary recommendations: The recommendations of experts in health and nutrition concerning your dietary intake.

Discriminate: Treating someone or a group differently from others, often in a negative way.

Diversity: Recognising and understanding that every person is special and not the same as anyone else.

Effective: To work well.

Empowerment: Giving power to others so they can make their own decisions and control their lives.

Environment: Everything that surrounds a person, for example where they live, the work they do, the kind of house they live in and the social class to which they belong.

Ethnic group: A group whose members share a common culture.

Family: A group of people who are related to each other.

Fats: Nutrients which supply the body with a concentrated source of energy, storage of some vitamins and insulation of body organs.

Fibre: The non-digestible part of carbohydrates used to help maintain the regular functioning of the digestive system.

Financial resources: The money needed to be spent (outgoings) and received (income) so that an activity or event can take place.

Food groups: There are five commonly accepted food groups:

- Bread and other cereals and potatoes
- Fruit and vegetables
- Milk and dairy foods
- Meat, fish and alternatives
- Fatty and sugary food.

Food tables: Lists of foods and nutrients which show the recommended intake of foods for different age groups according to age, sex and occupation.

Function: To work or operate.

Gender: The roles that are expected of us through being either male or female.

Human resources: The people needed to carry out an activity or event.

Immunisation: A way of protecting people from some diseases by introducing a mild form of the disease into their body so that the body can develop antibodies to protect itself in the future.

Independence: The right to choose and control one's own lifestyle.

Infection: The spread of harmful bacteria and viruses and other micro-organisms.

Kilocalorie (kcal) or, more commonly, calorie: A unit used to measure the energy of food.

Kilojoule (kJ): The metric unit of measurement for energy. 1kcal = 4.2kJ.

Lifestages: Socially defined periods of time which are used to identify the development stages of people, for example infancy, childhood, adulthood.

Lifestyle: The way in which individuals live their lives.

MAFF: Ministry of Agriculture, Fisheries and Food.

Malnutrition: Weakness and ill-health caused by not having the correct balance of nutrients in the diet.

Material resources: The things needed to create an activity or event.

Minerals: Nutrients which are needed by the body in small amounts to help form bones, skin and body tissue and regulate body processes.

Mobility: The ability to move around independently.

Motivate/motivation: To stimulate interest in doing or achieving something.

NACNE: Nutritional Advisory Committee on Nutritional Education.

National Health Service (NHS): The government funded and managed service, which provides hospitals, doctors, nurses and community services.

Nutrient: The 'building blocks' of food that are essential to keep us healthy and our body functioning. The nutrients in food are protein, carbohydrates, fats, vitamins and minerals.

Nutritious: Food or drink that is beneficial to health.

Obesity/obese: Gaining excessive weight.

Osteoporosis: A disease of the bones, where the bones become brittle due to loss of calcium.

Paraphrasing: To make something easier to understand by putting it into different words.

Pathogen: An organism that causes disease. In particular, bacteria (for example, salmonella) which cause diseases such as food poisoning.

PIES: Physical, Intellectual, Emotional and Social needs. PIES is a way of remembering them.

Prejudice: An attitude which is based on judging individuals or groups according to stereotyped views. Prejudice is often based on ignorance, with a negative effect on the person or group being targeted.

Priority: The order in which actions need to be taken, putting the most important first.

Promoting independence: To actively encourage an individual to choose an independent lifestyle. This is also a key part of the care value base.

Protein: Nutrients used by the body for growth and repair.

Racial prejudice: An unfavourable attitude towards another because they belong to a particular race.

Resources: The materials, money or people that are available for a particular task or action.

Reviewing: Looking back over what has taken place.

Role: What you have to do in a given situation.

Sedentary: Inactive.

Self-esteem: The way a person sees himself or herself. High self-esteem means a person feels good about himself or herself and that they are likely to be happy and self-confident. Low self-esteem means that he or she feels badly about themselves and this can lead to unhappiness or depression.

Social class: The status given to the people who work in certain jobs, for example a doctor is social class I or A and a teacher is social class II or B.

Source: Where things come from, for example one source of protein is meat.

Stereotyping: Assuming an individual will behave in a certain way or think in a certain way because of his appearance or other characteristics such as gender, age or ethnic background. People who have been stereotyped are expected to behave as 'typical' members of that group.

Team: A group of people working together to achieve a common goal.

Therapeutic: Something that cures or improves certain conditions.

Values: What you believe to be valuable in life. This may include the actions or attitudes you believe to be right or wrong.

Vegetarian/vegetarian diet: An individual who has a diet that does not contain any meat or fish products. A vegetarian may or may not include dairy products or eggs in the diet, according to preference.

Vitamins: Nutrients which are needed in small amounts for regulating and maintaining the growth of the body and functioning of body cells.

Ready to move on?

This is exactly what you need for the GNVQ Intermediate Health and Social Care award

● ●

Choose from two student books

1. *The Student Book without Options* covers all of the compulsory units, making it ideal for your Part One GNVQ.

2. *The Student Book with Edexcel Options* covers the compulsory units and options units, so it's ideal if you are taking the full award.

Learn how to achieve the grade you want

● Straightforward and user-friendly, the books will show you exactly how to achieve the success you want at Intermediate level. They clearly explain the skills you need to show in assessments to achieve a pass, merit or distinction grade.

Use the books easily

● Units and sub-sections in the book match the headings in the GNVQ award specification, so it's easy to find your way around the text.

Heinemann GNVQ Intermediate Health and Social Care without options – ideal for Part One GNVQs
ISBN: 0 435 45293 2

Heinemann GNVQ Intermediate Health and Social Care with Edexcel options
ISBN: 0 435 45600 8

Order from your local bookshop or call (01865) 888068.
● ●
There's an easy way to find out all the latest information about GNVQs.
Just visit www.heinemann.co.uk/gnvq

S 999 ADV 08

E566